LANGUAGE, PHILOSOPHY AND LOGIC

Clifford R. Paulson

KALA INFORMATION SERVICES
P.O. BOX 6245
SILVER SPRING, MARYLAND 20916-0245

Date of this Composition: 1989/05/20

This book has been composed on the Univac 1100/90 and Linotron, each at the University of Maryland, College Park.

PREFACE

This little monograph is the result of a feeling over several years that some unstated relationships existed among language, philosophy and logic and that relationships stated by one person were disregarded by others who were using them (perhaps) unconsciously.

An intimate relationship exists among logic, language, number and philosophy. This is our major thesis. This presentation attempts to explore that relationship. It further attempts to make explicit some of the underlying assumptions within our language which are usually left implicit, at least with respect to logic. In the process of demonstrating this, we shall develop a logic with both a deductive and an inductive side. The sequence of this presentation is structured primarily for purposes of the argument and will at times be different from the sequence more usually found in presentations.

After an introduction, we discuss intension and establish a calculus of intension as a basis for later analysis. This calculus is then used throughout the remainder of the text. We then develop number and its algebra in one of the conventional approaches. It is necessary to establish intension and number prior to the development of a calculus of classes since our "usual" definition of class involves each. Classes are then defined in a straightforward manner.

A brief discussion of the relationship between philosophy and truth leads then to an introduction to induction and probability. As a final section we have an overview of our English language, though predeeding sections were dependent upon it. An anomoly of our civilization and this book is that though they depend on language, we place language last.

This presentation is a mere framework. It provides a basis for further constructions. Within this serious limitation, the major ideas have been set forth for consideration and as a base from which to proceed. The purpose of this presentation is, hopefully, to stimulate thought in this area. To the extent that such stimulation occurs, to that extent the presentation will have been a success.

Note that bibliographic references herein are all of the form, (a,b), or of the form, (a). The first number, a, refers to the number of the reference in the Section,

Bibliography. The second number, b, is the page number in the referenced document.

Within the text, as discussed on page 36 numerical values are shown in binary form with a leading zero. Decimal numbers are used for other purposes. This should not be construed as the advocacy of binary numbers; these conventions are merely to help denote the different uses of number in an unambiguous manner.

C.R.P.

Table of Contents

1 INTRODUCTION 1
2 PRIMARY CONCEPTS AND SYMBOLS 4
2.1 Symbols 4
2.2 Quantities Related to a Symbol 5
2.3 Classes 7
2.4 Other Approaches 8
2.5 Assertions 8
2.6 Cross-Reference 12
3 INTENSION 14
3.1 Nouns 15
3.2 Morphemes 16
3.3 Identity Elements 23
3.4 Theorems 24
4 NUMBER 31
4.1 Nouns, Number 32
4.2 Verbs, Number 32
4.3 Conjunctions 34
4.4 Natural Numbers 35
4.5 Difference and Quotient 37
4.6 Additional Verbs 40
4.7 Theorems 40
5 EXTENSION 42
5.1 Nouns 43
5.2 Verbs 44
5.3 Conjunctions 47
5.4 Descriptors, Extension 51
5.5 Cardinality of a Class 54
5.6 Disjunction of Intensions 56
5.7 Other Definitions 59
5.8 Theorems 60
6 DEDUCTION 68
6.1 Types of Proofs 69
6.2 Conditions of Deduction 71
7 PHILOSOPHY AND TRUTH 74
7.1 Philosophies 74
7.2 Truth 77
7.3 Traditional Logic 90
8 INDUCTION 97
8.1 Truth and Induction 99
8.2 Changes to a Philosophy 100
9 LANGUAGE 108
9.1 Semiotics 109

9.2 Sentences 112
9.3 Descriptors 114
9.4 Verbs 124
9.5 Adverbs 130
9.6 Morphemes 132

10 SUMMARY OF STATEMENTS 138
10.1 Summary of Statements, Intension 138
10.2 Summary of Statements, Number 140
10.3 Summary of Statements, Extension 143
10.4 Summary of Statements, Deduction 148
10.5 Summary of Statements, Truth 148
10.6 Summary of Statements, Induction 150

BIBLIOGRAPHY 151

INDEX 153

1. INTRODUCTION

A major purpose of this work is to examine the foundations of Logic and to explicitly delineate those bases required in the foundation of Logic. Historically, we have tended to say that Logic rests on a small number of fundamental hypotheses, that is, that all Logic has been developed from or deduced from a few assumptions. The problem within this approach is that we first assume the use of a language (such as English); each language has numerous assumptions and conventions which have been established during the development of that language over time. We must, here, try to determine a base from which Logic may proceed without these implicit assumptions; all aspects of that base should be explicit.

Formal logic has been studied and used at least since the time of Aristotle. When we include mathematics as a formal logic, it is difficult to conceive our present civilization existing without its foundation of formal logic. Thus, the development of that logic and the knowledge of its foundations and limitations still holds great interest and utility for us today.

It is perhaps trivial to say that modern languages have developed over the millenia and that, in this development, customs and beliefs have been reflected so completely yet so implicitly in these languages that their presence is often not recognized. However, in such a situation we must realize that, with these same languages, we attempt to construct philosophies and logics as though they were independent of and different from the implicit forms imbedded in the language. Language thus applies constraints (if not distortions) to such constructions.

There is no reason to believe that our language is any more "God-given" than any other language, Eastern or Western. And there is no reason to believe that our conventional Logic is any more correct than some other Logic. Yet our comprehension of other philosophies, other logics and, thus, other languages is inhibited because our language and our Logic and our philosophy are inter-related to a significant degree and bias or limit our comprehension of these other calculi.

As an example (which we shall discuss later), the indefinite article, a (or an), is a contraction of the etymological ancestor of the word, one, and thus reflects a theory of number, even before we develop a theory of number. In like manner the limiting adjective, no, denotes the concept, zero; a common usage of the adverb, not, often assumes a dichotomy. Such words can bias a synthesis of a system of numbers or a philosophy in its formative stages.

Another part of the problem with our language is that it physically is one-dimensional in its spoken form and in its written form. That the written form is one-dimensional is obvious from the fact that complete representation can be made in ASCII (or other) codes on a telephone or teletype circuit. In like manner the spoken word is a longitudinal pressure wave, varying along a radial line from the source. Time is a second dimension along which the variations occur. Such one-dimensional forms limit the information which can be conveyed by the language. Though two- and three-dimensional forms are also in use (engineering drawings and maps are examples of such a language) their use is much less extensive than the use of ordinary language.

The one-dimensional form influences our thought processes. For example, the copula is dichotomic, and its name reflects the connection of the parts of the dichotomy.

Related to this last point, our language might also be a reflection of our mental limitations. We find it easy (and thus normal) to equate or compare two concepts or two objects, but (compounded further by the limitations of our one-dimensional language) the simultaneous consideration of more than two becomes more involved. These factors appear to be reflected in our logics, mathematics and traditional propositional logic.

Our philosophical beliefs also influence our Logic, though much of this is imbedded in our language. However, within the same language differences of philosophy can lead to different results.

Thus we are saying that, having a language, a philosophy can be defined. An important piece of that philosophy is the definition of a Logic. Without a language and a philosophy there is no Logic.

To repeat, some work in Logic has proceeded on the basis of what we might call inherent assumptions rather than on the basis of a foundation, each part of which has been carefully developed without circularity or with explicitly stated circularity. The use of our existing language in itself allows, encourages or forces the use of inherent assumptions. As mentioned above, the natural numbers (especially zero and one) are implied or explicit in many words of English. The use of such words in the development of Logic before we have defined the numbers does lead us in a circular path.

This presentation attempts to set forth an orderly progression of the development of the foundations of logic and mathematics. The presentation is unrelated to the temporal or historic development of a language of Logic. It is by no means the only progression which could be developed toward this goal.

In Section 9 we discuss a written language, specifically English, and it might be useful to refer to that Section during review of the intervening Sections. Of course, we are only concerned with language as used for scientific or logical purposes; other types of written language use forms which will not be considered. In this connection, we might observe that Weinreich (24,11) doubts that there is any point to semantic theories which are restricted to "... humorless, prosaic, banal prose ...".

But such an accusation is often applied to scientific or technical literature, and these are our only area of concern herein.

Our approach here will be that, with recognition of the conditions in a "living" language, we must look into more rigid forms of symbolism than normal English writing so that variations can be eliminated and differences can be recognized more easily. These forms will represent the concepts and classes. Necessary definitions will be made and axioms will be postulated, with the attendant problems noted. After establishment of a foundation we can then discuss truth.

2. PRIMARY CONCEPTS AND SYMBOLS

In Logic it is normally a requirement (and good practice) that a concept or symbol not be used until it has been properly defined. However, at some level the definition of a concept or symbol in terms of more elementary concepts or symbols ceases to be possible. The definition of a new symbol (e.g., word) in a written language can not proceed if there is no language. Thus, at the elementary level, definitions (if they exist at all) tend to become circular or based on another language (metalanguage?).

Because of this situation, in the next chapter a degree of circularity in definition will be explicitly admitted. Symbolic definitions will reference statements which appear initially in the text and again in Chapter 10, Summary. After the early chapters we shall then adhere to the policy of defining new symbols in terms of existing symbols.

We will define a calculus of operations on concepts with formality similar to that which appears in the calculus of operations on classes. In a sense this will be a codification of the communications used in the processes of Logic. By doing so we should be able to clearly point out those statements which are underlying our daily use of Logic.

We shall be postulating three concepts herein: intension, extension, number. These will be developed in Chapters 3, 5 and 4 respectively. We will also notice many similarities or parallel approaches among these three Chapters, for example, in the definitions of verbs, conjunctions and nouns for each concept. These similarities would appear to be more than mere coincidence; they possibly reflect a prior structuring of our thought processes. An interesting conjecture might be a study of variations of these developments, by the use of axioms other than those specified herein and in conventional texts. However since the present axioms are those which are reflected in our present English language to a great extent, some problems in exposition of such variations might well be expected.

2.1. Symbols

All printed characters, and spaces, are symbols. In the case of the printed word, aggregations of symbols (the individual letters) comprise a symbol (the word). In this Section we review some special symbols.

2.1.1. Braces, Brackets and Parentheses

These symbols will be used in the definition of function-symbols. As such, they are delimiters much as spaces and punctuation are delimiters in English. They shall be used together, and a "matching rule" is:

Rule: Each opening brace, bracket or parenthesis shall be matched by a closing brace, bracket or parenthesis in the same term and of the same type. Such pairs may be "nested" within other pairs, and the first closing brace, bracket or parenthesis shall be construed as being matched with the last previous opening symbol of the same type.

2.1.2. Subscripts

Subscripts will be used herein to denote different (or possibly different) entities in a discussion. As an example, if S_α represents a symbolic string, S_β is (usually) a different string.

2.2. Quantities Related to a Symbol

As stated in Section 9, a descriptor is a symbol; in the most simple case, a descriptor is a noun. Associated with each descriptor is the object or concept itself which Carnap (4,9) has called the designatum, that which is designated. The descriptor has been called a designator. But, as we have indicated before, there are additional entities associated with that descriptor. For every descriptor, d_α, we shall postulate $\mathbf{C}\{d_\alpha\}$, the denotation or extension of the term, and $\mathfrak{M}\{d_\alpha\}$, the connotation or intension of the term. Reference, e.g., Alston (1,16). Depending on how the descriptor is used, in English it may be the symbol for the class of objects (the extension) or the composite of attributes or characteristics (the intension). This is to say that an assertion may be in the extensive form or the intensive form. In normal English usage we often do not distinguish between the two. However, in our symbolism herein, we must and will distinguish. As examples, we can define the symbol, running boy, by first defining the terms, boy and running, and then assign the description to the boy. We might, for example, define boy as

** $\mathfrak{M}\{\text{boy}\}:\mathfrak{M}\{\text{young homo sapiens}\}$

A related statement is

** $\mathfrak{M}\{\text{boy}\}\in\mathbf{C}\{\text{homo sapiens}\}$

This merely demonstrates that each intension is a member of one or more classes.

Now if we discuss a particular boy, "the boy", we might assert that he is running by

** $\mathfrak{M}\{\text{the boy}\}\in\mathbf{C}\{\text{running boys}\}$

We have defined the general member of the class by its intension and defined an aspect of "the boy" by stating inclusion in a specified population.

Note that when we postulate $\mathbf{C}\{d_\alpha\}$ it does not represent a class of the symbols d_α; rather it represents a class of the intensions $\mathfrak{M}\{d_\alpha\}$. As we shall define and discuss later, for example,

** $(\text{cat})\in\mathbf{C}\{\text{symbols}\}$

whereas

** $\mathfrak{M}\{\text{cat}\}\in\mathbf{C}\{\text{mammals}\}$

In like manner we shall use the word, John, as a symbol and $\mathfrak{M}$\{John\} as the individual or concept.

To some there seems to be an anomoly between intension and extension. In a sense, a more elaborate concept will often result in a smaller class (a class having fewer members).

As Quine (19,120) has pointed out, attributes or properties can be assigned by statements of inclusion in classes. For example, a statement that the Apostles were included in the class, pious humans, conveys the concept that the Apostles were pious. He then tends to minimize the need for separating class and attribute. Carnap (6) presents a lengthy discussion on whether separate symbols are needed for extension and intension and the conduct of logical discussions in the absence of one or the other. He (4,145) contends that, in a properly constructed language, the extension can be defined from the intension, but the converse may not be applicable.

An argument might be made that the symbols of English in themselves represent the intension of the statement and that, therefore, our symbolic structure $\mathfrak{M}\{\ldots\}$ is unnecessary. Often this argument is reasonable and valid, but the symbolism of English is used for all purposes (intension, extension, etc.), and so to remove ambiguity we shall use separate, explicit symbolisms.

Thus we proceed with

E2.01 $\mathbf{C}\{d_\alpha\}$ is the symbol for the extension of descriptors d_α, the class of $\mathfrak{M}\{d_\alpha\}$

E2.02 $\mathfrak{M}\{d_\alpha\}$ is the symbol for the intensions of descriptors d_α

Related to these two quantities we shall later also postulate a metric or measure for each. These will be discussed as we proceed. In the following material we shall first discuss intension and then extension for reasons of ease of definition.

As a result, the quantities which we have for discussion are:

** the object or concept
** the symbol (name) for the object or concept
** the intension or connotation
** the extension or denotation
** the metric of the intension
** the metric of the extension

In addition, related to the intension and its metric is one other major consideration, the philosophy, in which these quantities are imbedded. This philosophy is composed of relationships, some of which define these quantities.

2.3. Classes

Our discussions to this point may have created some questions about our use of the word, class. Herein, we shall use a special definition for that word, but let us consider the more general situation. The type of class which we propose for extension causes no problems for most students of the subject, but what we propose for intension might also, in a more general sense, be viewed as a type of class.

A class has no defined structure. Though it may be pictorially represented in two dimensions by a Venn diagram, there is no definition that it exists in one, two, three or more dimensions. Such a definition is also quite unnecessary for the relationships that we shall use herein.

A class has no specified ordering or sequencing of its members. The sequence in which the members are selected, for whatever purpose, is defined by separate criteria, and for any given class the next sequence of selection may be entirely different from the sequence last employed. For example, an "ordered set" is an ordered selection of the members of that set, where we have preciously defined what we mean by "ordered".

For some people, synonyms for the word, class, are collection and set. These terms are close to the definition which we shall use herein, such as in Chapter 5. Much work has been done in the study of this type of class and in the development of notation for such classes.

Our definition of "class" does include the definition of "set" in mathematics; our classes are classes of concepts while our sets will be stated as sets of numbers or sets of "points", that is, groups of numbers or ordered n'tuples of numbers. These are discussed in Section 5.4.4. As further definition, our sets are specialized forms of classes of concepts, adapted to and used only for discussions of numbers. Since a number is a noun (a descriptor) it denotes a concept. Thus our distinction between classes and sets is primarily for adaptation to our customs and habits. However, we shall use slightly different versions of the symbolism for each.

Since a general definition of class might be broader than the definition which we use, broad enough to include our definition of intension, how do the two types differ? One major difference is that the class **C** (or **S**) is denumerable; we shall apply a measure of cardinality to it. The "class" $\mathfrak{M}$ is not denumerable, in our view; it is not composed of discrete, delineated members. Yet many of the basic definitions and axioms are quite similar for both types. Thus, we treat the axioms for class as theorems to be derived from those for intension.

Herein we shall use the notations specified above for the nouns, intension and extension, and we shall intentionally develop a different notation for intension from that for extension. Such an approach will allow us to keep the distinctions explicit while demonstrating similarities.

2.4. Other Approaches

Others have already established the foundations of subjects discussed herein in slightly different manners. As an example, a more usual approach to set theory and theory of number is found in Tarski, Givant (26) and similar texts. Tarski, Givant presents a formal language and proceeds to develop set theory. Fom this, number theory evolves. It is an excellent presentation, but we feel that there are certain statements of foundation which could be strengthened. This area has been our major concern here.

2.5. Assertions

In Section 9.2 we discuss sentences in a conventional manner. Here we must be more specific about assertions, the one form with which we are concerned. Assertions can occur in one of three structures. These are:

1. descriptor-predicate
   Only the sentences in natural language can occur with this structure in our work here. The variations possible in this format are so great that to assign invariant rules this form must be restated in terms of either or both of the two forms below.

2. descriptor-copula-descriptor
   The statements in the study of classes and in the theory of numbers have been developed and are used in this structure. For these uses the copula is essential since, for historical reasons, it performs specific functions. In this form, the descriptors must belong to the same class, that is, the symbols for the descriptors must both represent classes or they must both represent numbers. Further, in this form the copula must be selected from the definitions which were made for the type of descriptors being used. We should also observe that this form is frequently used in English.

3. descriptor-descriptor
   Our formulations of assertions about intensions herein are of this form. Herein, the descriptors must each represent an intension. As mentioned elsewhere, this form can occur in English but is more common in other languages where the copula is not considered essential.

We shall recognize four types of assertions, this differentiation being determined by type of usage.

1. definitions
2. axioms
3. theorems
4. hypotheses

2.5.1. Definitions

A definition is a semantic relationship. At least two methods are in use for the establishment of definitions. These arise in technical papers as well as dictionaries. In the first method we define the new symbolism (or term) precisely in terms of existing symbolism. An example is:

** $\mathfrak{M}\{\text{cat}\}:\mathfrak{M}\{\text{gato}\}$

where the term on the left is stated as having the same intension as the term on the right. The second method is to provide all known (or at least a number of) examples without asserting that it is a complete definition. An example might be:

** $\mathbf{C}\{\text{real-number}\}\supset(\mathbf{C}\{\text{rational-number}\}\cup\mathbf{C}\{\text{irrational-number}\})$

The former is an explicit definition; the latter is an implicit definition. The former is the "intensive" form; the latter is the "extensive" form. The latter is also called definition by enumeration.

For further comparison, an intensive definition of "young person" might be

S_1 $\mathfrak{M}\{\text{young person}\}:\Delta[\mathfrak{M}\{\text{boy}\},\mathfrak{M}\{\text{girl}\}]$

Observe that this is a complete definition if "boy" and "girl" have been defined previously. An extensive definition might be approximated by

** $\mathbf{C}\{\text{young people}\}\supset\mathbf{C}\{\text{boys}\}$

** $\mathbf{C}\{\text{young people}\}\supset\mathbf{C}\{\text{girls}\}$

** $\mathbf{C}\{\text{young people}\}\subset\mathbf{C}\{\text{people}\}$

or we might say

S_2 $\mathbf{C}\{\text{young people}\}\equiv(\mathbf{C}\{\text{boys}\}\cup\mathbf{C}\{\text{girls}\}$

Observe that S_1 is a statement about those concepts or attributes which are common to a boy and a girl, these attributes being the attributes of a young person. On the other hand, S_2 is a statement about populations of concepts.

We must be aware that a definition is not an axiom or a hypothesis. We may, for example, establish a hypothesis that a particular element is a member of class $\mathbf{C}_1$. Such a hypothesis is not a definition, even though it has the same form as an extensive form of definition; it is adding (or perhaps adding) new information. This is the important point: a definition adds no new information or concepts; it merely defines a symbol or intension in terms of existing symbols or intensions.

Explicit definitions provide us with a tool which is used almost continuously in

Logic. The Rule of Substitution which is formulated by many writers is merely the replacement of symbolism from one side of an explicit definition by the symbolism from the other side of that definition. The Rules of Substitution will be explicitly referenced herein, in intension, extension and number.

Our dictionary defines the word, definition, as "a declaration of the signification". Another says that it is an explanation of meaning. This latter definition might be misconstrued in many cases where we define a word or other symbol by an identity statement but without other explicit explanation, merely as a short code to replace a more elaborate but frequently occurring structure. This may occur in algebraic statements, in statements involving classes and in English. A common example in the English language of the United States is the name which is often a distorted acronym or mnemonic and which is assigned to a Federal project, military or civilian. "NASA" is such a name. However, the newly defined symbol then acquires the intension of the structure which it replaces, and so such a statement is still an equivalence of intensions.

As a result we observe that a noun or descriptor is a symbol which represents the aggregation of statements (one or more) which "define" that term. This statement, of course, points up again the circularity which is inherent in a dictionary or other device of definition, since that noun is defined in terms of other nouns through the aggregation of statements. But the intension of the symbol (noun) is the intension of the assertion, or aggregation of assertions, which defines the symbol.

There is another type of definition which is useless in written communications but is very important in face-to-face communications. This is Ostensive Definition which is a partially non-verbal definition. The word which is being defined must be spoken or written. Thus, in complete form we have a copulative sentence in which the subject is the demonstrative pronoun, that, and "that" is equated to the word being defined. For example, we might point at the animal and simultaneously assert

** That is a platypus

thereby defining the word, platypus, to a degree. This definition is not, however, presented in words. Therefore its intension is a mental interpretation of a visual image.

We mentioned above the circularity of definitions in a dictionary. In such a situation, an "artificial" language must resort to a metalanguage for its foundations. Yet each "living" language which is in use has not been derived from a metalanguage. Rather, each modern language has a spoken form, and we use ostensive definition in conjunction with the spoken form. Ostensive definition provides a "starting point" from which these languages can be developed.

Herein, those definitions for which the statement number is prefixed by an E are definitions of terms or phrases in English. They provide a form of reference between our developed symbols and the symbols of our English language. Note that our intent is that the "E" statements do not define the symbols in terms of English but, rather, define the English in terms of our symbols. Those statements for which the statement number is prefixed by a D are definitions of symbols in our system. "E" statements may be explicit definitions or pieces of an enumeration. All "D" statements will be explicit definitions.

We must note here that identity of the class or metric symbols for a pair of entities does not necessarily imply identity of the related intensions. However, we shall postulate that equivalence of intension includes equivalence of extension and equivalence of metrics. This will be stated in symbolic form in later chapters. This is in agreement with Carnap (6,145). We shall also treat as equivalent in use, in all respects except symbolic, the definiendum and the definiens. Definienda herein include the A, C, D, E and P tags or labels which we apply to the assertions. These labels, including the temporary use of S_α, are nouns, each of which represents the corresponding assertion, and, as stated above, the intension of the tag is the intension of the assertion.

A few situations arise in the work herein where symbols are used before definition. These are of two types:

1. In the early stages of definition of intension some circularity is necessary.
2. For continuity of thought some assertions which use the singular inclusion (ϵ) are included in Sections prior to the definition of the symbol. To be entirely correct these instances should all be moved to where they follow the definition of that symbol; they could be moved, except for the possible loss of continuity.

These deviations are specifically noted when used.

2.5.2. Axioms

The dictionary defines the word, axiom, as "a self-evident proposition" or as "a universally conceded principle". It defines the word, postulate, as "a fundamental condition". An axiom can not be "proved"; it is a piece of the "foundation" of our structure of logic. By changing the "foundation" (by postulating different axioms) we can build a different structure. However, the axioms which we postulate in this text will be those which are necessary for "conventional" results. But we might also observe that, where one person postulates an axiom X and then derives a theorem Y from it, another person might be able to postulate Y as an axiom and derive theorem X from it. That is, there may be a degree of interchangeability of roles between axioms and theorems, some of which will produce no substantive change in other results. Once chosen, axioms are the statements which comprise the philosophy of Logic; this philosophy of Logic then becomes a subclass of our philosophy $\mathfrak{P}$.

Axioms will be denoted by an "A" followed by arabic decimal digits.

Postulates may occur as temporary conditions during a discussion and will be denoted merely as another "S" assertion.

2.5.3. Theorems

Our dictionary defines the word, theorem, as a statement that has been proved. We will define the word slightly differently here as "a statement which has been deduced from axioms, definitions and other theorems". In some instances our definition may be more restrictive than that of the dictionary.

Theorems will be denoted by a "P" followed by arabic decimal digits.

Within the symbolic language which we develop one prior axiom or constraint is needed. All calculi need a constraint of this type.

** In deductions, only those A, D or P statements may be used which have previously been stated in this calculus.

This rule would be automatically ensured in our deductions if we did not have recourse to the English language. Deductions within English do, on occasion, inadvertently utilize symbols or axioms or theorems which have not been previously developed in the discourse.

2.5.4. Hypotheses

A hypothesis is a conjecture which is assumed but which is not as yet accepted. It might be viewed as a tentatively accepted axiom for purposes of the discussions involved in its evaluation or confirmation. The results of such confirmation determine its acceptance, modification or rejection. Hypotheses are discussed in greater depth in Section 8.

2.5.5. Auxiliary Assertions

These assertions are included only for convenience. In themselves they are of no importance; their purpose is to be the statements which appear as clauses in A, D or P assertions. For example, a theorem might be a conditional statement relating a pair of these auxiliary assertions, and the reference number of each auxiliary assertion would then appear in the statement of that theorem.

Auxiliary assertions will be denoted by a "C" followed by arabic decimal digits.

2.6. Cross-Reference

Underlying axioms will, as stated above, be denoted by A_α, and, for example, A3.07 will always refer to the same assertion wherever it is referenced in this paper. In like manner D_α will have invariant reference. However, assertions referenced only within a discussion will be denoted by S_α, as we stated for postulates, above. Thus, S_1 may occur as a symbol in many discussions, but in each discussion it will only apply to an assertion within that discussion, not to the other uses of that symbol.

We shall also use the symbol $\mathfrak{M}_\mu$ or $\mathbf{C}_\mu$ as an undefined concept or class in several discussions; the appearance and value, if any, in one subsection is unrelated to those in any other subsection.

3. INTENSION

We have defined intension as the composite of attributes or characteristics of the object or concept denoted by the descriptor. In a sense it is the concept which is represented by the descriptor. Some call it the connotation. When we discuss a particular animal we may confuse the concept of the animal with the physical entity. But discussions can only be about concepts, even when we are standing beside the physical entity. Touch, sight, smell, hearing and taste are part of a philosophy of physiology and physics, and such a philosophy may define "reality" for us, but our discussions are still about concepts. The situation appears to be somewhat different with those quantities which exist only in our minds. For example, we speak of electrons and photons so frequently that these entities are almost as familiar to us as a pet dog. But these entities only exist in our minds as pieces of a reasonably comprehensive and consistent physical theory. They are concepts which can not be directly observed, but the concepts are highly correlated with our "secondary" forms of observation. Thus, our concept, the electron, has attributes and characteristics; there is an intension associated with the descriptor, electron. And so, to refer back to our opening sentence here, intension is represented by a symbol which is a descriptor (a noun or a phrase which acts as a noun).

All sentences are, or can be restated as, one or more assertions. We have said that a noun denotes a particular concept. An assertion then provides a variation (such as, e.g., specialization or combination) of that concept. The sentence structure is the means of stating or presenting that variation, but the result is again a symbolism which represents the new or varied intension. A symbolic assertion (in English or some other calculus of symbols) which states that a specified element is a member of a given class is merely part of the definition of the concept represented by the symbol. Thus, as asserted in Section 2.5.1, each noun or descriptor merely represents the aggregation of assertions which define that symbol. In this view the meaning of a sentence and the meaning of a word which it defines are synonomous. And as we discuss in Section 9, each piece of the structures (sentences) and their parts which accomplish this have been analyzed and labeled.

The sentence, "The boy is running", requires a statement of definition by intensions and an assertion by classes. Each sentence (the definition and the assertion) carries or has an implied label. The label is a noun. Therefore, the intension of the sentence is represented by that label. As a result, we will be concerned with the intension of sentences (which we discuss in terms of their labels) as well as the intension of more simple descriptors. This is not a new concept. Some define the intension of an assertion as the proposition expressed by the assertion, and thus a propositional calculus can be a calculus of intensions. More frequently, however, it is viewed as a calculus of the truth-values of intensions. We discuss truth-values in Section 7.2.1 et seq.

Our use of intension and extension, above, places our discussions herein in a specific theory of meaning. Perhaps we must recognize the psychological or emotional aspect of language in common usage. This is discussed in, e.g., Alston (1,47) concerning the "emotive meaning" as opposed to the "cognitive meaning". We postulate that "emotive meaning" has no place in scientific or logical discussions except as a subject of discussion.

One of the common approaches to the analysis of a statement is to consider it to be composed of a subject and a predicate. The predicate may be a simple intransitive verb or it may be a lengthy clause. As we have stated before, the predicate modifies the subject; it "narrows" or "expands" the intension of the subject. That most verbs connote intension is reflected in all languages. Most verbs are formed from nouns, and often it is by the addition of, for example, a suffix, as we frequently do in English. In other languages the structure which is used as a noun in one situation is also used as a verb in another, the difference being only that of position in the sentence. See Tozzer (27,35) regarding Mayan in this respect. Each verb can, therefore, be defined in terms of and replaced by the copula and descriptors.

Repeating what we delineate elsewhere, each adjective represents a statement (which may be an aggregation) which defines the adjective in terms of known descriptors. Each sentence thus becomes an aggregation of copulative relationships of descriptors, an aggregation of elementary sentences. These elementary sentences are relationships of either intensions or classes or numbers.

With respect to intensions of descriptors, both those of simple and those of elaborate structure, we shall discuss each of a class of relationships. This class of relationships includes: identity, inclusion, conjunction (coincidence), conjunction (aggregate), exclusion, disjunction (exclusive), disjunction (inclusive). We shall note that other relationships exist and seem to be necessary in normal languages, while Traditional Logic has been limited to the use of these relationships. Such a limitation does not seem to cause any problems other than, perhaps, an expansion in the number of assertions required for accurate presentation.

Assertions in our notation for intensions will be constructed of nouns and morphemes. These will now be discussed.

3.1. Nouns

As stated in the last Chapter,

E2.02 $\mathfrak{M}\{d_\alpha\}$ is the symbol for the intensions of descriptors d_α

In this Section we are discussing intension and the symbolism for intension. For convenience of notation, in many cases we shall use

** $\mathfrak{M}_\alpha : \mathfrak{M}\{d_\alpha\}$

or, as stated in Section 2.5.1,

** $\mathfrak{M}_\alpha : \mathfrak{M}\{S_\alpha\}$

where S_α is the label of an assertion and $\mathfrak{M}_\alpha$ is the intension of that assertion. We might again question what the symbol $\mathfrak{M}\{d_\alpha\}$ can accomplish that the designator d_α does not. In addition to keeping ambiguity to a minimum, the former symbolism allows us to discuss situations in which the intensions are identical but the symbols are different. For example, we may equate the word, tabby, with the word, housecat; as a statement of intension this is allowable, but the symbols (tabby; housecat) are certainly not equivalent, such as from the standpoint of our computers.

We must also note that, for a given designator d_α, two different people may have two different concepts, $\mathfrak{M}_1\{d_\alpha\}$ and $\mathfrak{M}_2\{d_\alpha\}$. With our notation such differences can be represented. However, such a situation makes the above form invalid as a definition. We shall continue to use this form merely for the ease of symbolism which it allows, but we must always keep in mind that it is not a completely valid representation of "living" languages. Herein, if multiple definitions of the same symbol arise we shall explicitly state the differences.

We must comment that, just as "living" languages frequently assign multiple intensions to the same symbol, we find the languages of science often guilty of the same confusion. Thus we must be restrained in our criticism.

As in any language which is being used to discuss itself (that language), questions or ambiguities may arise. Consider the form, $\mathfrak{M}\{\mathfrak{M}_\alpha\}$, which appears, for example, in C3.01 below. This term represents the intension of the symbol $\mathfrak{M}_\alpha$. If, as we discussed above, $\mathfrak{M}_\alpha$ is the intension which is associated with descriptor d_α then here we are talking about the intension of a symbol which represents the intension of another symbol. Therefore, as a further specification we postulate that

A3.01 $\mathfrak{M}\{\mathfrak{M}_\alpha\}:\mathfrak{M}_\alpha$

To a degree this defines $\mathfrak{M}_\alpha$; the other axioms which we discuss also define characteristics of $\mathfrak{M}_\alpha$. Therefore we say

D3.01 $\mathfrak{M}\{\mathfrak{M}\}:\nabla[\nabla[\nabla[\mathfrak{M}\{A3.01\},\mathfrak{M}\{A3.17\}],$
$\nabla[\mathfrak{M}\{D3.02\},\mathfrak{M}\{D3.03\}]],\mathfrak{M}\{D3.04\}]$

3.2. Morphemes

Morphemes are discussed in more detail in Section 9. They include conjunctions, prepositions, articles, negation and copulas.

3.2.1. Verbs

The verbs used here are particular applications of the copula, to be, as it appears in common usage. As we mention in Section 9.4.1, the need for a copula as an explicit symbol in a sentence is questionable, especially if its interpretation is precisely defined. The verbs which appear in discussions of intension are those of identity and inclusion. But, as we shall show below, the latter is merely a special case of the former. Thus, our sentences (which might be called equations by some students) consist of two descriptors, simple or complex, without further symbolism other than grouping symbols and a symbol to show the point of division. We shall use a colon as that symbol; though it is not truly necessary, because the forms are self-delineating, it does assist in more immediate recognition.

The symbol, tomcat, in English and the symbol, gato, in Spanish represent the same concept. To state the identity of intensions of these symbols we postulate an identity format.

** $\mathfrak{M}\{\text{tomcat}\}:\mathfrak{M}\{\text{gato}\}$

This concept of identity means only that the two intensions being compared are identical. The term does not imply that the right side is the only reformulation of the left side (and vice versa).

This identity is stated as

A3.02 $\mathfrak{M}_\alpha:\mathfrak{M}_\alpha$

that is, the intension on the left side is (i.e., is identical to) the intension on the right. This statement is not trivial. In many of our symbolic systems (languages) the symbols on the left side of the "equation" are not precisely the same as the symbols on the right side. Consider the case of

** $(x^2\text{-}y^2)=(x+y)(x\text{-}y)$

The symbols on the two sides are not identical, but the intensions are the same. Therefore, we use the equality sign and "understand" that the intensions are the same, that is, that the two sides are "identical".

Assertion A3.02 is often classified as being reflexive.

E3.01 $\mathfrak{M}\{\text{identity format}\}\epsilon\mathbf{C}\{\text{reflexive relationships}\}$

As a note of explanation, this last assertion is a statement about class and member, and the symbols will not be defined until later Sections. It is included here only for the purpose of showing the statement of classification in proximity to the operation itself, rather than at some later point. Since the statement is made only for convenience and since later work is not dependent on it this particular irregularity will be continued throughout.

To repeat, this symbolism of identity can be used to define a symbol in terms of other symbols. Thus,

C3.01 $\mathfrak{M}\{\mathfrak{M}_\alpha\}:\mathfrak{M}\{\mathfrak{M}_\beta\}$

C3.02 Intension $\mathfrak{M}_\alpha$ is identical to intension $\mathfrak{M}_\beta$

E3.02 $\mathfrak{M}\{\text{C3.01}\}:\mathfrak{M}\{\text{C3.02}\}$

We observe here that, to be redundant, C3.01 is merely an example of A3.02.

We further postulate that

C3.03 $\mathfrak{M}\{\mathfrak{M}_\beta\}:\mathfrak{M}\{\mathfrak{M}_\alpha\}$

A3.03 $\mathfrak{M}\{\text{C3.01}\}:\mathfrak{M}\{\text{C3.03}\}$

This assertion is of use in symbolic manipulations as well as in the definition of identity. We might note that this assertion is also classified.

E3.03 $\mathfrak{M}\{\text{identity format}\}\in\mathbf{C}\{\text{symmetric relationships}\}$

3.2.2. Conjunctions

Conjunctions, as a class, join assertions or terms together. The joined terms may be any part of speech discussed in Chapter 9; the only requirement is that the joined terms be of like kind. The conjunction used most frequently in classical Logic has been the word, and. "Or" occurs nearly as frequently. However, from the standpoint of Logic each of these words can have at least two different meanings in different usages.

Here we discuss two uses of the word, and, and define them in terms of the axioms which specify their syntactic relationships. Most of these relationships are identical between the two definitions, D3.02 and D3.03. Compare the following pairs of axioms for verification of this statement: A3.04 and A3.08; A3.05 and A3.09; A3.07 and A3.11; A3.06 and A3.10. To define the unique characteristics of each we must also refer to the axioms of distribution, A3.15 and A3.16, which are not symmetric in the use of these symbols. This forces us to define these two symbols together.

We assert here that a conjunction of intensions is an intension; therefore, as special cases of A3.01 we have

C3.04 $\mathfrak{M}\{\nabla[\mathfrak{M}_\alpha,\mathfrak{M}_\beta]\}:\nabla[\mathfrak{M}_\alpha,\mathfrak{M}_\beta]$

C3.05 $\mathfrak{M}\{\Delta[\mathfrak{M}_\alpha,\mathfrak{M}_\beta]\}:\Delta[\mathfrak{M}_\alpha,\mathfrak{M}_\beta]$

3.2.2.1. Conjunction (Aggregate) of Intension

The "broadening" of a concept can be accomplished by the conjunction (aggregate) of this concept with another. This type of conjunction is one use of the word, and. The representation of the conjunction (aggregate) of $\mathfrak{M}_1$ and $\mathfrak{M}_2$ to produce the broader concept $\mathfrak{M}_4$ is:

** $\mathfrak{M}\{\nabla[\mathfrak{M}_1,\mathfrak{M}_2]\}:\mathfrak{M}\{\mathfrak{M}_4\}$

For example, the aggregate conjunction $\nabla[\mathfrak{M}\{\text{boy}\},\mathfrak{M}\{\text{girl}\}]$ is a broader concept than that of boy or girl or of young person. However, it includes each of these. As is evidenced by our definitions in this chapter, this type of conjunction is used to bring together independent concepts as may be necessary for some purpose of discussion.

E3.04 $\mathfrak{M}\{\nabla[\mathfrak{M}_\alpha,\mathfrak{M}_\beta]\}:\mathfrak{M}\{\text{the aggregation of concepts } \mathfrak{M}_\alpha \text{ and } \mathfrak{M}_\beta\}$

We now assert that

A3.04 $\mathfrak{M}\{\nabla[\mathfrak{M}_\alpha,\mathfrak{M}_\beta]\}:\mathfrak{M}\{\nabla[\mathfrak{M}_\beta,\mathfrak{M}_\alpha]\}$

This asserts that change in sequence of the internal symbols is unimportant in the use of this conjunction. Thus

E3.05 $\mathfrak{M}\{\text{conjunction } \nabla\} \epsilon \mathbf{C}\{\text{commutative relationships}\}$

To further define the conjunction we state that

A3.05 $\mathfrak{M}\{\nabla[\nabla[\mathfrak{M}_\alpha,\mathfrak{M}_\beta],\mathfrak{M}_\gamma]\}:\mathfrak{M}\{\nabla[\mathfrak{M}_\alpha,\nabla[\mathfrak{M}_\beta,\mathfrak{M}_\gamma]]\}$

This axiom states that groupings of sequences of this conjunction are interchangeable. This leads us to say

E3.06 $\mathfrak{M}\{\text{conjunction } \nabla\} \epsilon \mathbf{C}\{\text{associative relationships}\}$

The inclusion of an intension $\mathfrak{M}_\beta$ as a subconcept of another intension $\mathfrak{M}_\alpha$ can be represented by:

C3.06 $\mathfrak{M}_\alpha:\nabla[\mathfrak{M}_\beta,\mathfrak{M}_\mu]$

Here we state that $\mathfrak{M}_\alpha$ is composed of $\mathfrak{M}_\beta$ and some undefined concept $\mathfrak{M}_\mu$. This form is important in deductive logic, where S_α implies S_β. Using an analogy, we might state this as the situation where $\mathfrak{M}_\alpha$ contains $\mathfrak{M}_\beta$. The dictionary defines the verb, to imply, as: to indicate or suggest without express statement; to involve or require as a necessary condition; to involve logically. Logical implication is formally stated in the conditional form, "If ... then ...", though in actual discourse even the form may be implied. Form C3.06 above thus states that either

** $\mathfrak{M}_\alpha$ implies $\mathfrak{M}_\beta$ in light of aggregation $\mathfrak{M}_\mu$

or

** $\mathfrak{M}_\beta$ and aggregation $\mathfrak{M}_\mu$ are equivalent to $\mathfrak{M}_\alpha$

In each theorem, later, one or the other type of statement will occur. Therefore, we state

E3.07 $\mathfrak{M}\{\text{C3.06}\}:\mathfrak{M}\{\text{logical implication}\}$

The subjunctive mood is another instance of the use of implication in which the hypothesis is not fact. This will be discussed later when we discuss truth-values.

It might be observed that it has been customary to assign a separate word (verb form) to represent inclusion. For example, see Section 5.3.2 concerning classes. Our point here is that such a verb form is logically unnecessary, and in this instance (intension) it would not actually provide any additional convenience of symbolic operation. Thus we shall proceed in the manner stated above.

We further assert that

C3.07 $\mathfrak{M}\{\nabla[\mathfrak{M}_\alpha,\mathfrak{M}_\gamma]\}:\mathfrak{M}\{\nabla[\mathfrak{M}_\beta,\mathfrak{M}_\gamma]\}$

A3.06 $\mathfrak{M}\{\text{C3.01}\}:\mathfrak{M}\{\text{C3.07}\}$

Aggregation of a concept with itself (repetition) produces only that concept, from the standpoint of Logic.

A3.07 $\mathfrak{M}\{\nabla[\mathfrak{M}_\alpha,\mathfrak{M}_\alpha]\}:\mathfrak{M}\{\mathfrak{M}_\alpha\}$

We might recognize the fact, however, that in the common usage of many languages repitition is used for emphasis.

3.2.2.2. Conjunction (Coincident) of Intension

The "improvement" or "narrowing" or "sharpening" of a concept is done by the conjunction (coincident) of this concept with another related concept. This type of conjunction is another use of the word, and. The representation of this type of conjunction of $\mathfrak{M}_1$ and $\mathfrak{M}_2$ to produce the narrower concept $\mathfrak{M}_3$ is:

** $\mathfrak{M}\{\Delta[\mathfrak{M}_1,\mathfrak{M}_2]\}:\mathfrak{M}\{\mathfrak{M}_3\}$

As previously mentioned,

** $\mathfrak{M}\{\Delta[\mathfrak{M}\{\text{boy}\},\mathfrak{M}\{\text{girl}\}]\}:\mathfrak{M}\{\mathfrak{M}\{\text{young-person}\}\}$

that is, the attributes of a "young person" occur in either boys or girls.

In more formal statements,

E3.08 $\mathfrak{M}\{\Delta[\mathfrak{M}_\alpha,\mathfrak{M}_\beta]\}:\mathfrak{M}\{$the coincident portion of intensions $\mathfrak{M}_\alpha$ and $\mathfrak{M}_\beta\}$

Again, with this conjunction, sequence of the internal symbols is unimportant.

A3.08 $\mathfrak{M}\{\Delta[\mathfrak{M}_\alpha,\mathfrak{M}_\beta]\}:\mathfrak{M}\{\Delta[\mathfrak{M}_\beta,\mathfrak{M}_\alpha]\}$

E3.09 $\mathfrak{M}\{\text{conjunction } \Delta\}\in\mathbf{C}\{\text{commutative relationships}\}$

and

A3.09 $\mathfrak{M}\{\Delta[\Delta[\mathfrak{M}_\alpha,\mathfrak{M}_\beta],\mathfrak{M}_\gamma]\}:\mathfrak{M}\{\Delta[\mathfrak{M}_\alpha,\Delta[\mathfrak{M}_\beta,\mathfrak{M}_\gamma]]\}$

E3.10 $\mathfrak{M}\{\text{conjunction } \Delta\}\in\mathbf{C}\{\text{associative relationships}\}$

In addition,

C3.08 $\mathfrak{M}\{\Delta[\mathfrak{M}_\alpha,\mathfrak{M}_\gamma]\}:\mathfrak{M}\{\Delta[\mathfrak{M}_\beta,\mathfrak{M}_\gamma]\}$

A3.10 $\mathfrak{M}\{\text{C3.01}\}:\mathfrak{M}\{\text{C3.08}\}$

Furthermore, coincidence of a concept with itself produces only that concept.

A3.11 $\mathfrak{M}\{\Delta[\mathfrak{M}_\alpha,\mathfrak{M}_\alpha]\}:\mathfrak{M}\{\mathfrak{M}_\alpha\}$

In addition, the coincident portion is included in each of the original concepts, as stated in C3.11 below.

3.2.2.3. Applications of Conjunctions

We now proceed to another important assertion.

C3.09 $\mathfrak{M}\{\mathfrak{M}_\beta\}:\mathfrak{M}\{\mathfrak{M}_\gamma\}$

C3.10 $\mathfrak{M}\{\mathfrak{M}_\alpha\}:\mathfrak{M}\{\mathfrak{M}_\gamma\}$

A3.12 $\Delta[\mathfrak{M}\{\text{C3.01}\},\mathfrak{M}\{\text{C3.09}\}]:\mathfrak{M}\{\text{C3.10}\}$

This is viewed by many as

E3.11 $\mathfrak{M}\{\text{A3.12}\}\in\mathbf{C}\{\text{Rules of Substitution}\}$

In their view $\mathfrak{M}_\gamma$ is "substituted" for $\mathfrak{M}_\beta$ from C3.09 into C3.01 so as to produce C3.10. Whether it is viewed as substitution or viewed as merely the application of an axiom is not of great concern; the axiom or rule, as the choice may be, is necessary for deduction.

To cite a formality, we may observe that A3.12 also provides a classification.

E3.12 $\mathfrak{M}\{\text{identity format}\}\in\mathbf{C}\{\text{transitive relationships}\}$

One source of possible confusion in this and future sections on verbs is a dual definition of the adjective, transitive. In the discussion of syntax of language the term, transitive, refers to a verb which requires a direct object; in mathematics it denotes a relationship among three or more descriptors using two or more copulas. For example, see E3.18 below. We must apologize for perpetuating this situation.

As a Rule of Substitution, we can see that A3.12 is limited to usage in pure identities; if the symbol which is to be replaced is one term in a conjunction then A3.12 provides no means of accomplishment. For this we need an additional assertion for each type of conjunction.

A3.13 $\Delta[\mathfrak{M}\{\nabla[\mathfrak{M}_{\alpha},\mathfrak{M}_{\beta}]\},\mathfrak{M}\{\text{C3.09}\}]:\mathfrak{M}\{\nabla[\mathfrak{M}_{\alpha},\mathfrak{M}_{\gamma}]\}$

E3.13 $\mathfrak{M}\{\text{A3.13}\}\in\mathbf{C}\{\text{Rules of Substitution}\}$

A3.14 $\Delta[\mathfrak{M}\{\Delta[\mathfrak{M}_{\alpha},\mathfrak{M}_{\beta}]\},\mathfrak{M}\{\text{C3.09}\}]:\mathfrak{M}\{\Delta[\mathfrak{M}_{\alpha},\mathfrak{M}_{\gamma}]\}$

E3.14 $\mathfrak{M}\{\text{A3.14}\}\in\mathbf{C}\{\text{Rules of Substitution}\}$

Further relationships between the two conjunctions are the distributive relationships.

A3.15 $\mathfrak{M}\{\Delta[\mathfrak{M}_{\alpha},\nabla[\mathfrak{M}_{\beta},\mathfrak{M}_{\gamma}]]\}:\mathfrak{M}\{\nabla[\Delta[\mathfrak{M}_{\alpha},\mathfrak{M}_{\beta}],\Delta[\mathfrak{M}_{\alpha},\mathfrak{M}_{\gamma}]]\}$

A3.16 $\mathfrak{M}\{\nabla[\mathfrak{M}_{\alpha},\Delta[\mathfrak{M}_{\beta},\mathfrak{M}_{\gamma}]]\}:\mathfrak{M}\{\Delta[\nabla[\mathfrak{M}_{\alpha},\mathfrak{M}_{\beta}],\nabla[\mathfrak{M}_{\alpha},\mathfrak{M}_{\gamma}]]\}$

Thus we can define aggregate conjunction by

D3.02 $\mathfrak{M}\{\nabla\}:\Delta[\mathfrak{M}_{\nabla},\Delta[\mathfrak{M}\{\text{A3.15}\},\mathfrak{M}\{\text{A3.16}\}]]$

where

** $\mathfrak{M}\{\mathfrak{M}_{\nabla}\}:\Delta[\Delta[\mathfrak{M}\{\text{A3.04}\},\mathfrak{M}\{\text{A3.05}\}],\mathfrak{M}_{\nabla 1}]$

** $\mathfrak{M}\{\mathfrak{M}_{\nabla 1}\}:\Delta[\Delta[\mathfrak{M}\{\text{A3.06}\},\mathfrak{M}\{\text{A3.07}\}],\mathfrak{M}\{\text{A3.13}\}]$

and we can define coincident conjunction by

D3.03 $\mathfrak{M}\{\Delta\}:\Delta[\mathfrak{M}_{\Delta},\Delta[\mathfrak{M}\{\text{A3.15}\},\mathfrak{M}\{\text{A3.16}\}]]$

where

** $\mathfrak{M}\{\mathfrak{M}_{\Delta}\}:\Delta[\Delta[\mathfrak{M}\{\text{A3.08}\},\mathfrak{M}\{\text{A3.09}\}],\mathfrak{M}_{\Delta 1}]$

** $\mathfrak{M}\{\mathfrak{M}_{\Delta 1}\}:\Delta[\Delta[\mathfrak{M}\{\text{A3.10}\},\mathfrak{M}\{\text{A3.11}\}],\mathfrak{M}\{\text{A3.14}\}]$

In addition, we can also form a definition of the identity of intensions.

D3.04 $\mathfrak{M}\{\text{identity-format}\}:\Delta[\Delta[\mathfrak{M}\{\text{A3.02}\},\mathfrak{M}\{\text{A3.03}\}],\mathfrak{M}\{\text{A3.12}\}]$

An additional rule of substitution must be stated since it appears as a form in some theorems.

A3.17 $\Delta[\mathfrak{M}\{\mathfrak{M}_{\alpha}\},\mathfrak{M}\{\text{C3.01}\}]:\mathfrak{M}\{\mathfrak{M}_{\beta}\}$

Thus,

E3.15 $\mathfrak{M}\{\text{A3.17}\}\in\mathbf{C}\{\text{Rules of Substitution}\}$

3.2.2.4. Exclusion of Intension

Exclusion of an intension is the omission of that part of an intension which is included in another specified intension. In a sense it is the "opposite" of the coincident conjunction of the two intensions. Many discussions have used negation of a concept as a concept, but the complete negative of a concept seems to be unbounded or undefined, as discussed in Section 3.2.3, below. This "limited" negation, however, is a defined intension, even if null.

We shall use

C3.11 $\mathfrak{M}\{\mathfrak{M}_\alpha\}:\mathfrak{M}\{\nabla[\Delta[\mathfrak{M}_\alpha,\mathfrak{M}_\beta],\blacksquare[\mathfrak{M}_\alpha,\mathfrak{M}_\beta]]\}$

Note that this is also an assertion about the whole of M_α and its parts. The first term is the coincidence of $\mathfrak{M}_\alpha$ and $\mathfrak{M}_\beta$. The second term is the remainder of $\mathfrak{M}_\alpha$. We must take care that we do not interpret the second term as being $\mathfrak{M}_\alpha$ without the "occurrance" of $\mathfrak{M}_\beta$; occurrance is observed truth, but here we are only concerned with intension. We notice also that C3.11 by itself does not uniquely define the term $\blacksquare[\mathfrak{M}_\alpha,\mathfrak{M}_\beta]$; a restriction on the term is also needed. This restriction is that the two terms in C3.11 are independent. The word, independent, is defined in E5.25 later.

C3.12 $\Delta[\Delta[\mathfrak{M}_\alpha,\mathfrak{M}_\beta],\blacksquare[\mathfrak{M}_\alpha,\mathfrak{M}_\beta]]:\mathfrak{O}$

This assertion uses a symbol $\mathfrak{O}$ which is defined in D3.06. Thus, more properly the conjunction, exclusion, should be defined after the descriptor, null intension, but we include "exclusion" here with the other morphemes merely for purposes of continuity of the subject. Thus we will define the symbol $\blacksquare$ by

D3.05 $\mathfrak{M}\{\blacksquare\}:\Delta[\mathfrak{M}\{\text{C3.11}\},\mathfrak{M}\{\text{C3.12}\}]$

E3.16 $\mathfrak{M}\{\blacksquare[\mathfrak{M}_\alpha,\mathfrak{M}_\beta]\}:\mathfrak{M}\{\mathfrak{M}_\alpha$ excluding any and all of $\mathfrak{M}_\beta\}$

Here we should state that this conjunction is a version of the English negative conjunction, and not; the statement, $\blacksquare[\mathfrak{M}\{d_1\},\mathfrak{M}\{d_2\}]$, frequently is stated as, "d_1 and not d_2" , in the vernacular.

3.2.3. Negation

As we discuss in Section 3.3.2 it might be possible to establish an $\mathfrak{M}_I$ as the aggregation of all $\mathfrak{M}_\alpha$ for any α. Having such an $\mathfrak{M}_I$ we then might define

** $\mathfrak{M}\{\blacksquare[\mathfrak{M}_I,\mathfrak{M}_\alpha]\}:\mathfrak{M}\{\text{not-}\mathfrak{M}_\alpha\}$

Though not-d_α, not-S_α and not-$\mathfrak{M}_\alpha$ are discussed frequently in the literature, such an aggregation of almost all intensions, true or false, would seem to be awkward to use and of little actual utility, as mentioned in the referenced Section.

3.2.4. Disjunction

Selection from alternative concepts is accomplished by the use of disjunction or, more properly, disjunctive conjunction. These alternatives may or may not be entirely independent; they may or may not be mutually exclusive. And in common usage of the language we may intend either inclusive or exclusive disjunction while, because we are using the same words for each, our audience is not sure which was intended.

In the definition of disjunction there is a requirement for the concepts of class and number. Thus, disjunctions will be developed later in Section 5.6.

3.3. Identity Elements

The term, identity element, is a misnomer in that here we are not discussing elements of a set but, rather, intensions which, in conjunction with another, leave that other intension unchanged.

3.3.1. Descriptor, Null Intension

Our definition is that the null intension is the "identity element" for the conjunction (aggregate).

C3.13 $\mathfrak{M}\{\nabla[\mathfrak{M}_\alpha,\mathfrak{O}]\}:\mathfrak{M}\{\mathfrak{M}_\alpha\}$

D3.06 $\mathfrak{M}\{\mathfrak{O}\}:\mathfrak{M}\{C3.13\}$

A question might be raised about whether this definition can be applicable for all $\mathfrak{M}_\alpha$; for our definition of $\mathfrak{M}_\alpha$ we shall use this definition of $\mathfrak{O}$.

We further note, the null intension can be viewed as the result of a situation which produces nonsense, that is, nonsense is an absence of meaning. This situation may arise, for example, as a result of manipulations of symbolic forms.

E3.17 $\mathfrak{M}\{\mathfrak{O}\}:\mathfrak{M}\{\text{nonsense}\}$

Statements which are composed of nonsense can arise in a variety of ways. We might even say that there are forms of "logical nonsense" and "illogical nonsense". In English, one type of logical nonsense is a result of the great flexibility of our language in which we do not differentiate among the categories of sentences which are allowed. As a result we find speakers and writers mixing parts of different categories within the same sentence. Herein, as mentioned above, we shall formulate and discuss three categories of assertions: intensional, extensional, numerical. Each assertion shall be restricted to one category. However, within an assertion we can imply other assertions of different category. For example, a statement about the metric of an intension is a numerical statement, but it refers to the intensional statement which is separate. We shall use different symbolism for each category, and by this means we can minimize the type of nonsense which can arise in English by a mixture of such categories.

One type of nonsense arises in English by the improper use of a limiting adjective. Limiting adjectives are derived from nouns and, for example, a "square circle" is actually a mixture of two nouns of the same class, plane geometric figures. The adjective, square, is defined in terms of the noun, square, and by the definitions of each member the members of the class are mutually exclusive.

"Illogical nonsense" can be much more difficult to restrict. Some examples of this can result from a mixture of types of philosophy in the same clause. Using the normal definitions of words, a "blue convolution" is meaningless; "blue" is a part of our philosophy of physics while "convolution" is a part of our philosophy of logic (a type of integral in mathematics). In this area it would appear that care in formulation is the only cure. Of course, mixtures of philosophical concepts which we now categorize as nonsense might later be viewed as "creativity". We shall discuss this in a later chapter.

3.3.2. Identity Element for Conjunction (Coincident)

By the nature (i.e., definition) of this conjunction an identity element with respect to it must encompass all possible concepts such that, in coincident conjunction with any simple concept, the result is that same simple concept. If we were to attempt to define an identity element $\mathfrak{M}_I$ such that for any α

** $\mathfrak{M}\{\Delta[\mathfrak{M}_\alpha,\mathfrak{M}_I]\}:\mathfrak{M}\{\mathfrak{M}_\alpha\}$

then we can study it as we do other similar structures. A form of this type can arise in deduction occasionally, such as

C3.18 $\mathfrak{M}\{\Delta[\mathfrak{M}_\alpha,\mathfrak{M}_\beta]\}:\mathfrak{M}\{\mathfrak{M}_\beta\}$

In the next Section we develop the theorem which states,

P3.08 $\mathfrak{M}\{C3.18\}:\mathfrak{M}\{\nabla[\mathfrak{M}\{C3.06\},\mathfrak{M}_\rho]\}$

where

C3.06 $\mathfrak{M}_\alpha:\nabla[\mathfrak{M}_\beta,\mathfrak{M}_\mu]$

Thus, $\mathfrak{M}_I$ in the above structure must have the form

** $\mathfrak{M}_I:\nabla[\mathfrak{M}_\alpha,\mathfrak{M}_\mu]$

that is, it is composed of the aggregate conjunction of all possible concepts since it is a "universal" factor which would be applicable to all possible concepts. The utility of such an aggregation would seem to be non-existent. For an analogous discussion of a similar approach for classes, see Section 5.4.2.

3.4. Theorems

As stated before, theorems are assertions which have been deduced from (are included in) prior definitions, axioms and other theorems. See Chapter 6 for a more complete discussion of deduction.

3.4.1. Coincident Conjunction and Identity Element

** $\Delta[\mathfrak{M}\{C3.13\},\mathfrak{M}\{A3.13\}]:\mathfrak{M}\{S_1\}$

S_1 $\mathfrak{M}\{\nabla[\mathfrak{M}_\beta,\Phi]\}:\mathfrak{M}\{\mathfrak{M}_\beta\}$

** $\mathfrak{M}\{A3.02\}:\mathfrak{M}\{S_2\}$

S_2 $\Delta[\mathfrak{M}_\alpha,\mathfrak{M}_\beta]:\Delta[\mathfrak{M}_\alpha,\mathfrak{M}_\beta]$

** $\nabla[\nabla[\mathfrak{M}\{S_1\},\mathfrak{M}\{S_2\}],\mathfrak{M}\{A3.14\}]:\mathfrak{M}\{S_3\}$

S_3 $\Delta[\mathfrak{M}_\alpha,\nabla[\mathfrak{M}_\beta,\Phi]]:\Delta[\mathfrak{M}_\alpha,\mathfrak{M}_\beta]$

** $\nabla[\mathfrak{M}\{S_3\},\mathfrak{M}\{A3.15\}]:\mathfrak{M}\{S_4\}$

S_4 $\nabla[\Delta[\mathfrak{M}_\alpha,\mathfrak{M}_\beta],\Delta[\mathfrak{M}_\alpha,\Phi]]:\Delta[\mathfrak{M}_\alpha,\mathfrak{M}_\beta]$

Since $\Delta[\mathfrak{M}_\alpha,\mathfrak{M}_\beta]$ appears on both sides of this identity format, whether it is Φ or not, we can say

**	$\nabla[\mathfrak{M}\{S_4\},\mathfrak{M}\{C3.13\}]:\mathfrak{M}\{P3.01\}$
P3.01	$\Delta[\mathfrak{M}_\alpha,\mathfrak{O}]:\mathfrak{O}$

3.4.2. Exclusion and the Identity Element

**	$\Delta[\mathfrak{M}\{C3.20\},\Delta[\mathfrak{M}\{C3.11\},\mathfrak{M}\{P3.10\}]]:\mathfrak{M}\{S_1\}$
S_1	$\mathfrak{M}\{\mathfrak{M}_\alpha\}:\mathfrak{M}\{\nabla[\Delta[\mathfrak{M}_\alpha,\mathfrak{O}],\blacksquare[\mathfrak{M}_\alpha,\mathfrak{O}]]\}$
**	$\Delta[\mathfrak{M}\{S_1\},\Delta[\mathfrak{M}\{P3.01\},\mathfrak{M}\{A3.13\}]]:\mathfrak{M}\{S_2\}$
S_2	$\mathfrak{M}\{\mathfrak{M}_\alpha\}:\mathfrak{M}\{\nabla[\mathfrak{O},\blacksquare[\mathfrak{M}_\alpha,\mathfrak{O}]]\}$
**	$\Delta[\mathfrak{M}\{S_2\},\Delta[\mathfrak{M}\{A3.04\},\mathfrak{M}\{A3.12\}]]:\mathfrak{M}\{S_3\}$
S_3	$\mathfrak{M}\{\mathfrak{M}_\alpha\}:\mathfrak{M}\{\nabla[\blacksquare[\mathfrak{M}_\alpha,\mathfrak{O}],\mathfrak{O}]\}$
**	$\Delta[\mathfrak{M}\{S_3\},\Delta[\mathfrak{M}\{C3.13\},\mathfrak{M}\{A3.12\}]]:\mathfrak{M}\{S_4\}$
S_4	$\mathfrak{M}\{\mathfrak{M}_\alpha\}:\mathfrak{M}\{\blacksquare[\mathfrak{M}_\alpha,\mathfrak{O}]\}$
**	$\Delta[\mathfrak{M}\{S_4\},\mathfrak{M}\{A3.03\}]:\mathfrak{M}\{P3.02\}$
P3.02	$\mathfrak{M}\{\blacksquare[\mathfrak{M}_\alpha,\mathfrak{O}]\}:\mathfrak{M}\{\mathfrak{M}_\alpha\}$

Thus the null intension is the "identity element" with respect to exclusion also.

3.4.3. Transitivity of Logical Implication

We have termed C3.06 as logical implication.

C3.14	$\mathfrak{M}_\beta:\nabla[\mathfrak{M}_\gamma,\mathfrak{M}_\nu]$
S_a	$\Delta[\Delta[\mathfrak{M}\{C3.06\},\mathfrak{M}\{C3.14\}],\mathfrak{M}\{A3.13\}]:\mathfrak{M}\{S_1\}$
S_1	$\mathfrak{M}_\alpha:\nabla[\nabla[\mathfrak{M}_\gamma,\mathfrak{M}_\nu],\mathfrak{M}_\mu]$
S_b	$\Delta[\Delta[\mathfrak{M}\{S_1\},\mathfrak{M}\{A3.05\}],\mathfrak{M}\{A3.13\}]:\mathfrak{M}\{C3.15\}$
C3.15	$\mathfrak{M}_\alpha:\nabla[\mathfrak{M}_\gamma,\mathfrak{M}_\rho]$

where we have

**	$\mathfrak{M}_\rho:\nabla[\mathfrak{M}_\nu,\mathfrak{M}_\mu]$

We now combine two statements.

**	$\Delta[\Delta[\mathfrak{M}\{S_a\},\mathfrak{M}\{S_b\}],\Delta[\mathfrak{M}\{A3.14\},\mathfrak{M}\{A3.09\}]]:\mathfrak{M}\{P3.03\}$
P3.03	$\Delta[\Delta[\mathfrak{M}\{C3.06\},\mathfrak{M}\{C3.14\}],\mathfrak{M}_\eta]:\mathfrak{M}\{C3.15\}$

where

**	$\mathfrak{M}_\eta:\nabla[\mathfrak{M}\{A3.13\},\mathfrak{M}\{A3.05\}]$

This states (as a parallel to A3.12) that if S_α implies S_β and if S_β implies S_γ then, with certain conditions (axioms) which we have already accepted, S_α implies S_γ. Thus it is possible to say that

E3.18	$\mathfrak{M}$\{logical implication\}$\epsilon\mathbf{C}$\{transitive relationships\}

3.4.4. A Theorem on Aggregate Conjunction

C3.16	$\nabla[\mathfrak{M}_\alpha,\mathfrak{M}_\gamma]:\nabla[\nabla[\mathfrak{M}_\beta,\mathfrak{M}_\gamma],\mathfrak{M}_\mu]$
S_1	$\Delta[\mathfrak{M}\{C3.16\},\mathfrak{M}\{A3.04\}]:\mathfrak{M}\{S_a\}$
S_a	$\nabla[\mathfrak{M}_\alpha,\mathfrak{M}_\gamma]:\nabla[\mathfrak{M}_\mu,\nabla[\mathfrak{M}_\beta,\mathfrak{M}_\gamma]]$
S_2	$\Delta[\mathfrak{M}\{S_a\},\mathfrak{M}\{A3.05\}]:\mathfrak{M}\{S_b\}$
S_b	$\nabla[\mathfrak{M}_\alpha,\mathfrak{M}_\gamma]:\nabla[\nabla[\mathfrak{M}_\mu,\mathfrak{M}_\beta],\mathfrak{M}_\gamma]$
S_3	$\Delta[\mathfrak{M}\{S_b\},\Delta[\mathfrak{M}\{A3.04\},\mathfrak{M}\{A3.13\}]]:\mathfrak{M}\{S_c\}$

S_c $\nabla[\mathfrak{M}_\alpha,\mathfrak{M}_\gamma]:\nabla[\nabla[\mathfrak{M}_\beta,\mathfrak{M}_\mu],\mathfrak{M}_\gamma]$

S_4 $\Delta[\mathfrak{M}\{S_c\},\mathfrak{M}\{A3.06\}]:\mathfrak{M}\{C3.06\}$

** $\Delta[\Delta[\mathfrak{M}\{S_3\},\mathfrak{M}\{S_4\}],\mathfrak{M}\{A3.14\}]:\mathfrak{M}\{S_5\}$

S_5 $\Delta[\Delta[\mathfrak{M}\{S_b\},\mathfrak{M}_1],\mathfrak{M}\{A3.06\}:\mathfrak{M}\{C3.06\}$

where

** $\mathfrak{M}_1:\Delta[\mathfrak{M}\{A3.04\},\mathfrak{M}\{A3.13\}]$

** $\Delta[\mathfrak{M}\{S_5\},\mathfrak{M}\{A3.09\}]:\mathfrak{M}\{S_6\}$

S_6 $\Delta[\mathfrak{M}\{S_b\},\mathfrak{M}_2]:\mathfrak{M}\{C3.06\}$

where

** $\mathfrak{M}_2:\Delta[\mathfrak{M}_1,\mathfrak{M}\{A3.06\}]$

** $\Delta[\Delta[\mathfrak{M}\{S_2\},\mathfrak{M}\{S_6\}],\nabla[\mathfrak{M}\{A3.09\},\mathfrak{M}\{A3.14\}]]:\mathfrak{M}\{S_7\}$

S_7 $\Delta[\mathfrak{M}\{S_a\},\mathfrak{M}_3]:\mathfrak{M}\{C3.06\}$

where

** $\mathfrak{M}_3:\Delta[\mathfrak{M}\{A3.05\},\mathfrak{M}_2]$

** $\Delta[\Delta[\mathfrak{M}\{S_1\},\mathfrak{M}\{S17\}],\nabla[\mathfrak{M}\{A3.09\},\mathfrak{M}\{A3.14\}]]:\mathfrak{M}\{S_8\}$

S_8 $\Delta[\mathfrak{M}\{C3.16\},\mathfrak{M}_\rho]:\mathfrak{M}\{C3.06\}$

where

** $\mathfrak{M}_\rho:\Delta[\mathfrak{M}\{A3.04\},\mathfrak{M}_3]$

** $\Delta[\mathfrak{M}\{S_8\},\mathfrak{M}\{A3.03\}]:\mathfrak{M}\{P3.04\}$

P3.04 $\mathfrak{M}\{C3.06\}:\nabla[\mathfrak{M}\{C3.16\},\mathfrak{M}_\rho]$

This states that if $\mathfrak{M}_\alpha$ logically implies $\mathfrak{M}_\beta$ then the aggregation of $\mathfrak{M}_\alpha$ and $\mathfrak{M}_\gamma$ logically implies the aggregation of $\mathfrak{M}_\beta$ and $\mathfrak{M}_\gamma$.

3.4.5. A Further Theorem on Conjunction

** $\mathfrak{M}\{C3.11\}:\mathfrak{M}\{S_1\}$

S_1 $\mathfrak{M}\{\mathfrak{M}_\beta\}:\mathfrak{M}\{\nabla[\Delta[\mathfrak{M}_\beta,\mathfrak{M}_\alpha],\blacksquare[\mathfrak{M}_\beta,\mathfrak{M}_\alpha]]\}$

** $\Delta[\mathfrak{M}\{S_1\},\nabla[\mathfrak{M}\{A3.08\},\mathfrak{M}\{A3.13\}]]:\mathfrak{M}\{S_2\}$

S_2 $\mathfrak{M}\{\mathfrak{M}_\beta\}:\mathfrak{M}\{\nabla[\Delta[\mathfrak{M}_\alpha,\mathfrak{M}_\beta],\blacksquare[\mathfrak{M}_\beta,\mathfrak{M}_\alpha]]\}$

** $\Delta[\nabla[\mathfrak{M}\{C3.11\},\mathfrak{M}\{S_2\}],\mathfrak{M}\{A3.13\}]:\mathfrak{M}\{S_3\}$

S_3 $\mathfrak{M}\{\nabla[\mathfrak{M}_\alpha,\mathfrak{M}_\beta]\}:\mathfrak{M}\{\nabla[\nabla[\Delta[\mathfrak{M}_\alpha,\mathfrak{M}_\beta],\blacksquare[\mathfrak{M}_\alpha,\mathfrak{M}_\beta]],$
$\nabla[\Delta[\mathfrak{M}_\alpha,\mathfrak{M}_\beta],\blacksquare[\mathfrak{M}_\beta,\mathfrak{M}_\alpha]]]\}$

** $\Delta[\nabla[\mathfrak{M}\{S_3\},\mathfrak{M}\{A3.13\}],\nabla[\mathfrak{M}\{A3.04\},\mathfrak{M}\{A3.05\}]]:\mathfrak{M}\{S_4\}$

S_4 $\mathfrak{M}\{\nabla[\mathfrak{M}_\alpha,\mathfrak{M}_\beta]\}:\mathfrak{M}\{\nabla[\nabla[\Delta[\mathfrak{M}_\alpha,\mathfrak{M}_\beta],\Delta[\mathfrak{M}_\alpha,\mathfrak{M}_\beta]],$
$\nabla[\blacksquare[\mathfrak{M}_\alpha,\mathfrak{M}_\beta],\blacksquare[\mathfrak{M}_\beta,\mathfrak{M}_\alpha]]]\}$

** $\Delta[\mathfrak{M}\{S_4\},\nabla[\mathfrak{M}\{A3.07\},\mathfrak{M}\{A3.13\}]]:\mathfrak{M}\{P3.05\}$

P3.05 $\mathfrak{M}\{\nabla[\mathfrak{M}_\alpha,\mathfrak{M}_\beta]\}:\mathfrak{M}\{\nabla[\Delta[\mathfrak{M}_\alpha,\mathfrak{M}_\beta],\nabla[\blacksquare[\mathfrak{M}_\alpha,\mathfrak{M}_\beta],\blacksquare[\mathfrak{M}_\beta,\mathfrak{M}_\alpha]]]\}$

This provides another relationship among the conjunctions, which we shall use now.

** $\Delta[\mathfrak{M}\{P3.05\},\mathfrak{M}\{A3.05\}]:\mathfrak{M}\{S_5\}$

S_5 $\mathfrak{M}\{\nabla[\mathfrak{M}_\alpha,\mathfrak{M}_\beta]\}:\mathfrak{M}\{\nabla[\nabla[\Delta[\mathfrak{M}_\alpha,\mathfrak{M}_\beta],\blacksquare[\mathfrak{M}_\alpha,\mathfrak{M}_\beta]],\blacksquare[\mathfrak{M}_\beta,\mathfrak{M}_\alpha]]\}$

** $\Delta[\mathfrak{M}\{S_5\},\nabla[\mathfrak{M}\{C3.11\},\mathfrak{M}\{A3.13\}]]:\mathfrak{M}\{P3.06\}$

P3.06 $\mathfrak{M}\{\nabla[\mathfrak{M}_\alpha,\mathfrak{M}_\beta]\}:\mathfrak{M}\{\nabla[\mathfrak{M}_\alpha,\blacksquare[\mathfrak{M}_\beta,\mathfrak{M}_\alpha]]\}$

This states that the aggregation includes each member. It is a statement about the whole of the aggregation, though it is of the form

** $\nabla[\mathfrak{M}_\alpha,\mathfrak{M}_\beta]:\nabla[\mathfrak{M}_\alpha,\mathfrak{M}_\mu]$

3.4.6. A Theorem about Exclusion

C3.17 $\blacksquare[\mathfrak{M}_\alpha,\mathfrak{M}_\gamma]:\blacksquare[\mathfrak{M}_\beta,\mathfrak{M}_\gamma]$

S_1 $\Delta[\mathfrak{M}\{C3.17\},\mathfrak{M}\{A3.06\}]:\mathfrak{M}\{S_a\}$

S_a $\nabla[\blacksquare[\mathfrak{M}_\alpha,\mathfrak{M}_\gamma],\Delta[\mathfrak{M}_\alpha,\mathfrak{M}_\gamma]]:\nabla[\blacksquare[\mathfrak{M}_\beta,\mathfrak{M}_\gamma],\Delta[\mathfrak{M}_\alpha,\mathfrak{M}_\gamma]]$

S_2 $\Delta[\mathfrak{M}\{S_a\},\mathfrak{M}\{A3.04\}]:\mathfrak{M}\{S_b\}$

S_b $\nabla[\Delta[\mathfrak{M}_\alpha,\mathfrak{M}_\gamma],\blacksquare[\mathfrak{M}_\alpha,\mathfrak{M}_\gamma]]:\nabla[\Delta[\mathfrak{M}_\alpha,\mathfrak{M}_\gamma],\blacksquare[\mathfrak{M}_\beta,\mathfrak{M}_\gamma]]$

S_3 $\nabla[\mathfrak{M}\{S_b\},\nabla[\mathfrak{M}\{A3.10\},\mathfrak{M}\{A3.13\}]]:\mathfrak{M}\{S_c\}$

S_c $\nabla[\Delta[\mathfrak{M}_\alpha,\mathfrak{M}_\gamma],\blacksquare[\mathfrak{M}_\alpha,\mathfrak{M}_\gamma]]:\nabla[\Delta[\mathfrak{M}_\beta,\mathfrak{M}_\gamma],\blacksquare[\mathfrak{M}_\beta,\mathfrak{M}_\gamma]]$

S_4 $\nabla[\mathfrak{M}\{S_c\},\nabla[\mathfrak{M}\{C3.11\},\mathfrak{M}\{A3.12\}]]:\mathfrak{M}\{C3.01\}$

** $\nabla[\nabla[\mathfrak{M}\{S_4\},\mathfrak{M}\{S_3\}],\mathfrak{M}\{A3.13\}]:\mathfrak{M}\{S_5\}$

S_5 $\nabla[\nabla[\mathfrak{M}\{S_b\},\mathfrak{M}_{5a}],\mathfrak{M}_{5b}]:\mathfrak{M}\{C3.01\}$

where

** $\mathfrak{M}_{5a}:\nabla[\mathfrak{M}\{A3.10\},\mathfrak{M}\{A3.13\}]$

** $\mathfrak{M}_{5b}:\nabla[\mathfrak{M}\{C3.11\},\mathfrak{M}\{A3.13\}]$

** $\nabla[\mathfrak{M}\{S_5\},\mathfrak{M}\{A3.05\}]:\mathfrak{M}\{S_6\}$

S_6 $\nabla[\mathfrak{M}\{S_b\},\mathfrak{M}_\rho]:\mathfrak{M}\{C3.01\}$

where

** $\mathfrak{M}_\rho:\nabla[\nabla[\mathfrak{M}\{A3.10\},\mathfrak{M}\{A3.13\}],\nabla[\mathfrak{M}\{C3.11\},\mathfrak{M}\{A3.13\}]]$

** $\nabla[\nabla[\mathfrak{M}\{S_6\},\mathfrak{M}\{S_2\}],\mathfrak{M}\{A3.13\}]:\mathfrak{M}\{S_7\}$

S_7 $\nabla[\nabla[\mathfrak{M}\{S_a\},\mathfrak{M}\{A3.04\},\mathfrak{M}_\rho]:\mathfrak{M}\{C3.01\}$

** $\nabla[\mathfrak{M}\{S_7\},\mathfrak{M}\{A3.05\}]:\mathfrak{M}\{S_8\}$

S_8 $\nabla[\mathfrak{M}\{S_a\},\mathfrak{M}_\nu]:\mathfrak{M}\{C3.01\}$

where

** $\mathfrak{M}_\nu:\nabla[\mathfrak{M}\{A3.04\},\mathfrak{M}_\rho]$

** $\nabla[\nabla[\mathfrak{M}\{S_8\},\mathfrak{M}\{S_1\}],\mathfrak{M}\{A3.13\}]:\mathfrak{M}\{S_9\}$

S_9 $\nabla[\nabla[\mathfrak{M}\{C3.17\},\mathfrak{M}\{A3.06\}],\nabla[\mathfrak{M}\{A3.13\},\mathfrak{M}_\nu]]:\mathfrak{M}\{C3.01\}$

** $\nabla[\mathfrak{M}\{S_9\},\mathfrak{M}\{A3.05\}]:\mathfrak{M}\{S_{10}\}$

S_{10} $\nabla[\mathfrak{M}\{C3.17\},\mathfrak{M}_\mu]:\mathfrak{M}\{C3.01\}$

where

** $\mathfrak{M}_\mu:\nabla[\mathfrak{M}\{A3.06\},\nabla[\mathfrak{M}\{A3.13\},\mathfrak{M}_\nu]]$

** $\nabla[\mathfrak{M}\{S_{10}\},\mathfrak{M}\{A3.03\}]:\mathfrak{M}\{P3.07\}$

P3.07 $\mathfrak{M}\{C3.01\}:\nabla[\mathfrak{M}\{C3.17\},\mathfrak{M}_\mu]$

3.4.7. Implication from Coincident Identity

S_{11} $\nabla[\mathfrak{M}\{C3.06\},\mathfrak{M}\{A3.10\}]:\mathfrak{M}\{S_a\}$

S_a $\Delta[\mathfrak{M}_\alpha,\mathfrak{M}_\beta]:\Delta[\nabla[\mathfrak{M}_\beta,\mathfrak{M}_\mu],\mathfrak{M}_\beta]$

S_{12} $\nabla[\mathfrak{M}\{S_a\},\mathfrak{M}\{A3.08\}]:\mathfrak{M}\{S_b\}$

S_b $\Delta[\mathfrak{M}_\alpha,\mathfrak{M}_\beta]:\Delta[\mathfrak{M}_\beta,\nabla[\mathfrak{M}_\beta,\mathfrak{M}_\mu]]$

S_{13} $\nabla[\mathfrak{M}\{S_b\},\mathfrak{M}\{A3.15\}]:\mathfrak{M}\{S_c\}$

S_c $\Delta[\mathfrak{M}_\alpha,\mathfrak{M}_\beta]:\nabla[\Delta[\mathfrak{M}_\beta,\mathfrak{M}_\beta],\Delta[\mathfrak{M}_\beta,\mathfrak{M}_\mu]]$

S_{14} $\nabla[\mathfrak{M}\{S_c\},\mathfrak{M}_{14a}]:\mathfrak{M}\{S_d\}$

where

** $\mathfrak{M}_{14a}:\nabla[\mathfrak{M}\{A3.11\},\mathfrak{M}\{A3.13\}]$

S_d $\Delta[\mathfrak{M}_\alpha,\mathfrak{M}_\beta]:\nabla[\mathfrak{M}_\beta,\Delta[\mathfrak{M}_\beta,\mathfrak{M}_\mu]]$

We shall here specify C5.88 as a condition on $\mathfrak{M}_\beta$ and $\mathfrak{M}_\mu$, as asserted in S_f; thus they are independent or nonsense, as stated in E5.25. Again, note that as stated for E5.25 in the text, the singular inclusion symbol has not been defined yet, and this derivation actually belongs after that definition.

S_f $\Delta[\mathfrak{M}_\beta,\mathfrak{M}_\mu]:\mathfrak{O}$

S_{15} $\nabla[\mathfrak{M}\{S_d\},\mathfrak{M}_{15a}]:\mathfrak{M}\{S_e\}$

where

** $\mathfrak{M}_{15a}:\nabla[\mathfrak{M}\{S_f\},\mathfrak{M}\{A3.13\}]$

S_e $\Delta[\mathfrak{M}_\alpha,\mathfrak{M}_\beta]:\nabla[\mathfrak{M}_\beta,\mathfrak{O}]$

S_{16} $\nabla[\mathfrak{M}\{S_e\},\mathfrak{M}\{C3.13\}]:\mathfrak{M}\{C3.18\}$

C3.18 $\Delta[\mathfrak{M}_\alpha,\mathfrak{M}_\beta]:\mathfrak{M}_\beta$

** $\nabla[\nabla[\mathfrak{M}\{S_{16}\},\mathfrak{M}\{S_{15}\}],\mathfrak{M}\{A3.13\}]:\mathfrak{M}\{S_{17}\}$

S_{17} $\nabla[\nabla[\mathfrak{M}\{S_d\},\mathfrak{M}_{15a}],\mathfrak{M}\{C3.13\}]:\mathfrak{M}\{C3.18\}$

** $\nabla[\mathfrak{M}\{S_{17}\},\mathfrak{M}\{A3.05\}]:\mathfrak{M}\{S_{18}\}$

S_{18} $\nabla[\mathfrak{M}\{S_d\},\mathfrak{M}_{18a}]:\mathfrak{M}\{C3.18\}$

where

** $\mathfrak{M}_{18a}:\nabla[\mathfrak{M}_{15a},\mathfrak{M}\{C3.13\}]$

** $\nabla[\nabla[\mathfrak{M}\{S_{18}\},\mathfrak{M}\{S_{14}\}],\mathfrak{M}\{A3.13\}]:\mathfrak{M}\{S_{19}\}$

S_{19} $\nabla[\nabla[\mathfrak{M}\{S_c\},\mathfrak{M}_{14a}],\mathfrak{M}_{18a}]:\mathfrak{M}\{C3.18\}$

** $\nabla[\mathfrak{M}\{S_{19}\},\mathfrak{M}\{A3.05\}]:\mathfrak{M}\{S_{20}\}$

S_{20} $\nabla[\mathfrak{M}\{S_c\},\mathfrak{M}_{20a}]:\mathfrak{M}\{C3.18\}$

where

** $\mathfrak{M}_{20a}:\nabla[\mathfrak{M}_{14a},\mathfrak{M}_{18a}]$

** $\nabla[\nabla[\mathfrak{M}\{S_{20}\},\mathfrak{M}\{S_{13}\}],\mathfrak{M}\{A3.13\}]:\mathfrak{M}\{S_{21}\}$

S_{21} $\nabla[\nabla[\mathfrak{M}\{S_b\},\mathfrak{M}\{A3.15\}],\mathfrak{M}_{20a}]:\mathfrak{M}\{C3.18\}$

** $\nabla[\mathfrak{M}\{S_{21}\},\mathfrak{M}\{A3.05\}]:\mathfrak{M}\{S_{22}\}$

S_{22} $\nabla[\mathfrak{M}\{S_b\},\mathfrak{M}_{22a}]:\mathfrak{M}\{C3.18\}$

where

** $\mathfrak{M}_{22a}:\nabla[\mathfrak{M}\{A3.15\},\mathfrak{M}_{20a}]$

** $\nabla[\nabla[\mathfrak{M}\{S_{22}\},\mathfrak{M}\{S_{12}\}],\mathfrak{M}\{A3.13\}]:\mathfrak{M}\{S_{23}\}$

S_{23} $\nabla[\nabla[\mathfrak{M}\{S_a\},\mathfrak{M}\{A3.08\}],\mathfrak{M}_{22a}]:\mathfrak{M}\{C3.18\}$

** $\nabla[\mathfrak{M}\{S_{23}\},\mathfrak{M}\{A3.05\}]:\mathfrak{M}\{S_{24}\}$

S_{24} $\nabla[\mathfrak{M}\{S_a\},\mathfrak{M}_{24a}]:\mathfrak{M}\{C3.18\}$

where

** $\mathfrak{M}_{24a}:\nabla[\mathfrak{M}\{A3.08\},\mathfrak{M}_{22a}]$

** $\nabla[\nabla[\mathfrak{M}\{S_{24}\},\mathfrak{M}\{S_{11}\}],\mathfrak{M}\{A3.13\}]:\mathfrak{M}\{S_{25}\}$

S_{25} $\nabla[\nabla[\mathfrak{M}\{C3.06\},\mathfrak{M}\{A3.14\}],\mathfrak{M}_{24a}]:\mathfrak{M}\{C3.18\}$

** $\nabla[\mathfrak{M}\{S_{25}\},\mathfrak{M}\{A3.05\}]:\mathfrak{M}\{S_{26}\}$

S_{26} $\nabla[\mathfrak{M}\{C3.06\},\mathfrak{M}_\rho]:\mathfrak{M}\{C3.18\}$

where

** $\mathfrak{M}_\rho:\nabla[\mathfrak{M}\{A3.14\},\mathfrak{M}_{24a}]$

** $\nabla[\mathfrak{M}\{S_{26}\},\mathfrak{M}\{A3.03\}]:\mathfrak{M}\{P3.08\}$

P3.08 $\mathfrak{M}\{C3.18\}:\nabla[\mathfrak{M}\{C3.06\},\mathfrak{M}_\rho]$

Thus, C3.18 implies C3.06, with conditions $\mathfrak{M}_\rho$.

3.4.8. Another Theorem about Exclusion

** $\nabla[\nabla[\mathfrak{M}\{C3.01\},\mathfrak{M}\{C3.11\}],\nabla[\mathfrak{M}\{A3.13\},\mathfrak{M}\{A3.14\}]]:\mathfrak{M}\{S_1\}$

S_1 $\mathfrak{M}_\alpha:\nabla[\Delta[\mathfrak{M}_\alpha,\mathfrak{M}_\alpha],\blacksquare[\mathfrak{M}_\alpha,\mathfrak{M}_\alpha]]$

** $\nabla[\mathfrak{M}\{S_1\},\nabla[\mathfrak{M}\{A3.11\},\mathfrak{M}\{A3.13\}]]:\mathfrak{M}\{S_2\}$

S_2 $\mathfrak{M}_\alpha:\nabla[\mathfrak{M}_\alpha,\blacksquare[\mathfrak{M}_\alpha,\mathfrak{M}_\alpha]]$

** $\nabla[\mathfrak{M}\{S_2\},\nabla[\mathfrak{M}\{A3.03\},\mathfrak{M}\{A3.12\}]]:\mathfrak{M}\{S_3\}$

S_3 $\nabla[\mathfrak{M}_\alpha,\blacksquare[\mathfrak{M}_\alpha,\mathfrak{M}_\alpha]]:\mathfrak{M}_\alpha$

** $\nabla[\mathfrak{M}\{S_3\},\nabla[\mathfrak{M}\{C3.13\},\mathfrak{M}\{A3.13\}]]:\mathfrak{M}\{P3.09\}$

P3.09 $\blacksquare[\mathfrak{M}_\alpha,\mathfrak{M}_\alpha]:\mathfrak{O}$

3.4.9. Substitution in Exclusion

By the development of these theorems we demonstrate that substitution can also apply to the conjunction, exclusion.

** $\mathfrak{M}\{C3.12\}:\mathfrak{M}\{S_1\}$

S_1 $\Delta[\Delta[\mathfrak{M}_\alpha,\mathfrak{M}_\gamma],\blacksquare[\mathfrak{M}_\alpha,\mathfrak{M}_\gamma]]:\mathfrak{O}$

** $\mathfrak{M}\{C3.12\}:\mathfrak{M}\{S_2\}$

S_2 $\Delta[\Delta[\Delta[\mathfrak{M}_\alpha,\mathfrak{M}_\beta],\blacksquare[\mathfrak{M}_\alpha,\mathfrak{M}_\beta]],\mathfrak{M}\{C3.09\}]:\Delta[\mathfrak{O},\mathfrak{M}\{C3.09\}]$

** $\Delta[\mathfrak{M}\{S_2\},\mathfrak{M}\{P3.01\}]:\mathfrak{M}\{S_3\}$

S_3 $\Delta[\Delta[\Delta[\mathfrak{M}_\alpha,\mathfrak{M}_\beta],\blacksquare[\mathfrak{M}_\alpha,\mathfrak{M}_\beta]],\mathfrak{M}\{C3.09\}]:\mathfrak{O}$

** $\Delta[\mathfrak{M}\{S_3\},\mathfrak{M}\{A3.11\}]:\mathfrak{M}\{S_4\}$

S_4 $\Delta[\Delta[\Delta[\mathfrak{M}_\alpha,\mathfrak{M}_\beta],\blacksquare[\mathfrak{M}_\alpha,\mathfrak{M}_\beta]],\Delta[\mathfrak{M}\{C3.09\},\mathfrak{M}\{C3.09\}]]:\mathfrak{O}$

** $\Delta[\mathfrak{M}\{S_4\},\mathfrak{M}\{A3.09\}]:\mathfrak{M}\{S_5\}$

S_5 $\Delta[\Delta[\Delta[\mathfrak{M}_\alpha,\mathfrak{M}_\beta],\mathfrak{M}\{C3.09\}],\Delta[\blacksquare[\mathfrak{M}_\alpha,\mathfrak{M}_\beta],\mathfrak{M}\{C3.09\}]]:\mathfrak{O}$

** $\Delta[\mathfrak{M}\{S_5\},\mathfrak{M}\{A3.14\}]:\mathfrak{M}\{S_6\}$

S_6 $\Delta[\Delta[\mathfrak{M}_\alpha,\mathfrak{M}_\gamma],\Delta[\blacksquare[\mathfrak{M}_\alpha,\mathfrak{M}_\beta],\mathfrak{M}\{C3.09\}]]:\mathfrak{O}$

** $\Delta[\mathfrak{M}\{S_6\},\mathfrak{M}\{A3.03\}]:\mathfrak{M}\{S_7\}$

** $\Delta[\mathfrak{M}\{S_1\},\mathfrak{M}\{A3.03\}]:\mathfrak{M}\{S_8\}$

S_7 $\Delta[\Delta[\blacksquare[\mathfrak{M}_\alpha,\mathfrak{M}_\beta],\mathfrak{M}\{C3.09\}],\Delta[\mathfrak{M}_\alpha,\mathfrak{M}_\gamma]]:\mathfrak{O}$

S_8 $\Delta[\blacksquare[\mathfrak{M}_\alpha,\mathfrak{M}_\gamma],\Delta[\mathfrak{M}_\alpha,\mathfrak{M}_\gamma]]:\mathfrak{O}$

** $\Delta[\nabla[\mathfrak{M}\{S_7\},\mathfrak{M}\{S_8\}],\mathfrak{M}\{A3.12\}]:\mathfrak{M}\{S_9\}$

S_9 $\Delta[\Delta[\blacksquare[\mathfrak{M}_\alpha,\mathfrak{M}_\beta],\mathfrak{M}\{C3.09\}],\Delta[\mathfrak{M}_\alpha,\mathfrak{M}_\gamma]]:\Delta[\blacksquare[\mathfrak{M}_\alpha,\mathfrak{M}_\gamma],\Delta[\mathfrak{M}_\alpha,\mathfrak{M}_\gamma]]$

** $\Delta[\mathfrak{M}\{S_9\},\mathfrak{M}\{A3.10\}]:\mathfrak{M}\{P3.10\}$

P3.10 $\Delta[\blacksquare[\mathfrak{M}_\alpha,\mathfrak{M}_\beta],\mathfrak{M}\{C3.09\}]:\blacksquare[\mathfrak{M}_\alpha,\mathfrak{M}_\gamma]$

Therefore, we say

E3.19 $\mathfrak{M}\{P3.10\}\epsilon\mathbf{C}\{\text{Rules of Substitution}\}$

With an almost identical process we can develop the theorem which is parallel to this.

P3.11 $\Delta[\blacksquare[\mathfrak{M}_\alpha,\mathfrak{M}_\beta],\mathfrak{M}\{C3.10\}]:\blacksquare[\mathfrak{M}_\gamma,\mathfrak{M}_\beta]$

E3.20 $\mathfrak{M}\{\mathrm{P3.11}\}\in\mathbf{C}\{\text{Rules of Substitution}\}$

3.4.10. A Theorem about Identity Element

S_a $\nabla[\mathfrak{M}\{\mathrm{A3.02}\},\mathfrak{M}\{\mathrm{A3.10}\}]:\mathfrak{M}\{S_1\}$

S_1 $\nabla[\mathfrak{M}_\alpha,\mathfrak{M}_\beta]:\nabla[\mathfrak{M}_\alpha,\mathfrak{M}_\beta]$

C3.19 $\mathfrak{M}_\alpha:\mathfrak{O}$

C3.20 $\mathfrak{M}_\beta:\mathfrak{O}$

S_b $\Delta[\nabla[\mathfrak{M}\{\mathrm{C3.19}\},\mathfrak{M}\{\mathrm{C3.20}\}],\nabla[\mathfrak{M}\{S_1\},\mathfrak{M}\{\mathrm{A3.13}\}]]:\mathfrak{M}\{S_2\}$

S_2 $\nabla[\mathfrak{M}_\alpha,\mathfrak{M}_\beta]:\nabla[\mathfrak{O},\mathfrak{O}]$

S_c $\Delta[\mathfrak{M}\{S_2\},\mathfrak{M}\{\mathrm{A3.07}\}]:\mathfrak{M}\{\mathrm{C3.21}\}$

C3.21 $\nabla[\mathfrak{M}_\alpha,\mathfrak{M}_\beta]:\mathfrak{O}$

** $\Delta[\Delta[\mathfrak{M}\{S_b\},\mathfrak{M}\{S_c\}],\mathfrak{M}\{\mathrm{A3.14}\}]:\mathfrak{M}\{S_d\}$

S_d $\Delta[\nabla[\mathfrak{M}\{\mathrm{C3.19}\},\mathfrak{M}\{\mathrm{C3.20}\}],\mathfrak{M}_\mu]:\mathfrak{M}\{\mathrm{C3.21}\}$

where

** $\mathfrak{M}_\mu:\Delta[\nabla[\mathfrak{M}\{S_1\},\mathfrak{M}\{\mathrm{A3.13}\}],\mathfrak{M}\{\mathrm{A3.07}\}]$

** $\Delta[\nabla[\mathfrak{M}\{S_d\},\mathfrak{M}\{S_a\}],\nabla[\mathfrak{M}\{\mathrm{A3.14}\},\mathfrak{M}\{\mathrm{A3.13}\}]]:\mathfrak{M}\{S_e\}$

S_e $\Delta[\nabla[\mathfrak{M}\{\mathrm{C3.19}\},\mathfrak{M}\{\mathrm{C3.20}\}],\mathfrak{M}_\rho]:\mathfrak{M}\{\mathrm{C3.21}\}$

where

** $\mathfrak{M}_\rho:\Delta[\nabla[\mathfrak{M}\{\mathrm{A3.02}\},\mathfrak{M}\{\mathrm{A3.13}\}],\mathfrak{M}\{\mathrm{A3.07}\}]$

** $\Delta[\mathfrak{M}\{S_e\},\mathfrak{M}\{\mathrm{A3.03}\}]:\mathfrak{M}\{\mathrm{P3.12}\}$

P3.12 $\mathfrak{M}\{\mathrm{C3.21}\}:\Delta[\nabla[\mathfrak{M}\{\mathrm{C3.19}\},\mathfrak{M}\{\mathrm{C3.20}\}],\mathfrak{M}_\rho]$

This states that if the aggregate conjunction of two intensions is null then each is null.

4. NUMBER

The concept of number enters into all of our discussions, especially the concepts of zero and one. The concept, zero, enters as, for example, "I have no time today". The concept, one, appears as, for example, "You may take a guest with you", since the article, a, is a contraction of "one". Number enters in many other aspects also. The word, many, in the last sentence denotes "large number". These have been examples of the natural numbers. There are other types of numbers also, all of great importance in our daily lives, directly or indirectly.

In the general situation, a number need not be an integer or even be able to be represented by finite groups of integers. Number is, after all, a postulated entity as are intension and class, and its primary points of subdivision (the integers) are determined by arbitrary definitions. These definitions are then used in more general relationships which constitute an algebra of number. A relationship which is valid over a wide range of numbers is what we have, for example, in the following quadratic form.

** $y=(x^2+x-2)$

In this example, when a number is specified for x (the "value" of x) then a number is known for y.

Number has myriad uses. Herein, number will be used as "metric" or measure for our other postulated entities, intension and class. A metric which can assume any value within a specified range will be assigned to intension whereas a natural number (a non-negative integer) will be assigned to classes. That these metrics occur in the daily conduct of our lives has been discussed already to some extent and will be exhibited further in our discussions as we proceed.

An algebra is a system of notation adapted to the study of a system of relationships, that is, an algebra is merely another special language. The term, algebra, with no further designation, refers usually to the algebra of number, which in our case is a subclass of our symbolism and syntax.

In several texts on the theory of number, the foundations are not presented, they are assumed to have been developed elsewhere. No definitions are given for the nouns, verbs or conjunctions in these texts. Here we shall attempt to define each noun, each verb and each conjunction in a manner parallel to that which we use for intension and classes. Thus, rather than assuming a set of, e.g., natural number we shall construct the members of that set.

In the algebra of number, customs have evolved in the representation of each noun, verb and conjunction. These customs do not directly fit in with the notation which we have developed to this point, and we feel that the use of a different and slightly more explicit notation is worth the extra effort involved. Later, we shall revert to customary symbollism.

4.1. Nouns, Number

The symbol for a number will initially be a letter of the lower case Roman alphabet. Certain specialized symbols will also be used, such as for the integers. Each of these symbols represents a noun, but we must observe that it is common practice to use these nouns as adjectives also. This ambiguity is discussed more in Section 9.3.3.2.1.

In the general case, a number is composed of a "real" part and an "imaginary" part; in the customary presentation the number is developed as a sum of the "real" and "imaginary" parts, the latter being shown as a product of a "real" number and an "operator" i. Actually, the symbols for the "imaginary" part also represent numbers. The symbols refer to a concept which is derived from the algebra as other numbers are. Many authors have commented that the use of these adjectives ("real" and "imaginary") is unfortunate but prevalent. We shall first consider only "real" numbers.

In conventional notation, the symbol for a real number (1, 5, -7, etc.) is composed of two parts; it is composed of a magnitude and a sign. This is merely an arbitrary (but convenient) form of symbolism since there is no more importance attached to +5 than to -7. Each number is a point or a member in a sequence or "continuum" which has no specified beginning and no specified end.

In common practice, a number is not written with explicit sign unless that number is negative (e.g., -27). This practice is efficient, but for our present discussions we prefer to be less efficient and more explicit so as to remove any ambiguity. Thus, for this Section we shall use symbols other than + and -. A postivie 0100 will be represented as 0100» while a negative 010 will be represented as 010«. These conventions are more explicitly stated below, where we specify the symbols for these nouns.

4.2. Verbs, Number

The verbs used in algebra are: identity (equality); sequencing (greater than or less than); inequality.

4.2.1. Identity

Different symbols for the same number convey the same concept of number. For this purpose we define the symbol = . This diadic relationship appears in all mathematical analysis. It is another use of the verb, to be. As we have discussed previously, this copula is necessary only as a convenient convention.

Some texts use the term, identity, for equations such as

**	$(x^2-1)=(x+1)(x-1)$

and use the term, equality, for equations such as

**	$(x^2+1)=-2x$

Both of these are identities, one for a "continuum" and one for a point.

In a more formal manner,

C4.01	$x=y$
C4.02	The number x is identical to the number y
E4.01	$\mathfrak{M}\{C4.01\}:\mathfrak{M}\{C4.02\}$

As a definition of this symbol, we assert

C4.03	$\mathfrak{M}\{x\}:\mathfrak{M}\{y\}$
C4.04	$\mathfrak{M}\{C4.03\}:\mathfrak{M}\{C4.01\}$
D4.01	$\mathfrak{M}\{=\}:\mathfrak{M}\{C4.04\}$

Specifically,

**	$\mathfrak{M}\{A3.02\}:\nabla[\mathfrak{M}\{S_1\},\mathfrak{M}_\mu]$
S_1	$\mathfrak{M}\{x\}:\mathfrak{M}\{x\}$
**	$\Delta[\mathfrak{M}\{S_1\},\mathfrak{M}\{C4.04\}]:\mathfrak{M}\{P4.01\}$
P4.01	$x=x$
E4.02	$\mathfrak{M}\{\text{copula} =\}\in\mathbf{C}\{\text{reflexive relationships}\}$

To demonstrate symmetry,

C4.05	$y=x$
C4.06	$\mathfrak{M}\{y\}:\mathfrak{M}\{x\}$
**	$\mathfrak{M}\{A3.03\}:\mathfrak{M}\{S_1\}$
S_1	$\mathfrak{M}\{C4.03\}:\mathfrak{M}\{C4.06\}$
**	$\nabla[\nabla[\mathfrak{M}\{S_1\},\mathfrak{M}\{C4.04\}],\mathfrak{M}\{A3.12\}]:\mathfrak{M}\{P4.02\}$
P4.02	$\mathfrak{M}\{C4.01\}:\mathfrak{M}\{C4.05\}$
E4.03	$\mathfrak{M}\{\text{copula} =\}\in\mathbf{C}\{\text{symmetric relationships}\}$

To show transitivity of this verb,

**	$\mathfrak{M}\{C4.03\}:\mathfrak{M}\{S_1\}$
S_1	$\mathfrak{M}\{y\}:\mathfrak{M}\{z\}$
**	$\Delta[\mathfrak{M}\{S_1\},\mathfrak{M}\{C4.04\}]:\mathfrak{M}\{C4.07\}$
C4.07	$y=z$
**	$\mathfrak{M}\{C4.03\}:\mathfrak{M}\{S_2\}$
S_2	$\mathfrak{M}\{x\}:\mathfrak{M}\{z\}$
**	$\Delta[\mathfrak{M}\{S_2\},\mathfrak{M}\{C4.04\}]:\mathfrak{M}\{C4.08\}$
C4.08	$x=z$
**	$\mathfrak{M}\{A3.12\}:\mathfrak{M}\{S_3\}$
S_3	$\Delta[\mathfrak{M}\{C4.03\},\mathfrak{M}\{S_1\}]:\mathfrak{M}\{S_2\}$
**	$\Delta[\mathfrak{M}\{S_3\},\nabla[\mathfrak{M}\{C4.04\},\mathfrak{M}\{A3.14\}]]:\mathfrak{M}\{P4.03\}$
P4.03	$\Delta[\mathfrak{M}\{C4.01\},\mathfrak{M}\{C4.07\}]:\mathfrak{M}\{C4.08\}$
E4.04	$\mathfrak{M}\{\text{copula} =\}\in\mathbf{C}\{\text{transitive relationships}\}$
E4.05	$\mathfrak{M}\{P4.03\}\in\mathbf{C}\{\text{Rules of Substitution}\}$

Again, observe that this Rule P4.03 is only applicable, as stated, to the symbolism of equalities. A separate statement would seem to be needed for forms composed of numbers and other symbols which represent numbers so as to reflect the change in symbolism. If f(x) is such a form, composed of numbers and conjunctions of numbers then we must assert that

A4.01 $\Delta[\mathfrak{M}\{f(x)\},\mathfrak{M}\{C4.03\}]:\mathfrak{M}\{f(y)\}$

Again we classify this as

E4.06 $\mathfrak{M}\{A4.01\}\epsilon\mathbf{C}\{\text{Rules of Substitution}\}$

4.2.2. Verb, Inequality

This verb can be defined by the following:

C4.09 $x \neq y$

C4.10 $\Delta[\mathfrak{M}\{x\},\mathfrak{M}\{y\}]:\mathfrak{O}$

C4.11 $\mathfrak{M}\{C4.10\}:\mathfrak{M}\{C4.09\}$

D4.02 $\mathfrak{M}\{\neq\}:\mathfrak{M}\{C4.11\}$

4.2.3. Verb, Sequencing

In our definition of these verbs we use concepts which have not been developed yet. Thus, they are defined in Section 4.6.

4.3. Conjunctions

Four conjunctions are normally defined with respect to number. These result in sum, product, difference and quotient. The first will be discussed here; the latter will be discussed in Section 4.5. Our notation here for sum and product will differ from the conventional notation, for the purpose of avoiding pre-established habits in their use. In later Sections we shall revert to the use of + and •. We also observe here that a conjunction of like entities has the character of those entities; thus a conjunction of numbers is a number.

4.3.1. Conjunction, Sum

We shall now define a relationship between numbers, the conjunction for sum. This conjunction is another common (but truncated) usage of the word, and.

E4.07 $\mathfrak{M}\{\mathfrak{s}[x,y]\}:\mathfrak{M}\{\text{the sum of numbers x and y}\}$

We specify commutivity and associativity of sum.

A4.02 $\mathfrak{M}\{\mathfrak{s}[x,y]\}:\mathfrak{M}\{\mathfrak{s}[y,x]\}$

E4.08 $\mathfrak{M}\{\text{conjunction } \mathfrak{s}\}\epsilon\mathbf{C}\{\text{commutative relationships}\}$

A4.03 $\mathfrak{M}\{\mathfrak{s}[\mathfrak{s}[x,y],z]\}:\mathfrak{M}\{\mathfrak{s}[x,\mathfrak{s}[y,z]]\}$

E4.09 $\mathfrak{M}\{\text{conjunction } \mathfrak{s}\}\epsilon\mathbf{C}\{\text{associative relationships}\}$

C4.12 $\mathfrak{s}[x,z]=\mathfrak{s}[y,z]$

A4.04 $\mathfrak{M}\{C4.01\}:\mathfrak{M}\{C4.12\}$

These axioms are customarily accepted in the establishment of the characteristics of the sum of arbitrary numbers.

4.3.2. Conjunction, Product

E4.10 𝕸{𝔭[x,y]}:𝕸{the product of numbers x and y}
Requirements on the definition of 𝔭 are:
A4.05 𝕸{𝔭[x,y]}:𝕸{𝔭[y,x]}
This statement is classified as
E4.11 𝕸{conjunction 𝔭}ϵ**C**{commutative relationships}
A4.06 𝕸{𝔭[𝔭[x,y],z]}:𝕸{𝔭[x,𝔭[y,z]]}
This assertion is classified as
E4.12 𝕸{conjunction 𝔭}ϵ**C**{associative relationships}
C4.13 𝔭[x,z]=𝔭[y,z]
A4.07 𝕸{C4.01}:𝕸{C4.13}

An important part of the definitions of product and sum is a statement of distribution which is a relationship between product and sum.
A4.08 𝕸{𝔭[x,𝔰[y,z]]}:𝕸{𝔰[𝔭[x,y],𝔭[x,z]]}

Therefore, as a definition of 𝔰 we state
D4.03 𝕸{𝔰}:∇[∇[𝕸{A4.02},𝕸{A4.03}],∇[𝕸{A4.04},𝕸{A4.08}]]
and as a definition of 𝔭 we state
D4.04 𝕸{𝔭}:∇[∇[𝕸{A4.05},𝕸{A4.06}],∇[𝕸{A4.07},𝕸{A4.08}]]

4.4. Natural Numbers

We shall now begin to define the members of the set, natural-number. All natural numbers, except for the digit 1», are defined with respect to the conjunction 𝔰.

We define the number 0 as the "identity element" for the conjunction 𝔰.
C4.14 𝔰[x,0]=x
D4.05 𝕸{0}:𝕸{C4.14}
This definition applies for all values of x, real or complex.

We define the number 1» as the "identity element" for the conjunction 𝔭.
C4.15 𝔭[x,1»]=x
D4.06 𝕸{1»}:𝕸{C4.15}

The two "values", 0 and 1», from the "continuum", number, provide two arbitrary points of reference in that "continuum" and are the basis of the members of the set, natural-number, **N**.

In our discussions about each of the nouns in the class, natural-number, we shall use binary representations. We shall assume that the reader knows the necessary definitions for the algorithm of binary representations, such as the significance of position. Though these definitions will be used herein, we will not present them.

Thus, we are now able to define the symbols for the next few natural numbers.

D4.07 𝔐{010»}:𝔐{𝔰[1»,1»]}

D4.08 𝔐{011»}:𝔐{𝔰[010»,1»]}

D4.09 𝔐{0100»}:𝔐{𝔰[011»,1»]}

D4.10 𝔐{0101»}:𝔐{𝔰[0100»,1»]}

This process of definition can continue without bound; that is, for any such member of the class we can define the next member (the successor) in the progression by this process. Here we are defining the members of a class (or set) by a recursion formula of intensions of symbols, using the algorithm which links these symbols together in a sequence. Again, the important point is that each symbol is unique. The symbol 011» is different from the symbol 010», but the intensions of these symbols are related by the definition (above). These definitions, as a sequence, are discussed further in Section 5.5. A recursive definition, as applied above, is equivalent to the use of a successor function as defined in Kunen (16,18).

** 1=S(0), 2=S(1), 3=S(2), 4=S(3), ..., (n+1)=S(n), etc.

Note, however, that these forms of the successor function also constitute a process of definition of a sequence of symbols. Our symbol for this sequence is seq(0,N); in this example N is the last number considered and 0 is the first. That is,

D4.11 𝔐{seq(0,N)}:∇[𝔐{D4.05},∇[𝔐{D4.06},∇[𝔐{D4.07},∇[...

We shall, from here on, be using decimal digits as arbitrary symbols or as adjectives. As stated above we shall use binary digits to represent nouns. To aid in decreasing some potential confusion and ambiguity of symbolism, we shall precede each binary number by a zero. Thus, a decimal two is the symbol 2; a binary two is the symbol 010». A decimal ten is 10; a binary ten is 01010».

These last definitions are also the basis of an "addition table" by which we teach the algorithm, arithmetic. For example,

** ∇[𝔐{D4.10},𝔐{C4.04}]:𝔐{S_1}

S_1 0101»=𝔰[0100»,1»]

** ∇[𝔐{D4.09},𝔐{C4.04}]:𝔐{S_2}

S_2 0100»=𝔰[011»,1»]

** ∇[∇[𝔐{S_1},𝔐{S_2}],𝔐{A4.01}]:𝔐{S_3}

S_3 0101»=𝔰[𝔰[011»,1»],1»]

** ∇[𝔐{S_3},𝔐{A4.03}]:𝔐{S_4}

S_4 0101»=𝔰[011»,𝔰[1»,1»]]

** ∇[𝔐{D4.07},𝔐{C4.04}]:𝔐{S_5}

S_5 010»=𝔰[1»,1»]

** ∇[∇[𝔐{S_4},𝔐{S_5}],𝔐{A4.01}]:𝔐{P4.04}

P4.04 0101»=𝔰[011»,010»]

This same process can be used to construct sums of all other combinations of numbers.

4.5. Difference and Quotient

Difference, or subtraction, is sometimes viewed as the antonym of sum (Section 4.3.1), but it is merely one of the possible relationships among numbers. On the other hand, it is one of the relationships which is defined in terms of sum. Difference is defined in terms of negative numbers.

The members of the set **S**{negative-integer} are defined in terms of the members of the set **N** . For example, consider the following sequence of assertions (equations):

S_1	𝔰[x,1»]=010»
S_2	𝔰[x,1»]=1»
S_3	𝔰[x,1»]=0

We might, then, have no difficulty in deciding that

S_4	𝔐{S_1}:𝔐{x=1»}
S_5	𝔐{S_2}:𝔐{x=0}

However, for S_3, we have no rule of determination. We therefore define

C4.16	𝔰[x,1»]=0
C4.17	x=(1«)
C4.18	𝔐{C4.16}:𝔐{C4.17}
D4.12	𝔐{1«}:𝔐{C4.18}

For every positive number a negative number of the same magnitude can be defined. This is discussed somewhat more in Section 5.4.4.

With the negative integer 1« we can define subtraction.

C4.19	𝔰[x,𝔭[y,1«]]=z
C4.20	x=𝔰[y,z]
C4.21	𝔐{C4.19}:𝔐{C4.20}
D4.13	𝔐{𝔰[x,𝔭[y,1«]]}:𝔐{C4.21}
E4.13	𝔐{𝔰[x,𝔭[y,1«]]}:𝔐{the difference of x and y}

It is possible to deduce from these and prior statements that subtraction is not commutative, and it is associative only among two of the three factors. Note here that "1«" is a single symbol.

Symbolism which implies division is often a convenience when performing the processes of analysis. We define

C4.22	x=b/ a
C4.23	a≠0
C4.24	𝔭[a,x]=b
C4.25	Δ[𝔐{C4.24},𝔐{C4.23}]:𝔐{C4.22}
D4.14	𝔐{x/ y}:𝔐{C4.25}

E4.14 $\mathfrak{M}\{x/y\}:\mathfrak{M}\{\text{the quotient of x and y}\}$

4.5.1. Function of a Variable

Earlier in this Chapter we spoke of f(x) where x was a number, real or complex, to be determined and f(x) was a function of x. A function of x is some formulation or series in which the variable x appears explicitly or implicitly in some manner. This definition does not presuppose the type of formulation, nor does it limit the characteristics of that formulation with various values of x. Further, a function may be defined on the basis of several variables rather than only one. We must state that as x is a number so the function of x is a number, real or complex.

4.5.2. Real Numbers

From our processes to this point it can be seen that we have defined real numbers by a form

** $f(x)=0$

where for rational numbers

** $f(x)=\mathfrak{s}[\mathfrak{p}[a,x],b]$

This latter form has been termed "linear"; the exponent of x by its omission is considered to be unity. We define the next level of exponential symbols by

** $\mathfrak{p}[x,x]=x^{010»}$

and

D4.15 $\mathfrak{M}\{\mathfrak{p}[x,x^n]\}:\mathfrak{M}\{x^{\mathfrak{s}[n,1»]}\}$

If we choose an f(x) which has been formed of the sum of products $\mathfrak{p}[a_n,x^n]$ for various values of n then for certain forms of f(x) we can define "irrational number" and "transcendental number". For convenience we shall define that

D4.16 $\mathfrak{M}\{x^0\}:\mathfrak{M}\{1»\}$

for any non-zero value of x. Then any real number x is algebraic if it satisfies the following assertions:

C4.26 $f(x)=\sum_{n=0}^{N}\mathfrak{p}[a_n,x^n]$

C4.27 $f(x)=0$

C4.28 Number

E4.15 $\Delta[\mathfrak{M}\{C4.26\},\mathfrak{M}\{C4.27\}]:\mathfrak{M}\{C4.28\}$

To restate, using this form, rational numbers result if N=1». Irrational numbers may result if N>1», a_0 is negative and all other a_n are zero except for the N'th which is positive. Transcendental numbers can also be defined from this form but with much more elaborate conditions. The definition D4.15 is usually expanded such that

D4.17 $\mathfrak{M}\{\mathfrak{p}[x^a,x^b]\}:\mathfrak{M}\{x^{\mathfrak{s}[a,b]}\}$

where a and b are any numbers.

4.5.3. Roots of Numbers

For the form x^a where 𝔭[n,a]=1» and where n is a positive integer we define that x^a is the n'th root of x. For example, if n=010» then x^a is termed the "square root" of x and is usually written as $\sqrt{x}$. We postulate that

A4.09 𝔐{𝔭[1«,1«]}:𝔐{1»}

Thus 𝔭[x,x] is a positive number for any real number, positive or negative, which may be used in place of the symbol x. Therefore, it becomes necessary to define in each case whether we are discussing a positive value or a negative value of x (a "positive root" or a "negative root").

4.5.4. Complex Numbers

Complex numbers may arise from any case of the above form which includes

** 𝔭[x,x]=1«

and, therefore, that

** x=i»

or

** x=i«

Thus the solutions of an equation such as

** (𝔭[x,x]+𝔭[a,a])=0

are

** x=𝔭[a,i»]

and

** x=𝔭[a,i«]

where

D4.18 𝔐{𝔭[i»,i»]}:𝔐{1«}

Since the symbol i» is defined by our algebra, it also represents a number and is a part of what we call a complex number. Complex numbers have limited or no application in the discourse of the average person, but they are vital to all forms of mathematical analysis and applications thereof.

As a root of a polynomial we usually represent a complex number x as, e.g.,

** x=𝔰[u,𝔭[v,i»]]

where u and v are each real numbers. Thus complex numbers are merely an extension of the class of real numbers and contain the real numbers as the case where v=0. As will be noticed in the ensuing work, a complex number 𝔰[u,𝔭[v,i»]] exhibits similar characteristics to an ordered pair of numbers (u,v) and in applications the two concepts are often interchanged.

4.6. Additional Verbs

The verb, greater than, or the verb, less than, is difficult to define for the general case in terms of existing concepts. We have defined inequality, but we note that inequality can be defined as the condition of being either less than or greater than the specified number. If, from this, we try to define "greater than" in terms of natural numbers (certainly not a general case) such as

**	$\mathfrak{s}[x,1\text{»}]>x$

then anyone not familiar with the symbol $>$ could read it as "not equal to" . There is nothing inherent in the statement that carries the additional limiting conotation of "greater than" . Or we could devise a circular pair of definitions such as

**	$\mathfrak{M}\{x>y\}:\blacksquare[\mathfrak{M}\{x\neq y\},\mathfrak{M}\{x<y\}]$
**	$\mathfrak{M}\{x<y\}:\blacksquare[\mathfrak{M}\{x\neq y\},\mathfrak{M}\{x>y\}]$

These statements might be combined and augmented (to differentiate between the two types of inequality, less and greater) to produce the following definitions:

C4.29	$x>y$
C4.30	$\mathfrak{s}[x,1\text{»}]>x$
D4.19	$\mathfrak{M}\{C4.29\}:\Delta[\blacksquare[\mathfrak{M}\{C4.09\},\blacksquare[\mathfrak{M}\{C4.09\},\mathfrak{M}\{C4.29\}]],\mathfrak{M}\{C4.30\}]$
C4.31	$x<y$
C4.32	$x<\mathfrak{s}[x,1\text{»}]$
D4.20	$\mathfrak{M}\{C4.31\}:\Delta[\blacksquare[\mathfrak{M}\{C4.09\},\blacksquare[\mathfrak{M}\{C4.09\},\mathfrak{M}\{C4.31\}]],\mathfrak{M}\{C4.32\}]$

In the absence of more explicit definitions we shall use these.

4.7. Theorems

These theorems are presented merely for continuity of development.

4.7.1. Multiplication

With A4.08 we can develop a useful theorem. Consider the situation where

C4.33	$z=0$
**	$\nabla[\mathfrak{M}\{A4.08\},\mathfrak{M}\{C4.33\}]:\mathfrak{M}\{S_1\}$
S_1	$\mathfrak{M}\{\mathfrak{p}[x,\mathfrak{s}[y,0]]\}:\mathfrak{M}\{\mathfrak{s}[\mathfrak{p}[x,y],\mathfrak{p}[x,0]]\}$
**	$\nabla[\mathfrak{M}\{S_1\},\mathfrak{M}\{C4.14\}]:\mathfrak{M}\{S_2\}$
S_2	$\mathfrak{M}\{\mathfrak{p}[x,y]\}:\mathfrak{M}\{\mathfrak{s}[\mathfrak{p}[x,y],\mathfrak{p}[x,0]]\}$
**	$\nabla[\mathfrak{M}\{S_2\},\mathfrak{M}\{C4.04\}]:\mathfrak{M}\{S_3\}$
S_3	$\mathfrak{p}[x,y]=\mathfrak{s}[\mathfrak{p}[x,y],\mathfrak{p}[x,0]]$
**	$\nabla[\mathfrak{M}\{S_3\},\mathfrak{M}\{C4.14\}]:\mathfrak{M}\{P4.05\}$
P4.05	$\mathfrak{p}[x,0]=0$

From C4.15 and A4.08 we can, with respect to integers, view multiplication as successive additions of the same quantity.

If we choose

C4.34 y=1»

C4.35 z=1»

then

** $\nabla[\mathfrak{M}\{A4.08\},\nabla[\mathfrak{M}\{C4.34\},\mathfrak{M}\{C4.35\}]]:\mathfrak{M}\{S_1\}$

S_1 $\mathfrak{M}\{\mathfrak{p}[x,\mathfrak{s}[1»,1»]]\}:\mathfrak{M}\{\mathfrak{s}[\mathfrak{p}[x,1»],\mathfrak{p}[x,1»]]\}$

** $\nabla[\mathfrak{M}\{S_1\},\nabla[\mathfrak{M}\{D4.07\},\mathfrak{M}\{C4.15\}]]:\mathfrak{M}\{P4.06\}$

P4.06 $\mathfrak{M}\{\mathfrak{p}[x,010»]\}:\mathfrak{M}\{\mathfrak{s}[x,x]\}$

This procedure may be continued through the set of natural numbers, such that, as the next example,

** $\mathfrak{p}$[x,011»]=$\mathfrak{s}[\mathfrak{s}$[x,x],x]

From C4.15 we can also see that

P4.07 $\mathfrak{p}$[1»,1»]=1»

Further,

P4.08 $\mathfrak{p}$[1«,1»]=1«

4.7.2. A Theorem about Greater Than

** $\nabla[\mathfrak{M}\{D4.02\},\mathfrak{M}\{D4.19\}]:\mathfrak{M}\{P4.09\}$

P4.09 $\mathfrak{M}\{C4.29\}:\nabla[\mathfrak{M}\{C4.10\},\mathfrak{M}\{C4.36\}]$

where

C4.36 $\delta>0$

5. EXTENSION

The extension of a descriptor is the class to which the connotation of that descriptor belongs. The class, cat, is composed of each concept, cat, which we may discuss. In other words, a class is composed of members or elements. A class is the aggregation of these members of like kind. The class is defined when the member is defined. The member is a concept; it may be the conceptualization of a physical object such as a chair; the member may be an abstract concept such as the concept of a number. Thus our conceptualization of the class $\mathbf{C}\{d_\alpha\}$ is that it is a collection of the concepts $\mathfrak{M}\{d_\alpha\}$, for each allowable value of α. This will become especially obvious when we discuss disjunction (disjunctive conjunction) of intensions. Restated, our notation $\mathbf{C}\{d_\alpha\}$ will represent the class of intensions $\mathfrak{M}\{d_\alpha\}$ rather than the class of objects which are represented by d_α. This is the normal situation in our discussions even though we usually do not admit it. We discuss our concept of the object rather than the object. This last statement applies whether the object is, for example, a horse or a unicorn.

The members of a class may bc defined by other class statements or by statements of intension. Both will appear here. See the discussion in Section 2.2 and the early paragraphs of Section 3.

The notation used herein for classes and operations thereon will be very similar to that which is currently in use in other references. The structure of a class-assertion will be: descriptor, copula, descriptor. The study of operations on classes forms the algebra of classes. This algebra has many similarities to the algebra of number, but many differences will also be noted. To highlight the similarities many authors use the same notation in operations in both algebras. However, we feel that the differences are important, and we use different notations for the operations and nouns of the two algebras.

Class statements in English can usually be recognized by their structure. A general unspecified individual which is in singular form and preceded by the indefinite article is one example, such as

** A cat is a mammal

The plural form often is a class statement.

** Cats are mammals

Now consider two statements:

S_1 My dog is black

S_2 My dog is the black dog

The assertion S_1 is a general statement which might be restated as

S_1 My dog is a black dog

Thus to us the formulations of these statements would be

S_1 $\mathfrak{M}\{\text{my dog}\} \in \mathbf{C}\{\text{black dogs}\}$

** $\mathbf{C}\{\text{black dogs}\} \subset \mathbf{C}\{\text{dogs}\}$

S_2 $\mathfrak{M}\{\text{my dog}\} : \mathfrak{M}\{\text{the black dog}\}$

5.1. Nouns

The symbol for the extension of a descriptor or noun will be **C** .

A class is composed of distinct members, $\mathfrak{M}\{a_\alpha\}$. A class is usually assigned a name, and that name usually is indicative of the common characteristic, a, of each member in the class. These statements allow us to define "class" more precisely. However, we must recognize that class, subclass and sub-subclass each place conceptually similar but different constraints on a definition.

Consider a total population of all possible potential members $d_{\mu\alpha}$ where the range of values of μ is

C5.01 $1» \le \mu \le M$

and that of α is

C5.02 $1» \le \alpha \le N(\mu)$

that is, there may be a different range N for each μ. From this population we are interested in those members which have the attribute, a. Thus we perform a selection for which our criterion is

C5.03 $\Delta[\mathfrak{M}\{a\},\mathfrak{M}\{d_{\mu\alpha}\}]:\mathfrak{M}\{a\}$

The form of this selection and theorem A3.10 indicate that the selected members have the form

C5.04 $\mathfrak{M}\{a_\alpha\}:\nabla[\mathfrak{M}\{a\},\mathfrak{M}\{k_\alpha\}]$

This form indicates that all selected members have the characteristic or name, a, while the variations amoung the selected members are designated by k_α.

Note that a and k_α are independent for all values of α, that is,,

C5.05 $\Delta[\mathfrak{M}\{a\},\mathfrak{M}\{k_\alpha\}]:\oplus$

A controlling constraint is $\blacksquare[\mathfrak{M}\{C5.06\},\mathfrak{M}\{C5.07\}]$ where

C5.06 $\Delta[\mathfrak{M}\{a_\beta\},\mathfrak{M}\{a_\gamma\}]:\oplus$

C5.07 $\beta=\gamma$

An apparent conflict arises with this last constraint, for example, in sets of observations in which we may have observed the same values more than once; however, the time of each observation is different, thus making each one unique.

Having defined each member a_α above, we assert that we have defined the class. Our definition is

D5.01 $\mathfrak{M}\{\mathbf{C}\{a\}\}:\nabla[\mathfrak{M}\{a_\alpha\},\mathfrak{M}_{\mathbf{C}}]$

where

** $\mathfrak{M}_{\mathbf{C}}:\nabla[\nabla[\mathfrak{M}\{C5.02\},\mathfrak{M}\{C5.03\}],\blacksquare[\mathfrak{M}\{C5.06\},\mathfrak{M}\{C5.07\}]]$

As a simplified example, we might say

** $\mathfrak{M}\{\text{apples}\}\in\mathbf{C}\{\text{apples}\}$

where

** $\mathfrak{M}\{\text{apples}\}:\Delta[\mathfrak{M}\{\text{fruit}\},\Delta[\mathfrak{M}\{\text{apple}\},\mathfrak{M}\{k_\alpha\}]]$

with the notation that k_α are more detailed specifications for each type of apple, etc.

The name or designation of a class can vary in practice.

> Our normal practice is to name the class on the basis of the common characteristic, a. An alternative notation for a class is to show an enumeration of the symbols a_α which represent the members. That is, our notations might be $\mathbf{C}\{a\}$ or $\mathbf{C}\{a_\alpha\}$ or $\mathbf{C}\{a_1,a_2,\ldots,a_N\}$.

As a result, for one common format, we say

E2.01 $\mathfrak{M}\{\mathbf{C}\{d_\alpha\}\}:\mathfrak{M}\{\text{class of intensions of } d_\alpha\}$

Observe that if class $\mathbf{C}\{a\}$ has subclasses then

** $\mathfrak{M}\{k_\alpha\}:\Delta[\mathfrak{M}\{h_\nu\},\mathfrak{M}\{k_{\nu\alpha}\}]$

where ν represents any one subclass. As an example, the class of mammals, $\mathbf{C}\{\text{mammals}\}$, has subclasses such as the class of bovines and the class of canines. One major common factor is the presence of mammary glands for feeding the young. The class of bovines is partially defined by a specialized digestive system. Within the class, bovines, the class, Holstein, is defined by a particular configuration and coloration. Thus there is a factor, mammal, and a factor, bovine, and a factor, Holstein. Each defines a particular level or subclass in the hierarchy.

5.2. Verbs

As with intension, the verbs in use with classes are copulas, although in some discussions the forms may be inverted so as to appear as transitive verbs when stated in English.

5.2.1. Inclusion of a Member

When defining the class, we have asserted that $\mathfrak{M}\{a_\alpha\}$ form that class. As an implication of D5.01 we have

C5.08 $\Delta[\mathfrak{M}\{a_\alpha\},\mathfrak{M}\{\mathbf{C}\{a\}\}]:\mathfrak{M}\{a_\alpha\}$

In a conventional notation this appears as

C5.09 $\mathfrak{M}\{a_\alpha\}\epsilon\mathbf{C}\{a\}$

C5.10 $\mathfrak{M}\{\text{C5.09}\}:\mathfrak{M}\{\text{C5.08}\}$

We have termed this, singular inclusion, that is,

E5.01 $\mathfrak{M}\{\epsilon\}:\mathfrak{M}\{\text{singular inclusion}\}$

However, we note that C5.09 is not one assertion but several, one for each "value" of α (one for each separate symbol which is represented by α). Therefore, we state

D5.02 $\mathfrak{M}\{\epsilon\}:\mathfrak{M}\{\text{C5.10}\}$

It is obvious from the definitions of $\mathbf{C}$ and ϵ that singular inclusion is directly related to the natural number 1». The term, singular, here applies to the "count" of the subclass, in this case, of the member. See Section 5.5 re cardinality.

As a minor point which sometimes causes confusion, singular inclusion is merely a statement about a member and a class; that member is already included in the class; it is not a new member and does not increase the cardinality of the class.

At this point, we can now see that a class of classes $\mathbf{C}\{\mathbf{C}_\beta\}$ is not the same as the class of all the members $\mathbf{C}\{d_{\alpha\beta}\}$ of all those classes. The members of the former are intensions of classes, and the members of the latter are intensions of other descriptors; member is our smallest or lowest-level designation in the definition of a class. Thus, for a given value of β

** $\mathfrak{M}\{d_{\alpha\beta}\}\epsilon\mathbf{C}_\beta$

when collected for all values of α. The class of these classes is

** $\mathfrak{M}\{\mathbf{C}_\beta\}\epsilon\mathbf{C}\{c\}$

where c is a common factor of all classes $\mathbf{C}_\beta$. Note that $\mathbf{C}\{c\}$ is not the union of all the classes $\mathbf{C}_\beta$. On the other hand we might be able to define a class $\mathbf{C}\{h\}$ such that

** $\mathfrak{M}\{d\alpha\beta\}\epsilon\mathbf{C}\{h\}$

when collected for all allowable permutations of α and β. Class $\mathbf{C}\{h\}$ is then the union of all the classes $\mathbf{C}_\beta$.

5.2.2. Identity of Extensions

Different symbols for the same members must have the same extension. For this purpose we define the identity symbol $\equiv$.

** $\mathbf{C}\{\text{all cats}\}\equiv\mathbf{C}\{\text{todos gatos}\}$

C5.11 $\mathbf{C}\{a\}\equiv\mathbf{C}\{b\}$

C5.12 Class $\mathbf{C}\{a\}$ contains the same members as class $\mathbf{C}\{b\}$

E5.02 $\mathfrak{M}\{\text{C5.11}\}:\mathfrak{M}\{\text{C5.12}\}$

Consider another example of C5.08.

C5.13 $\Delta[\mathfrak{M}\{b_\beta\},\mathfrak{M}\{\mathbf{C}\{b\}\}]:\mathfrak{M}\{b_\beta\}$

Then the corresponding form of C5.09 is

C5.14 $\mathfrak{M}\{b_\beta\}\epsilon\mathbf{C}\{b\}$

If the range of α is

** $1\text{»}\leq\alpha\leq M$

and the range of β is

** $1\text{»}\leq\beta\leq N$

then a requirement for identity is that

C5.15 $M=N$

Thus

** $\nabla[\mathfrak{M}\{\text{C5.15}\},\mathfrak{M}\{\text{C5.14}\}]:\mathfrak{M}\{\text{C5.16}\}$

C5.16 $\mathfrak{M}\{b_\beta\}\epsilon\mathbf{C}\{b\}$

Another, more stringent, requirement is that an additional reselection and attendant relabeling of members be done on one of the populations (for example, the members of $\mathbf{C}\{b\}$) such that, for all allowable α

C5.17 $\mathfrak{M}\{a_\alpha\}:\mathfrak{M}\{b_\alpha\}$

We then assert that

** $\nabla[\nabla[\mathfrak{M}\{\text{C5.09}\},\mathfrak{M}\{\text{C5.16}\}],\mathfrak{M}\{\text{C5.15}\}]:\mathfrak{M}\{\text{C5.18}\}$

C5.18 $\mathfrak{M}\{C5.17\}:\mathfrak{M}\{C5.11\}$

D5.03 $\mathfrak{M}\{\equiv\}:\mathfrak{M}\{C5.18\}$

In particular,

** $\mathfrak{M}\{A3.02\}:\nabla[\mathfrak{M}\{S_1\},\mathfrak{M}_\mu]$

S_1 $\mathfrak{M}\{a_\alpha\}:\mathfrak{M}\{a_\alpha\}$

** $\Delta[\mathfrak{M}\{S_1\},\mathfrak{M}\{C5.08\}]:\mathfrak{M}\{S_2\}$

S_2 $\Delta[\mathfrak{M}\{a_\alpha\},\mathfrak{M}\{\mathbf{C}\{a\}\}]:\Delta[\mathfrak{M}\{a_\alpha\},\mathfrak{M}\{\mathbf{C}\{a\}\}]$

P5.01 $\mathbf{C}\{a\}\equiv\mathbf{C}\{a\}$

With this assertion we can classify the copula.

E5.03 $\mathfrak{M}\{\text{copula} \equiv\}\epsilon\mathbf{C}\{\text{reflexive relationships}\}$

In a similar manner we restate C5.18 as

C5.19 $\nabla[\nabla[\mathfrak{M}\{C5.09\},\mathfrak{M}\{C5.14\}],\nabla[\mathfrak{M}\{C5.15\},\mathfrak{M}\{C5.17\}]]:\mathfrak{M}\{C5.20\}$

where

C5.20 $\mathbf{C}\{b\}\equiv\mathbf{C}\{a\}$

Thus

** $\nabla[\nabla[\mathfrak{M}\{C5.18\},\mathfrak{M}\{C5.19\}],\mathfrak{M}\{A3.12\}]:\mathfrak{M}\{P5.02\}$

P5.02 $\mathfrak{M}\{C5.11\}:\mathfrak{M}\{C5.20\}$

E5.04 $\mathfrak{M}\{\text{copula} \equiv\}\epsilon\mathbf{C}\{\text{symmetric relationships}\}$

Another important theorem can be developed.

C5.21 $\mathbf{C}\{b\}\equiv\mathbf{C}\{c\}$

C5.22 $\mathbf{C}\{a\}\equiv\mathbf{C}\{c\}$

In a manner parallel to that presented above,

C5.23 $\mathfrak{M}\{c_\alpha\}\epsilon\mathbf{C}\{c\}$

C5.24 $\mathfrak{M}\{b_\alpha\}:\mathfrak{M}\{c_\alpha\}$

** $\nabla[\mathfrak{M}\{C5.14\},\mathfrak{M}\{C5.23\}]:\mathfrak{M}\{C5.25\}$

C5.25 $\mathfrak{M}\{C5.24\}:\mathfrak{M}\{C5.21\}$

and

C5.26 $\mathfrak{M}\{a_\alpha\}:\mathfrak{M}\{c_\alpha\}$

** $\nabla[\mathfrak{M}\{C5.09\},\mathfrak{M}\{C5.23\}]:\mathfrak{M}\{C5.27\}$

C5.27 $\mathfrak{M}\{C5.26\}:\mathfrak{M}\{C5.22\}$

We may further observe that

** $\nabla[\nabla[\mathfrak{M}\{C5.17\},\mathfrak{M}\{C5.24\}],\mathfrak{M}\{A3.12\}]:\mathfrak{M}\{S_1\}$

S_1 $\Delta[\mathfrak{M}\{C5.17\},\mathfrak{M}\{C5.24\}]:\mathfrak{M}\{C5.26\}$

** $\nabla[\nabla[\mathfrak{M}\{S_1\},\mathfrak{M}\{C5.27\}],\mathfrak{M}\{A3.12\}]:\mathfrak{M}\{S_2\}$

S_2 $\Delta[\mathfrak{M}\{C5.17\},\mathfrak{M}\{C5.24\}]:\mathfrak{M}\{C5.22\}$

** $\nabla[\nabla[\mathfrak{M}\{S_2\},\mathfrak{M}\{A3.14\}],\nabla[\mathfrak{M}\{C5.18\},\mathfrak{M}\{C5.25\}]]:\mathfrak{M}\{P5.03\}$

P5.03 $\nabla[\mathfrak{M}\{C5.11\},\mathfrak{M}\{C5.21\}]:\mathfrak{M}\{C5.22\}$

E5.05 $\mathfrak{M}\{\text{copula} \equiv\}\epsilon\mathbf{C}\{\text{transitive relationships}\}$

Here again we have

E5.06 $\mathfrak{M}\{P5.03\}\epsilon\mathbf{C}\{\text{Rules of Substitution}\}$

As with intension and number, this Rule does not state the situation for conjunctions. Again, as a result, we whall present the analogous assertions with the definition of the conjunction.

5.2.3. Inclusion of a Subclass

In a manner similar to C3.06, we will define inclusion by the use of the conjunction $\cup$ in Section 5.3.2.

5.3. Conjunctions

As with the conjunctions for intension, we shall discuss three analogous conjunctions: intersection, complement and union. Complement will be discussed in Section 5.4.3. Observe here that a conjunction of classes is a class.

For a discussion of conjunctions of classes, consider the situation where for a population $d_{\mu\alpha}$ we apply two different selections which are similar to that of C5.03.

C5.28 $\Delta[\mathfrak{M}\{a\},\mathfrak{M}\{d_{\mu\alpha}\}]:\mathfrak{M}\{a\}$

C5.29 $\Delta[\mathfrak{M}\{b\},\mathfrak{M}\{d_{\mu\alpha}\}]:\mathfrak{M}\{b\}$

We see that a_α is selected by C5.28 and b_β is selected by C5.29; we must, however, be aware that some members which are selected in one of these statements may be selected by both. We shall label these common members as g_ρ. No other members of $d_{\mu\alpha}$ meet either of the selection criteria. If we assume that class a and class b are each a subclass of a larger class h (why else would we be concerned about a conjunction of the two?) then as in C5.04, using A3.10,

C5.30 $\mathfrak{M}\{a_\alpha\}:\nabla[\mathfrak{M}\{h\},\nabla[\mathfrak{M}\{a\},\mathfrak{M}\{r_\alpha\}]]$

C5.31 $\mathfrak{M}\{b_\beta\}:\nabla[\mathfrak{M}\{h\},\nabla[\mathfrak{M}\{b\},\mathfrak{M}\{t_\beta\}]]$

For those particular a_α and b_β which are selected by both C5.28 and C5.29, we can say (with perhaps a renumbering of γ) that

C5.32 $\mathfrak{M}\{g_\rho\}:\Delta[\mathfrak{M}\{a_\alpha\},\mathfrak{M}\{b_\beta\}]$

and then the form of g_ρ would be

C5.33 $\mathfrak{M}\{g_\rho\}:\nabla[\nabla[\mathfrak{M}\{a\},\mathfrak{M}\{b\}],\nabla[\mathfrak{M}\{h\},\mathfrak{M}\{s_\rho\}]]$

In comparison with C5.09 we can deduce that

C5.09 $\mathfrak{M}\{a_\alpha\}\in\mathbf{C}\{a\}$

C5.34 $\mathfrak{M}\{g_\rho\}\in\mathbf{C}\{a\}$

C5.14 $\mathfrak{M}\{b_\beta\}\in\mathbf{C}\{b\}$

C5.35 $\mathfrak{M}\{g_\rho\}\in\mathbf{C}\{b\}$

and that

C5.36 $\mathfrak{M}\{a_\alpha\}\in\mathbf{C}\{h\}$

C5.37 $\mathfrak{M}\{g_\rho\}\in\mathbf{C}\{h\}$

C5.38 $\mathfrak{M}\{b_\beta\}\in\mathbf{C}\{h\}$

These latter statements assume that

** $\Delta[\mathfrak{M}\{a\},\mathfrak{M}\{b\}]:\mathfrak{O}$

** $\Delta[\mathfrak{M}\{a\},\mathfrak{M}\{r_\alpha\}]:\mathfrak{O}$

** $\Delta[\mathfrak{M}\{b\},\mathfrak{M}\{t_\beta\}]:\mathfrak{O}$

5.3.1. Conjunction, Union

The union of two classes includes all members of each class without duplication of those members which appear in both classes. The class $\mathbf{C}_4$ formed by the union of class $\mathbf{C}_1$ and class $\mathbf{C}_2$ is represented by

** $\mathbf{C}_4 \equiv (\mathbf{C}_1 \cup \mathbf{C}_2)$

In keeping with our definition of class, a union of two classes is a class which is named by the factor which is common to the two subclasses. To refer to a current cliche, a union (or "mix") of "apples and oranges" is only applicable as a class if they each have a common factor, e.g., fruit.

Thus, a_α, b_β and g_ρ are each members of the class $\mathbf{C}\{h\}$, and each is a member of some "smaller" class. Since we may not know all members of class h (e.g., fruit), we can only discuss that subclass of $\mathbf{C}\{h\}$ which is composed of classes a and b. As stated above, our notation for this subclass is $(\mathbf{C}\{a\} \cup \mathbf{C}\{b\})$. As the two classes are defined by C5.09 and C5.14 (under the conditions associated with D5.01) so we may state that

** $\mathfrak{M}\{p_\mu\}:\nabla[\mathfrak{M}\{a_\alpha\},\mathfrak{M}\{b_\beta\}]$

and that

C5.39 $\mathfrak{M}\{p_\mu\} \epsilon (\mathbf{C}\{a\} \cup \mathbf{C}\{b\})$

E5.07 $\mathfrak{M}\{(\mathbf{C}\{a\} \cup \mathbf{C}\{b\})\}:\mathfrak{M}\{$the union of class $\mathbf{C}\{a\}$ and class $\mathbf{C}\{b\}\}$

We may notice that the sequence of symbolism for this union is arbitrary, and as an application of A3.04 we recognize this arbitrariness by stating

C5.40 $\mathfrak{M}\{(\mathbf{C}\{a\} \cup \mathbf{C}\{b\})\}:\mathfrak{M}\{(\mathbf{C}\{b\} \cup \mathbf{C}\{a\})\}$

This allows us to say,

E5.08 $\mathfrak{M}\{$conjunction $\cup\} \epsilon \mathbf{C}\{$commutative relationships$\}$

As an extension of C5.09 and it establishment, we state that

C5.41 $\mathfrak{M}\{c_\gamma\} \epsilon \mathbf{C}\{c\}$

This statement, with C5.09 and C5.14, defines two new classes. As a parallel to C5.39 and with the conditions of D5.01, we now define that

** $\mathfrak{M}\{q_\nu\}:\nabla[\nabla[\mathfrak{M}\{a_\alpha\},\mathfrak{M}\{b_\beta\}],\mathfrak{M}\{c_\gamma\}]$

such that

C5.42 $\mathfrak{M}\{q_\nu\} \epsilon ((\mathbf{C}\{a\} \cup \mathbf{C}\{b\}) \cup \mathbf{C}\{c\})$

We also state that

** $\mathfrak{M}\{r_\rho\}:\nabla[\mathfrak{M}\{a_\alpha\},\nabla[\mathfrak{M}\{b_\beta\},\mathfrak{M}\{c_\gamma\}]]$

such that

C5.43 $\mathfrak{M}\{r_\rho\} \epsilon (\mathbf{C}\{a\} \cup (\mathbf{C}\{b\} \cup \mathbf{C}\{c\}))$

Thus, because of A3.05 and A3.12, we assert in C5.44 that the difference between its left and right sides is merely one of symbolic grouping.

C5.44 $\mathfrak{M}\{((\mathbf{C}\{a\} \cup \mathbf{C}\{b\}) \cup \mathbf{C}\{c\})\}:\mathfrak{M}\{(\mathbf{C}\{a\} \cup (\mathbf{C}\{b\} \cup \mathbf{C}\{c\}))\}$

E5.09 $\mathfrak{M}\{$conjunction $\cup\} \epsilon \mathbf{C}\{$associative relationships$\}$

We may observe that, in the event of C5.15 and C5.17, the term $(\mathbf{C}\{a\}\cup\mathbf{C}\{b\})$ becomes the term $(\mathbf{C}\{a\}\cup\mathbf{C}\{a\})$. But with A3.07 we assert that C5.09 defines only one class $\mathbf{C}\{a\}$ because of A3.07. Thus we say

C5.45 $\mathfrak{M}\{(\mathbf{C}\{a\}\cup\mathbf{C}\{a\})\}:\mathfrak{M}\{\mathbf{C}\{a\}\}$

This often proves to be a convenience in symbolic manipulations.

With these statements, our definition of $\cup$ is

D5.04 $\mathfrak{M}\{\cup\}:\Delta[\Delta[\mathfrak{M}\{C5.39\},\mathfrak{M}\{D5.01\}],\mathfrak{M}_{\cup}]$

where

** $\mathfrak{M}_{\cup}:\Delta[\Delta[\mathfrak{M}\{C5.40\},\mathfrak{M}\{C5.44\}],\mathfrak{M}\{C5.45\}]$

If c_γ is as defined above in C5.41 then by forms similar to C5.39 with D5.01 we have (with the re-use of p_μ and q_ν as symbols)

** $\Delta[\mathfrak{M}\{C5.39\},\mathfrak{M}\{D5.01\}]:\Delta[\mathfrak{M}\{S_1\},\mathfrak{M}\{C5.46\}]$

S_1 $\mathfrak{M}\{p_\mu\}:\nabla[\mathfrak{M}\{a_\alpha\},\mathfrak{M}\{c_\gamma\}]$

C5.46 $\mathfrak{M}\{p_\mu\}\in(\mathbf{C}\{a\}\cup\mathbf{C}\{c\})$

** $\Delta[\mathfrak{M}\{C5.39\},\mathfrak{M}\{D5.01\}]:\Delta[\mathfrak{M}\{S_2\},\mathfrak{M}\{C5.47\}]$

S_2 $\mathfrak{M}\{q_\nu\}:\nabla[\mathfrak{M}\{b_\beta\},\mathfrak{M}\{c_\gamma\}]$

C5.47 $\mathfrak{M}\{q_\nu\}\in(\mathbf{C}\{b\}\cup\mathbf{C}\{c\})$

** $\Delta[\nabla[\mathfrak{M}\{C5.17\},\mathfrak{M}\{A3.06\}],\nabla[\mathfrak{M}\{C5.46\},\mathfrak{M}\{C5.47\}]]:\mathfrak{M}\{C5.48\}$

C5.48 $(\mathbf{C}\{a\cup\mathbf{C}\{c)\equiv(\mathbf{C}\{b\cup\mathbf{C}\{c)$

** $\Delta[\mathfrak{M}\{C5.18\},\mathfrak{M}\{A3.12\}]:\mathfrak{M}\{P5.04\}$

P5.04 $\mathfrak{M}\{C5.11\}:\mathfrak{M}\{C5.48\}$

5.3.2. Inclusion of a Subclass

Though inclusion is a verb, it is an application of union; the inclusion of all members of one class $\mathbf{C}\{b\}$ in another class $\mathbf{C}\{a\}$ is represented by:

C5.49 $\mathbf{C}\{a\}\supset\mathbf{C}\{b\}$

C5.50 $\mathbf{C}\{a\}\equiv(\mathbf{C}\{b\}\cup\mathbf{C}_\mu)$

C5.51 $\mathfrak{M}\{C5.49\}:\mathfrak{M}\{C5.50\}$

D5.05 $\mathfrak{M}\{\supset\}:\mathfrak{M}\{C5.51\}$

C5.52 Class $\mathbf{C}\{a\}$ contains all members of class $\mathbf{C}\{b\}$

E5.10 $\mathfrak{M}\{C5.49\}:\mathfrak{M}\{C5.52\}$

This verb is used in two forms, $\supset$ and $\subset$, in a manner analogous to the active and passive forms of a transitive verb: includes; is included. Or one might be viewed as an inverted form of the other. The definition of the symbol $\subset$ directly parallels that which we have just completed for "$\supset$" , but with some of the sequences reversed. The inclusion of all members of one class $\mathbf{C}\{a\}$ in another class $\mathbf{C}\{b\}$ is represented by:

C5.53 $\mathbf{C}\{a\}\subset\mathbf{C}\{b\}$

C5.54 $\mathbf{C}\{b\}\equiv(\mathbf{C}\{a\}\cup\mathbf{C}_\nu)$

C5.55 $\mathfrak{M}\{C5.53\}:\mathfrak{M}\{C5.54\}$

D5.06 $\mathfrak{M}\{\subset\}:\mathfrak{M}\{C5.55\}$

C5.56 Class $\mathbf{C}\{b\}$ contains all members of class $\mathbf{C}\{a\}$

E5.11 $\mathfrak{M}\{C5.53\}:\mathfrak{M}\{C5.56\}$

5.3.3. Conjunction, Intersection

The intersection of class $\mathbf{C}_1$ and class $\mathbf{C}_2$ is that class $\mathbf{C}_3$ which contains only those members which appear in both of the classes.

** $(\mathbf{C}_1 \cap \mathbf{C}_2) \equiv \mathbf{C}_3$

The intersection of two classes is a class which is named by the factor which is unique to the intersection. The members of the intersection are defined by C5.32. With such a definition of member, we state

C5.57 $\mathfrak{M}\{g_\nu\} \epsilon (\mathbf{C}\{a\} \cap \mathbf{C}\{b\})$

E5.12 $\mathfrak{M}\{(\mathbf{C}\{a\} \cap \mathbf{C}\{b\})\}:\mathfrak{M}\{$the intersection of class $\mathbf{C}\{a\}$ and class $\mathbf{C}\{b\}\}$

The sequence of symbolism for this intersection is arbitrary; we recognize this arbitrariness, from A3.08, as part of our definition by asserting

C5.58 $\mathfrak{M}\{(\mathbf{C}\{a\} \cap \mathbf{C}\{b\})\}:\mathfrak{M}\{(\mathbf{C}\{b\} \cap \mathbf{C}\{a\})\}$

As a result, the classification of this symbolism is

E5.13 $\mathfrak{M}\{$conjunction $\cap\} \epsilon \mathbf{C}\{$commutative relationships$\}$

With the individual classes defined by C5.09, C5.14 and C5.41 and with the relationships shown by C5.32 and C5.57, we shall further define that

** $\mathfrak{M}\{p_\mu\}:\Delta[\Delta[\mathfrak{M}\{a_\alpha\},\mathfrak{M}\{b_\beta\}],\mathfrak{M}\{C1C\}]$

Note that here we are re-using the symbols p_μ and q_ν with new definitions.

C5.59 $\mathfrak{M}\{p_\mu\} \epsilon ((\mathbf{C}\{a\} \cap \mathbf{C}\{b\}) \cap \mathbf{C}\{c\})$

In like manner we shall define that

** $\mathfrak{M}\{q_\nu\}:\Delta[\mathfrak{M}\{a_\alpha\},\Delta[\mathfrak{M}\{b_\beta\},\mathfrak{M}\{c_\gamma\}]]$

C5.60 $\mathfrak{M}\{q_\nu\} \epsilon (\mathbf{C}\{a\} \cap (\mathbf{C}\{b\} \cap \mathbf{C}\{c\}))$

But A3.09 and A3.12 would lead us to establish C5.61 as a part of our definition.

C5.61 $\mathfrak{M}\{((\mathbf{C}\{a\} \cap \mathbf{C}\{b\}) \cap \mathbf{C}\{c\})\}:\mathfrak{M}\{(\mathbf{C}\{a\} \cap (\mathbf{C}\{b\} \cap \mathbf{C}\{c\}))\}$

E5.14 $\mathfrak{M}\{$conjunction $\cap\} \epsilon \mathbf{C}\{$associative relationships$\}$

Again, in the event of C5.15 and C5.17, the term $(\mathbf{C}\{a\} \cap \mathbf{C}\{b\})$ becomes the term $(\mathbf{C}\{a\} \cap \mathbf{C}\{a\})$. And with A3.11 we assert that C5.09 defines only one class $\mathbf{C}\{a\}$. Therefore,

C5.62 $\mathfrak{M}\{(\mathbf{C}\{a\} \cap \mathbf{C}\{a\})\}:\mathfrak{M}\{\mathbf{C}\{a\}\}$

With these statements, our definition of $\cap$ is

D5.07 $\mathfrak{M}\{\cap\}:\Delta[\Delta[\mathfrak{M}\{C5.32\},\mathfrak{M}\{C5.57\}],\Delta[\mathfrak{M}\{D5.01\},\mathfrak{M}_\cap]]$

where

** $\mathfrak{M}_\cap:\Delta[\Delta[\mathfrak{M}\{C5.58\},\mathfrak{M}\{C5.61\}],\mathfrak{M}\{C5.62\}]$

If c_γ is defined as in C5.41 then (with the re-definition of p_μ and q_ν)

** $\Delta[\Delta[\mathfrak{M}\{C5.32\},\mathfrak{M}\{C5.57\}],\mathfrak{M}\{D5.01\}]:\Delta[\mathfrak{M}\{S_1\},\mathfrak{M}\{C5.63\}]$

S_1 $\mathfrak{M}\{p_\mu\}:\Delta[\mathfrak{M}\{a_\alpha\},\mathfrak{M}\{c_\gamma\}]$

C5.63 $\mathfrak{M}\{p_\mu\}\in(\mathbf{C}\{a\}\cap\mathbf{C}\{c\})$

** $\Delta[\Delta[\mathfrak{M}\{C5.32\},\mathfrak{M}\{C5.57\}],\mathfrak{M}\{D5.01\}]:\Delta[\mathfrak{M}\{S_2\},\mathfrak{M}\{C5.64\}]$

S_2 $\mathfrak{M}\{q_\nu\}:\Delta[\mathfrak{M}\{b_\beta\},\mathfrak{M}\{c_\gamma\}]$

C5.64 $\mathfrak{M}\{q_\nu\}\in(\mathbf{C}\{b\}\cap\mathbf{C}\{c\})$

** $\Delta[\nabla[\mathfrak{M}\{C5.17\},\mathfrak{M}\{A3.10\}],\nabla[\mathfrak{M}\{C5.63\},\mathfrak{M}\{C5.64\}]]:\mathfrak{M}\{C5.65\}$

C5.65 $(\mathbf{C}\{a\}\cap\mathbf{C}\{c\})\equiv(\mathbf{C}\{b\}\cap\mathbf{C}\{c\})$

** $\Delta[\mathfrak{M}\{C5.18\},\mathfrak{M}\{A3.12\}]:\mathfrak{M}\{P5.05\}$

P5.05 $\mathfrak{M}\{C5.11\}:\mathfrak{M}\{C5.65\}$

5.3.4. Distribution Between Conjunctions

S_1 $\Delta[\Delta[\mathfrak{M}\{a_\alpha\},\nabla[\mathfrak{M}\{b_\beta\},\mathfrak{M}\{c_\gamma\}]],\nabla[\mathfrak{M}\{C5.39\},\mathfrak{M}\{C5.57\}]]:$
$\mathfrak{M}\{(\mathbf{C}\{a\}\cap(\mathbf{C}\{b\}\cup\mathbf{C}\{c\}))\}$

S_2 $\Delta[\nabla[\Delta[\mathfrak{M}\{a_\alpha\},\mathfrak{M}\{b_\beta\}],\Delta[\mathfrak{M}\{a_\alpha\},\mathfrak{M}\{c_\gamma\}]],\nabla[\mathfrak{M}\{C5.39\},\mathfrak{M}\{C5.57\}]]:$
$\mathfrak{M}\{((\mathbf{C}\{a\}\cap\mathbf{C}\{b\})\cup(\mathbf{C}\{a\}\cap\mathbf{C}\{c\}))\}$

** $\Delta[\nabla[\mathfrak{M}\{S_1\},\mathfrak{M}\{S_2\}],\nabla[\mathfrak{M}\{A3.10\},\mathfrak{M}\{A3.12\}]]:\mathfrak{M}\{P5.06\}$

P5.06 $\mathfrak{M}\{(\mathbf{C}\{a\}\cap(\mathbf{C}\{b\}\cup\mathbf{C}\{c\}))\}:\mathfrak{M}\{((\mathbf{C}\{a\}\cap\mathbf{C}\{b\})\cup(\mathbf{C}\{a\}\cap\mathbf{C}\{c\}))\}$

S_1 $\Delta[\nabla[\mathfrak{M}\{a_\alpha\},\Delta[\mathfrak{M}\{b_\beta\},\mathfrak{M}\{c_\gamma\}]],\nabla[\mathfrak{M}\{C5.39\},\mathfrak{M}\{C5.57\}]]:$
$\mathfrak{M}\{(\mathbf{C}\{a\}\cup(\mathbf{C}\{b\}\cap\mathbf{C}\{c\}))\}$

S_2 $\Delta[\Delta[\nabla[\mathfrak{M}\{a_\alpha\},\mathfrak{M}\{b_\beta\}],\nabla[\mathfrak{M}\{a_\alpha\},\mathfrak{M}\{c_\gamma\}]],\nabla[\mathfrak{M}\{C5.39\},\mathfrak{M}\{C5.57\}]]:$
$\mathfrak{M}\{((\mathbf{C}\{a\}\cup\mathbf{C}\{b\})\cap(\mathbf{C}\{a\}\cup\mathbf{C}\{c\}))\}$

** $\Delta[\nabla[\mathfrak{M}\{S_1\},\mathfrak{M}\{S_2\}],\nabla[\mathfrak{M}\{A3.10\},\mathfrak{M}\{A3.12\}]]:\mathfrak{M}\{P5.07\}$

P5.07 $\mathfrak{M}\{(\mathbf{C}\{a\}\cup(\mathbf{C}\{b\}\cap\mathbf{C}\{c\}))\}:\mathfrak{M}\{((\mathbf{C}\{a\}\cup\mathbf{C}\{b\})\cap(\mathbf{C}\{a\}\cup\mathbf{C}\{c\}))\}$

5.4. Descriptors, Extension

To further establish a parallel between extension and intension, we shall discuss some additional entities.

5.4.1. The Vacuous Class

The vacuous class **O** is often defined as a class which has no members. Or, referring back to our definition of union, we might be tempted to define it as a class for which all members are null. The latter is a very awkward concept, and the former might be more useful as a derived characteristic. The purpose of **O** seems to be entirely for convenience in the manipulations of symbolism in derivations. Therefore, we shall define a vacuous class **O** as the "identity element" for the conjunction $\cup$, that is, a class which has no members.

C5.66 $\mathfrak{M}\{(\mathbf{C}\{a\}\cup\mathbf{O})\}:\mathfrak{M}\{\mathbf{C}\{a\}\}$

D5.08 $\mathfrak{M}\{\mathbf{O}\}:\mathfrak{M}\{C5.66\}$

5.4.2. A "Unity" Class

Some students have also defined an "identity element" or "universal set" based on intersection $\cap$. This would perhaps appear in the form, for all α,

** $(\mathbf{C}_\alpha \cap \mathbf{C}_I) \equiv \mathbf{C}_\alpha$

As with intension, if this relationship holds for all classes then $\mathbf{C}_I$ must be the union of all conceivable classes: cats, dogs, numbers, point sets, apples, oranges, etc., etc. In more restricted discussions, such as the theory of number, the concept appears more frequently. For example, a "universal set" of the natural numbers,

** $\mathbf{N} \equiv \mathbf{C}\{\text{natural-number}\}$

might be used when discussing subjects which involve natural numbers. Then, for some set of natural numbers $\mathbf{S}\{n\}$

** $(\mathbf{S}\{n\} \cap \mathbf{N}) \equiv \mathbf{S}\{n\}$

Many who define such a "denumerably infinite" class seem to do so for the purpose of "operations" which are directly parallel to those for matrices. A matrix is a cartesian tensor. A matrix is a dimensioned array. It may be viewed, perhaps, as a special class, but classes are not necessarily dimensioned and are not, therefore, necessarily matrices. Further, matrices are defined in terms of the algebra of number and therefore are based on the axioms of that algebra.

We also may observe that it is often possible, with the use of the diagonal matrix (an identity element), to define an "inverse" matrix, under certain rigidly specified conditions. One condition is that the determinant of the original matrix can not be zero. In like manner some would define an "inverse" class, using a $\mathbf{C}_I$ as the identity element. Let us denote this "inverse" of class $\mathbf{C}\{a\}$ with the symbol $\mathbf{C}^i\{a\}$. Then we would have

** $(\mathbf{C}\{a\} \cap \mathbf{C}^i\{a\}) \equiv \mathbf{C}_I$

But observe that the maximum intersection with $\mathbf{C}\{a\}$ is $\mathbf{C}\{a\}$ which is in conflict with our previous comments about $\mathbf{C}_I$ being the union of all conceivable classes.

5.4.3. Complement of the Intersection

In the establishment of the intersection of a pair of classes we excluded members of either class which were not in both. The excluded members are our concern here. This class is, in some texts, denoted by a minus sign between two class symbols. To minimize the possible ambiguity in symbolism later on, we shall use a different symbol, **w**.

C5.67 $\mathfrak{M}\{\mathbf{C}\{a\}\}:\mathfrak{M}\{((\mathbf{C}\{a\}\mathbf{w}\mathbf{C}\{b\})\cup(\mathbf{C}\{a\}\cap\mathbf{C}\{b\}))\}$

C5.68 $((\mathbf{C}\{a\}\mathbf{w}\mathbf{C}\{b\})\cap(\mathbf{C}\{a\}\cap\mathbf{C}\{b\}))\equiv\mathbf{O}$

D5.09 $\mathfrak{M}\{\mathbf{w}\}:\Delta[\mathfrak{M}\{\text{C5.67}\},\mathfrak{M}\{\text{C5.68}\}]$

E5.15 $\mathfrak{M}\{(\mathbf{C}\{a\}\mathbf{w}\mathbf{C}\{b\})\}:\mathfrak{M}\{\mathbf{C}\{a\}\text{ excluding any member of }\mathbf{C}\{b\}\}$

5.4.4. Sets

As we have previously stated, a special type of class is frequently used, and we shall call this a "set". We shall denote it by **S**. Our definition is that a set is a collection of numbers or of ordered groups ("n-tuples" or "n dimensions") of numbers which are included in some prescribed definition. All elements of the set must conform to that definition. Unless a constraint is included within the prescribed definition of the set, a set is an unordered aggregation, and it may have any quantity of duplicate values; e.g., a set of observations may contain many identical values.

Since we view sets as special examples of classes, all of the definitions, axioms and theorems of Chapter 5 also apply to sets.

To conform with prevalent notation, the members of a set will be shown as the specific nouns, the numbers or points, rather than the intension which is represented by that noun, as we do in our notation for classes. However, it must be remembered that set notation is still only a "shorthand" for class notation, and we shall attempt to maintain parallels in these two notations.

To partially define the set **N** we state

** 0∈**N**
** 1»∈**N**
** 010»∈**N**
** 011»∈**N**
** 0100»∈**N**
** •
** •

We have previously defined the natural numbers as individual symbols. We also state

D5.10 **N**≡**S**{natural-numbers}

We shall now define a new set **S**{integer} . As mentioned before, integers are "reference points" in the "continuum" of number.

D5.11 **S**{integer}≡(**S**{natural-number}∪**S**{negative-integer})

As discussed earlier, we define the set of negative integers in the following manner.

C5.69 **S**{n}⊂**S**{natural-number}
C5.70 𝔰[x,n]=0
C5.71 **S**{x}⊂**S**{negative-integer}
D5.12 ∇[𝔐{C5.69},𝔐{C5.70}]:𝔐{C5.71}

Another definition to consider is

D5.13 **S**{natural-number}≡(**S**{0}∪**S**{positive-integer})

C5.72 **S**{a}⊂**S**{positive-integer}
C5.73 **S**{b}⊂**S**{integer}
C5.74 **S**{x}⊂**S**{rational-number}
D5.14 ∇[∇[𝕸{C4.24},𝕸{C5.72}],𝕸{C5.73}]:𝕸{C5.74}

Thus, depending on the values of a and b above, we can see that

D5.15 **S**{rational-number}⊃**S**{integer}

We now define the set, real-number, by

D5.16 **S**{real-number}≡(**S**{rational-number}∪(**S**{irrational-number}∪**S**{transcendental-number}))

5.5. Cardinality of a Class

As one of our uses of number we shall define the metric of a class. A metric is a measure, and there are several measures which might be defined with respect to a class. For our purposes we shall confine our discussion to one particular metric ƀ{**C**{a}}, the cardinality of the class. However, as examples for a set, another common measure is the arithmetic mean of the elements of the set, and another might be the length of interval which contains those elements.

Referring back to C5.01, C5.09 and related doscussions, we there stated in C5.02 that α had a "range" N. Thus, there we were assuming a labeling of members of a class by the use of natural numbers, though such an assumption is not a requirement of the definition or class or its attributes. In D4.06, D4.07, D4.08, etc., we defined numbers by what might be viewed as a recursion formula: each new member being defined as a sum of the "prior" member and 1». An aggregation of these definitions can then be defined as a sequence, seq(m,n), where "m" is the number with which we started and "n" is the ending number. More specifically, as an example,

** 𝕸{seq(1,3)}:∇[∇[𝕸{D4.06},𝕸{D4.07}],𝕸{D4.08}]

In the more general case, seq(1,M), each member of the sequence is defined from its predecessor, and the number M is the largest number defined for that sequence.

Each member a_α of a class **C**{a} is labeled once with a member from the sequence as that member of the sequence is defined. That is, if

** 𝕸{a_α}∊**C**{a}

then each α is defined by the next value from the recursion formula for seq(1,N). Each such value is a natural number. This labeling is the one-to-one relationship of which Russell spoke (21,133). And since seq(1,N) is a class (a set), it has a cardinality.

C5.75 ƀ{seq(1,N)}=N

Further, seq(1,N) constitutes the range of α. Therefore,

C5.76 𝔟{**C**{a}}=N
C5.77 𝔐{C5.75}:𝔐{C5.76}
D5.17 𝔐{𝔟}:Δ[Δ[𝔐{C5.09},𝔐{C5.02}],𝔐{C5.77}]
E5.16 𝔐{𝔟{**C**{a}}}:𝔐{cardinality of class **C**{a}}

We must interject a statement at this point about "counting". The one-to-one correspondence which is established above between the members of a general class and the members of seq(1,N), which is a subset of **N**, is the process which we call counting. The "count" of the members of the class is its cardinality. That is,

E5.17 𝔐{count}:𝔐{cardinality}

We note that counting does not define the natural numbers; the natural numbers are used in the definition of counting.

The word, similar, as applied to classes can now be defined.

C5.78 𝔟{**C**{a}}=𝔟{**C**{b}}
C5.79 Classes **C**{a} and **C**{b} are similar
E5.18 𝔐{C5.78}:𝔐{C5.79}

We must remember, however, that similarity of classes implies nothing more than that the quantity of members of each are the same.

If we consider two classes, **C**{a} and **C**{b}, and the intersection of these classes we can assign a value of cardinality to each.

C5.76 𝔟{**C**{a}}=N
S_1 𝔟{**C**{b}}=M
S_2 𝔟{(**C**{a}∩**C**{b})}=L

We can not specify that L is non-zero; that is, we do not specify the extent of intersection. By referring to our original definitions of class as a collection of related members, the cardinality of class (**C**{a}∪**C**{b}) can be stated as

S_3 𝔟{(**C**{a}∪**C**{b})}=𝔰[N,𝔰[M,𝔭[L,1«]]]

By substitution from the first three assertions we determine that

P5.08 𝔰[𝔟{(**C**{a}∪**C**{b})},𝔟{(**C**{a}∩**C**{b})}]=𝔰[𝔟{**C**{a}},𝔟{**C**{b}}]

From this statement it follows that

P5.09 𝔟{**O**}=0

5.5.1. Repeated Addition and Multiplication

For convenience of later symbolic manipulations we shall now define other forms of two conjunctions. In each case the new symbol represents a repetition of the previously defined conjunction. Each of these symbols represents an "operation" over the members of a class or set. Further, each assumes that the members of that class or set have already been labeled or relabeled (per Section 5.5) from the sequence, seq(1,M).

The definitions for repeated sum are:

D5.18 $\mathfrak{s}[\mathfrak{s}[x_1,x_{010}],x_{011}]=\sum_{\alpha=1}^{011} x_\alpha$

D5.19 $\sum_{\alpha=1»}^{\mathfrak{s}[n,1»]} x_\alpha=\mathfrak{s}[x_{\mathfrak{s}[n,1»]},\sum_{\alpha=1»}^{n} x_\alpha]$

The definitions for repeated product are:

D5.20 $\mathfrak{p}[\mathfrak{p}[x_1,x_{010}],x_{011}]=\prod_{\alpha=1}^{011} x_\alpha$

D5.21 $\prod_{\alpha=1}^{\mathfrak{s}[n,1»]} x_\alpha=\mathfrak{p}[x_{\mathfrak{s}[n,1»]},\prod_{\alpha=1}^{n} x_\alpha]$

With the use of repeated sum we can define the arithmetic mean of a set of numbers. If that set is $\mathbf{S}\{x_\alpha\}$ then

C5.80 $N=\mathfrak{h}\{\mathbf{S}\{x_\alpha\}\}$

C5.81 $\mathfrak{p}[N,X]=\sum_{\alpha=1}^{N} x_\alpha$

where

C5.82 $\mathfrak{M}\{X\}:\mathfrak{M}\{\text{arithmetic mean of } x_\alpha\}$

E5.19 $\nabla[\mathfrak{M}\{C5.80\},\mathfrak{M}\{C5.81\}]:\mathfrak{M}\{C5.82\}$

5.6. Disjunction of Intensions

At this point we can now consider one of the subjects which we alluded to earlier at several points. Disjunction (or disjunctive conjunction) is a selection from a collection of alternatives. As such it contains a facet which is external to Logic; the selection may be by choice or chance. In physical situations the selection occurs at a future time or is hypothetical for some reason. Examples of a future selection are:

** Either I shall go to the movies or I shall watch TV.

** He will take the suitcase and/or the handbag.

In each of these examples we have only two alternatives, but examples with many alternatives are common. Concerning the selection, it is not difficult to argue that even choice actually has all the elements of a biased chance selection, and thus the selection process (which is important in induction) becomes the foundation of the "frequency" view of probability. This is discussed in later Sections.

The situation of being hypothetical requires disjunction. Statements about known completed action are merely descriptive; statements about unknown completed action are conjectural. Thus the completed action in

** "Either he lit the fuse or lightning did"

is a probabilistic assertion about the poor soul and is handled by a disjunction. The truth-value developed for this statement is based on the circumstances. Restated, it might appear that disjunction could only be discussed after we have assumed a philosophy of physics since disjunction is a selection which seems to be a change with respect to time or a discussion of situation before and situation after some point in time. Of course, time and space are defined by the four variables which constitute the foundation of our physical philosophy. Though it often appears that all applications of disjunction are based on such physical philosophy, note that D5.22 and D5.23 are disjunctions which are not temporal or physical in any sense.

In common usage of the language, both of the forms

** Either A or B

** A and/or B

are often oversimplified and stated as

** A or B

where A and B are assertions. Such a simplification can create a serious ambiguity in the mind of the reader. Thus we must differentiate more carefully herein between the two types. To be more precise we define

E5.20 $\mathfrak{M}$\{inclusive disjunction\}:$\mathfrak{M}$\{the selection of at least N alternatives\}

E5.21 $\mathfrak{M}$\{exclusive disjunction\}:$\mathfrak{M}$\{the selection of exactly N alternatives\}

By the use of the above examples, these can be restated as

E5.20 $\mathfrak{M}$\{inclusive disjunction\}:$\mathfrak{M}$\{A and/or B\}

E5.21 $\mathfrak{M}$\{exclusive disjunction\}:$\mathfrak{M}$\{either A or B\}

These will be discussed separately.

5.6.1. Exclusive Disjunction

In this process we select exactly M options from the available N options. The most common situation is where M=1, as used in the example above.

C5.83 $\mathfrak{M}_1 \epsilon \mathbf{C}\{S_\alpha\}$

C5.84 $\mathfrak{M}_1$ is the selected concept from a class of $\mathfrak{M}_\alpha$

E5.22 $\mathfrak{M}$\{C5.83\}:$\mathfrak{M}$\{C5.84\}

Using the above example,

S_1 I shall go to the movies

S_2 I shall watch TV

S_3 $\mathfrak{M}\{S_1\} \epsilon \mathbf{C}\{S_\alpha\}$

S_4 $\mathfrak{M}\{S_2\} \epsilon \mathbf{C}\{S_\alpha\}$

S_5 $\mathfrak{b}\{\mathbf{C}\{S_\alpha\}\}=010$»

Note that S_3, S_4 and S_5 define $\mathbf{C}\{S_\alpha\}$. Therefore, if $\mathfrak{M}_\mu$ is the selected concept then

S_6 $\mathfrak{M}_\mu \epsilon \mathbf{C}\{S_\alpha\}$

and we state the interpretation that

** $\mathfrak{M}\{S_6\}:\mathfrak{M}\{S_7\}$

where

S_7 $\mathfrak{M}_\mu$:$\mathfrak{M}$\{either I shall go to the movies or I shall watch TV\}

In the above definition, E5.22, we have placed no requirement that the members $\mathfrak{M}_\alpha$ of the class $\mathbf{C}\{S_\alpha\}$ be independent. However, since only one member of the class can be selected, we define

C5.85 The members S_α of the class are mutually exclusive

E5.23 $\mathfrak{M}$\{C5.83\}:$\mathfrak{M}$\{C5.85\}

A case which appears to be more general than that which we have discussed above is the selection of exactly M members from a class having N members. For example,

** "2 of the 9 boys will win prizes"

The class from which we can select has nine members of the form

** $\mathfrak{M}$\{A will win a prize\}

** $\mathfrak{M}$\{B will win a prize\}

** •

** •

From this class we must select two members. The formulation of such a process is straightforward, if lengthy. An alternative formulation is to create a statement for each possible combination, of which there are 36 possibilities in this example. These would be of the form

** $\mathfrak{M}$\{A and B will each win a prize\}

** $\mathfrak{M}$\{A and C will each win a prize\}

** •

** •

The selection from a class containing these 36 members is a selection of exactly one member, which is the situation described at the beginning of this Section. Thus, exclusive disjunction can be restated in all cases as the selection of exactly one member. Note that in this last example the members of the class from which the selection is made are mutually exclusive, but they are certainly not independent.

5.6.2. Inclusive Disjunction

In this process we select at least M of the N options available. The possible selections are not mutually exclusive, but we usually assume that the options are exhaustive. If the members $\mathfrak{M}_\alpha$ are mutually exclusive then this selection degenerates to that of exclusive disjunction by definition.

As in the general case of exclusive disjunction, we here can take the class of N options and form a new class of all the possible selections and thus select only one from that new class. If M=1 with respect to the original class then the number of members in this new class would be Q, where Q is the number of possible selections. To define this number we must first define the term, factorial.

C5.86 $N!=\prod_{\alpha=1}^{N}\alpha$

C5.87 $\mathfrak{M}$\{N!\}:$\mathfrak{M}$\{N factorial\}

E5.24 $\mathfrak{M}$\{C5.86\}:$\mathfrak{M}$\{C5.87\}

With this definition we can define Q, above, as

** $Q=\sum_{M=1}^{N}(N!/\ \mathfrak{p}[\mathfrak{s}[N,\mathfrak{p}[M,1«]]!,M!])$

In the common situation of choosing one or both from a class having two members ($\mathfrak{M}_\alpha$ and $\mathfrak{M}_\beta$), there are three mutually exclusive options: $\mathfrak{M}_\alpha$, $\mathfrak{M}_\beta$, $\nabla[\mathfrak{M}_\alpha,\mathfrak{M}_\beta]$. Let us define

** $\mathfrak{M}_\alpha \epsilon \mathbf{C}_1$

** $\mathfrak{M}_\beta \epsilon \mathbf{C}_1$

** $\mathfrak{b}\{\mathbf{C}_1\}=010»$

and for our new class

** $\mathfrak{M}_\alpha \epsilon \mathbf{C}_2$

** $\mathfrak{M}_\beta \epsilon \mathbf{C}_2$

** $\nabla[\mathfrak{M}_\alpha,\mathfrak{M}_\beta] \epsilon \mathbf{C}_2$

** $\mathfrak{b}\{\mathbf{C}_2\}=011»$

Thus our selection is shown as

** $\mathfrak{M}_\mu \epsilon \mathbf{C}_2$

which is another case of exclusive disjunction.

5.7. Other Definitions

We are now in a position to define some other useful concepts.

5.7.1. Independence

With disjunction and the null intension we can define "independence".

C5.88 $\Delta[\mathfrak{M}_\alpha,\mathfrak{M}_\beta]:\mathfrak{O}$

E5.25 $\mathfrak{M}$\{C5.88\}$\epsilon\mathbf{C}$\{C5.89,C5.90,C5.91,C5.92\}

C5.89 S_α and S_β are independent

C5.90 S_α is nonsense

C5.91 S_β is nonsense

C5.92 Both S_α and S_β are nonsense

Independence of concepts is used in many areas of Logic and probability theory.

5.7.2. Disjoint Classes

Disjoint classes can be defined on the basis of the vacuous class and disjunction.

C5.93 $(\mathbf{C}\{a\}\cap\mathbf{C}\{b\})\equiv\mathbf{O}$

E5.26 $\mathfrak{M}$\{C5.93\}$\epsilon\mathbf{C}$\{C5.94,C5.95,C5.96,C5.97\}

C5.94 **C**{a} and **C**{b} are disjoint classes

C5.95 **C**{a} is a vacuous class

C5.96 **C**{b} is a vacuous class

C5.97 (**C**{a}∪**C**{b}) is a vacuous class

5.7.3. Sequencing, Number

By the use of previous verbs for number and of disjunction we can now define two other useful verbs.

C5.98 $x \leq y$

D5.22 $\mathfrak{M}\{C5.98\}\epsilon\mathbf{C}\{C4.01,C4.31\}$

C5.99 $x \geq y$

D5.23 $\mathfrak{M}\{C5.99\}\epsilon\mathbf{C}\{C4.01,C4.29\}$

We now intend to show that multiplying both sides of an inequality by a positive number does not change the inequality.

** $\mathfrak{M}\{C4.10\}:\mathfrak{M}\{S_{10}\}$

S_{10} $x=\mathfrak{s}[y,a]$

** $\nabla[\mathfrak{M}\{S_{10}\},\mathfrak{M}\{A4.07\}]:\mathfrak{M}\{S_{11}\}$

S_{11} $\mathfrak{p}[x,z]=\mathfrak{p}[\mathfrak{s}[y,a],z]$

** $\nabla[\mathfrak{M}\{S_{11}\},\mathfrak{M}\{A4.05\}]:\mathfrak{M}\{S_{12}\}$

S_{12} $\mathfrak{p}[x,z]=\mathfrak{p}[z,\mathfrak{s}[y,a]]$

** $\nabla[\mathfrak{M}\{S_{12}\},\mathfrak{M}\{A4.08\}]:\mathfrak{M}\{S_{13}\}$

S_{13} $\mathfrak{p}[x,z]=\mathfrak{s}[\mathfrak{p}[z,y],\mathfrak{p}[z,a]]$

** $\nabla[\mathfrak{M}\{S_{13}\},\mathfrak{M}\{A4.05\}]:\mathfrak{M}\{S_{14}\}$

S_{14} $\mathfrak{p}[x,z]=\mathfrak{s}[\mathfrak{p}[y,z],b]$

where

** $b=\mathfrak{p}[a,z]$

If we specify that

S_{15} $b>0$

then

** $\nabla[\nabla[\mathfrak{M}\{S_{14}\},\mathfrak{M}\{S_{15}\}],\mathfrak{M}\{C4.36\}]:\mathfrak{M}\{C5.100\}$

C5.100 $\mathfrak{p}[x,z]>\mathfrak{p}[y,z]$

By substituting back through this sequence in each of the deriving statements and into P4.09 we find that

P5.10 $\mathfrak{M}\{C4.29\}:\nabla[\mathfrak{M}\{C5.100\},\mathfrak{M}_{\nu}]$

Thus A4.07 and P5.10 can be used to redefine the members of the class from which we select in D5.23 and to demonstrate that

C5.101 $\mathfrak{p}[x,z]\geq\mathfrak{p}[y,z]$

P5.11 $\mathfrak{M}\{C5.99\}:\nabla[\mathfrak{M}\{C5.101\},\mathfrak{M}_{\rho}]$

In a similar manner we can develop

C5.102 $\mathfrak{p}[x,z]\leq\mathfrak{p}[y,z]$

P5.12 $\mathfrak{M}\{C5.98\}:\nabla[\mathfrak{M}\{C5.102\},\mathfrak{M}_{\rho}]$

5.8. Theorems

In this Section a few theorems are developed which may be useful. However, the purpose of this Section is to provide examples rather than to develop a complete set of theorems. Derivations are conducted in the same manner as in Section 3.4, except that explicit reference to the Rules of Substitution, A3.12 and P5.03, is not made in each usage. Though this is admittedly poor practice, it has been the custom in a number of references.

5.8.1. A Theorem about Distribution

**	$\mathfrak{M}\{P4.01\}:\mathfrak{M}\{S_1\}$
S_1	$\mathfrak{s}[\mathfrak{p}[x,n],x]=\mathfrak{s}[\mathfrak{p}[x,n],x]$
**	$\nabla[\mathfrak{M}\{S_1\},\mathfrak{M}\{C4.15\}]:\mathfrak{M}\{S_2\}$
S_2	$\mathfrak{s}[\mathfrak{p}[x,n],x]=\mathfrak{s}[\mathfrak{p}[x,N],\mathfrak{p}[x,1]]$
**	$\nabla[\mathfrak{M}\{S_2\},\mathfrak{M}\{A4.08\}]:\mathfrak{M}\{S_3\}$
S_3	$\mathfrak{s}[\mathfrak{p}[x,n],x]=\mathfrak{p}[x,\mathfrak{s}[n,1]]$
**	$\nabla[\mathfrak{M}\{S_3\},\mathfrak{M}\{A4.05\}]:\mathfrak{M}\{P5.13\}$
P5.13	$\mathfrak{s}[\mathfrak{p}[n,x],x]=\mathfrak{p}[\mathfrak{s}[n,1],x]$

This special form of the distribution relationship A4.08 provides a more explicit statement about addition and multipliers. Note, also, that P4.06 is a special example of this theorem.

5.8.2. A Theorem about the Vacuous Class

C5.103	$\mathbf{C}\{a\}\equiv\mathbf{O}$
C5.104	$\mathbf{C}\{b\}\equiv\mathbf{O}$
S_1	$\nabla[\nabla[\mathfrak{M}\{C5.103\},\mathfrak{M}\{C5.104\}],\mathfrak{M}\{C5.40\}]:\mathfrak{M}\{S_a\}$
S_a	$(\mathbf{C}\{a\}\cup\mathbf{C}\{b\})\equiv(\mathbf{O}\cup\mathbf{O})$
S_2	$\nabla[\mathfrak{M}\{S_a\},\mathfrak{M}\{C5.45\}]:\mathfrak{M}\{C5.105\}$
C5.105	$(\mathbf{C}\{a\}\cup\mathbf{C}\{b\})\equiv\mathbf{O}$
**	$\nabla[\mathfrak{M}\{S_1\},\mathfrak{M}\{S_2\}]:\mathfrak{M}\{S_b\}$
S_b	$\nabla[\nabla[\mathfrak{M}\{C5.103\},\mathfrak{M}\{C5.104\}],\mathfrak{M}_\rho]:\mathfrak{M}\{C5.105\}$

where

**	$\mathfrak{M}_\rho:\nabla[\mathfrak{M}\{C5.40\},\mathfrak{M}\{C5.45\}]$

and thus

**	$\nabla[\mathfrak{M}\{S_b\},\mathfrak{M}\{A3.03\}]:\mathfrak{M}\{P5.14\}$
P5.14	$\mathfrak{M}\{C5.105\}:\nabla[\nabla[\mathfrak{M}\{C5.103\},\mathfrak{M}\{C5.104\}],\mathfrak{M}_\rho]$

Thus if the union of the classes is vacuous then each class is vacuous.

5.8.3. Intersection and the Vacuous Class

**	$\mathfrak{M}\{C5.66\}:\mathfrak{M}\{S_1\}$
S_1	$\mathfrak{M}\{(\mathbf{C}\{b\}\cup\mathbf{O})\}:\mathfrak{M}\{\mathbf{C}\{b\}\}$
**	$\nabla[\mathfrak{M}\{P5.01\},\mathfrak{M}\{P5.05\}]:\mathfrak{M}\{S_2\}$
S_2	$(\mathbf{C}\{a\}\cap\mathbf{C}\{b\})\equiv(\mathbf{C}\{a\}\cap\mathbf{C}\{b\})$
**	$\nabla[\mathfrak{M}\{S_1\},\mathfrak{M}\{S_2\}]:\mathfrak{M}\{S_3\}$
S_3	$(\mathbf{C}\{a\}\cap(\mathbf{C}\{b\}\cup\mathbf{O}))\equiv(\mathbf{C}\{a\}\cap\mathbf{C}\{b\})$
**	$\nabla[\mathfrak{M}\{S_3\},\mathfrak{M}\{P5.06\}]:\mathfrak{M}\{S_4\}$
S_4	$((\mathbf{C}\{a\}\cap\mathbf{C}\{b\})\cup(\mathbf{C}\{a\}\cap\mathbf{O}))\equiv(\mathbf{C}\{a\}\cap\mathbf{C}\{b\})$

** $\nabla[\mathfrak{M}\{S_4\},\mathfrak{M}\{C5.66\}]:\mathfrak{M}\{P5.15\}$

P5.15 $(\mathbf{C}\{a\}\cap\mathbf{O})\equiv\mathbf{O}$

5.8.4. Exclusion and the Vacuous Class

From these we can form S_1.

** $\nabla[\mathfrak{M}\{C5.67\},\mathfrak{M}\{C5.104\}]:\mathfrak{M}\{S_1\}$

S_1 $\mathbf{C}\{a\}\equiv((\mathbf{C}\{a\}\mathbf{w}\mathbf{O})\cup(\mathbf{C}\{a\}\cap\mathbf{O}))$

** $\nabla[\mathfrak{M}\{S_1\},\mathfrak{M}\{P5.15\}]:\mathfrak{M}\{S_2\}$

S_2 $\mathbf{C}\{a\}\equiv((\mathbf{C}\{a\}\mathbf{w}\mathbf{O})\cup\mathbf{O})$

** $\nabla[\mathfrak{M}\{S_2\},\mathfrak{M}\{C5.66\}]:\mathfrak{M}\{S_3\}$

S_3 $\mathbf{C}\{a\}\equiv(\mathbf{C}\{a\}\mathbf{w}\mathbf{O})$

** $\nabla[\mathfrak{M}\{S_3\},\mathfrak{M}\{P5.02\}]:\mathfrak{M}\{P5.16\}$

P5.16 $(\mathbf{C}\{a\}\mathbf{w}\mathbf{O})\equiv\mathbf{C}\{a\}$

Thus, **O** is the "identity element" for **w**.

5.8.5. Transitivity of Inclusion

C5.106 $\mathbf{C}\{b\}\equiv(\mathbf{C}\{c\}\cup\mathbf{C}\{v\})$

C5.107 $\mathbf{C}\{a\}\equiv(\mathbf{C}\{c\}\cup\mathbf{C}\{r\})$

S_a $\nabla[\mathfrak{M}\{C5.50\},\mathfrak{M}\{C5.106\}]:\mathfrak{M}\{S_1\}$

S_1 $\mathbf{C}\{a\}\equiv((\mathbf{C}\{c\}\cup\mathbf{C}\{v\})\cup\mathbf{C}\{u\})$

S_b $\nabla[\mathfrak{M}\{S_1\},\mathfrak{M}\{C5.44\}]:\mathfrak{M}\{C5.53\}$

where we have

** $\mathbf{C}\{r\}\equiv(\mathbf{C}\{v\}\cup\mathbf{C}\{u\})$

** $\nabla[\mathfrak{M}\{S_a\},\mathfrak{M}\{S_b\}]:\mathfrak{M}\{P5.17\}$

P5.17 $\nabla[\nabla[\mathfrak{M}\{C5.50\},\mathfrak{M}\{C5.106\}],\mathfrak{M}_\eta]:\mathfrak{M}\{C5.53\}$

where

** $\mathfrak{M}_\eta:\mathfrak{M}\{C5.44\}$

We now note that

** $\mathfrak{M}\{C5.51\}:\mathfrak{M}\{S_2\}$

C5.108 $\mathbf{C}\{b\}\supset\mathbf{C}\{c\}$

S_2 $\mathfrak{M}\{C5.109\}:\mathfrak{M}\{C5.106\}$

** $\mathfrak{M}\{C5.51\}:\mathfrak{M}\{S_3\}$

C5.109 $\mathbf{C}\{a\}\supset\mathbf{C}\{c\}$

S_3 $\mathfrak{M}\{C5.109\}:\mathfrak{M}\{C5.53\}$

Thus a restatement of P5.17 is that

** $\nabla[\nabla[\mathfrak{M}\{P5.17\},\mathfrak{M}\{C5.51\}],\nabla[\mathfrak{M}\{S_2\},\mathfrak{M}\{S_3\}]]:\mathfrak{M}\{P5.18\}$

P5.18 $\nabla[\nabla[\mathfrak{M}\{C5.49\},\mathfrak{M}\{C5.108\}],\mathfrak{M}_\eta]:\mathfrak{M}\{C5.109\}$

This, then, states that

E5.27 $\mathfrak{M}\{\text{copula }\supset\}\epsilon\mathbf{C}\{\text{transitive relationships}\}$

Note that a similar statement can be derived for $\subset$.

5.8.6. A Theorem about Union in Inclusion

C5.110 $(\mathbf{C}\{a\}\cup\mathbf{C}\{c\})\equiv((\mathbf{C}\{b\}\cup\mathbf{C}\{c\})\cup\mathbf{C}\{u\})$

S_1 $\nabla[\mathfrak{M}\{C5.110\},\nabla[\mathfrak{M}\{C5.40\},\mathfrak{M}\{C5.44\}]]:\mathfrak{M}\{S_a\}$

S_a $(\mathbf{C}\{a\}\cup\mathbf{C}\{c\})\equiv((\mathbf{C}\{b\}\cup\mathbf{C}\{u\})\cup\mathbf{C}\{c\})$

S_2 $\nabla[\mathfrak{M}\{S_a\},\mathfrak{M}\{P5.04\}]:\mathfrak{M}\{C5.50\}$

** $\nabla[\mathfrak{M}\{S_1\},\mathfrak{M}\{S_2\}]:\mathfrak{M}\{S_3\}$

S_3 $\nabla[\nabla[\mathfrak{M}\{C5.110\},\mathfrak{M}_\nu],\mathfrak{M}\{P5.04\}]:\mathfrak{M}\{C5.50\}$

where

** $\mathfrak{M}_\nu:\nabla[\mathfrak{M}\{C5.40\},\mathfrak{M}\{C5.44\}]$

** $\nabla[\mathfrak{M}\{S_3\},\mathfrak{M}\{A3.05\}]:\mathfrak{M}\{S_4\}$

S_4 $\nabla[\mathfrak{M}\{C5.110\},\mathfrak{M}_\rho]:\mathfrak{M}\{C5.50\}$

** $\nabla[\mathfrak{M}\{S_4\},\mathfrak{M}\{A3.03\}]:\mathfrak{M}\{P5.19\}$

P5.19 $\mathfrak{M}\{C5.50\}:\nabla[\mathfrak{M}\{C5.110\},\mathfrak{M}_\rho]$

where

** $\mathfrak{M}_\rho:\nabla[\mathfrak{M}_\nu,\mathfrak{M}\{P5.04\}]$

We also have We shall now use

S_5 $\mathbf{C}_\delta\equiv(\mathbf{C}\{a\}\cup\mathbf{C}\{c\})$

S_6 $\mathbf{C}_\epsilon\equiv(\mathbf{C}\{b\}\cup\mathbf{C}\{c\})$

With these substitutions in C5.110 and the use of C5.51 we can derive that C5.110 is equivalent to

S_7 $(\mathbf{C}\{a\}\cup\mathbf{C}\{c\})\supset(\mathbf{C}\{b\}\cup\mathbf{C}\{c\})$

Thus we can establish that

P5.20 $\mathfrak{M}\{C5.49\}:\mathfrak{M}\{C5.110\}$

5.8.7. A Further Theorem on Conjunction

** $\mathfrak{M}\{C5.67\}:\mathfrak{M}\{S_1\}$

S_1 $\mathfrak{M}\{\mathbf{C}\{b\}\}:\mathfrak{M}\{((\mathbf{C}\{b\}\mathbf{w}\mathbf{C}\{a\})\cup(\mathbf{C}\{b\}\cap\mathbf{C}\{a\}))\}$

** $\nabla[\mathfrak{M}\{S_1\},\mathfrak{M}\{C5.58\}]:\mathfrak{M}\{S_2\}$

S_2 $\mathfrak{M}\{\mathbf{C}\{b\}\}:\mathfrak{M}\{((\mathbf{C}\{b\}\mathbf{w}\mathbf{C}\{a\})\cup(\mathbf{C}\{a\}\cap\mathbf{C}\{b\}))\}$

** $\nabla[\mathfrak{M}\{C5.67\},\mathfrak{M}\{S_2\}]:\mathfrak{M}\{S_3\}$

S_3 $\mathfrak{M}\{(\mathbf{C}\{a\}\cup\mathbf{C}\{b\})\}:$
$\mathfrak{M}\{(((\mathbf{C}\{a\}\mathbf{w}\mathbf{C}\{b\})\cup(\mathbf{C}\{a\}\cap\mathbf{C}\{b\}))\cup((\mathbf{C}\{b\}\mathbf{w}\mathbf{C}\{a\})\cup(\mathbf{C}\{a\}\cap\mathbf{C}\{b\})))\}$

** $\nabla[\mathfrak{M}\{S_3\},\nabla[\mathfrak{M}\{C5.40\},\mathfrak{M}\{C5.44\}]]:\mathfrak{M}\{S_4\}$

S_4 $\mathfrak{M}\{(\mathbf{C}\{a\}\cup\mathbf{C}\{b\})\}:$
$\mathfrak{M}\{(((\mathbf{C}\{a\}\cap\mathbf{C}\{b\})\cup(\mathbf{C}\{a\}\cap\mathbf{C}\{b\}))\cup((\mathbf{C}\{a\}\mathbf{w}\mathbf{C}\{b\})\cup(\mathbf{C}\{b\}\mathbf{w}\mathbf{C}\{a\})))\}$

** $\nabla[\mathfrak{M}\{S_4\},\mathfrak{M}\{C5.45\}]:\mathfrak{M}\{P5.21\}$

P5.21 $\mathfrak{M}\{(\mathbf{C}\{a\}\cup\mathbf{C}\{b\})\}:$
$\mathfrak{M}\{((\mathbf{C}\{a\}\cap\mathbf{C}\{b\})\cup((\mathbf{C}\{a\}\mathbf{w}\mathbf{C}\{b\})\cup(\mathbf{C}\{b\}\mathbf{w}\mathbf{C}\{a\})))\}$

A variation of this will now be developed.

** $\nabla[\mathfrak{M}\{P5.21\},\mathfrak{M}\{C5.44\}]:\mathfrak{M}\{S_5\}$

S_5 $\mathfrak{M}\{(\mathbf{C}\{a\}\cup\mathbf{C}\{b\})\}:$

$\mathfrak{M}\{(((\mathbf{C}\{a\}\mathbf{wC}\{b\})\cup(\mathbf{C}\{a\}\cap\mathbf{C}\{b\}))\cup(\mathbf{C}\{b\}\mathbf{wC}\{a\}))\}$

** $\nabla[\mathfrak{M}\{S_5\},\mathfrak{M}\{C5.67\}]:\mathfrak{M}\{P5.22\}$

P5.22 $\mathfrak{M}\{(\mathbf{C}\{a\}\cup\mathbf{C}\{b\})\}:\mathfrak{M}\{(\mathbf{C}\{a\}\cup(\mathbf{C}\{b\}\mathbf{wC}\{a\}))\}$

5.8.8. A Theorem about the Complement of Intersection

C5.111 $(\mathbf{C}\{a\}\mathbf{wC}\{c\})\equiv(\mathbf{C}\{b\}\mathbf{wC}\{c\})$

S_1 $\nabla[\mathfrak{M}\{C5.111\},\mathfrak{M}\{P5.04\}]:\mathfrak{M}\{S_a\}$

S_a $((\mathbf{C}\{a\}\mathbf{wC}\{c\})\cup(\mathbf{C}\{a\}\cap\mathbf{C}\{c\}))\equiv((\mathbf{C}\{b\}\mathbf{wC}\{c\})\cup(\mathbf{C}\{a\}\cap\mathbf{C}\{c\}))$

S_2 $\nabla[\mathfrak{M}\{S_a\},\mathfrak{M}\{P5.05\}]:\mathfrak{M}\{S_b\}$

S_b $((\mathbf{C}\{a\}\mathbf{wC}\{c\})\cup(\mathbf{C}\{a\}\cap\mathbf{C}\{c\}))\equiv((\mathbf{C}\{b\}\mathbf{wC}\{c\})\cup(\mathbf{C}\{b\}\cap\mathbf{C}\{c\}))$

S_3 $\nabla[\mathfrak{M}\{S_b\},\mathfrak{M}\{C5.67\}]:\mathfrak{M}\{C5.11\}$

** $\nabla[\mathfrak{M}\{S_2\},\mathfrak{M}\{S_3\}]:\mathfrak{M}\{S_4\}$

S_4 $\nabla[\mathfrak{M}\{S_a\},\mathfrak{M}_\rho]:\mathfrak{M}\{C5.11\}$

where

** $\mathfrak{M}_\rho:\nabla[\mathfrak{M}\{P5.05\},\mathfrak{M}\{C5.67\}]$

** $\nabla[\mathfrak{M}\{S_4\},\mathfrak{M}\{S_1\}]:\mathfrak{M}\{S_5\}$

S_5 $\nabla[\mathfrak{M}\{C5.111\},\mathfrak{M}_\mu]:\mathfrak{M}\{C5.11\}$

where

** $\mathfrak{M}_\mu:\nabla[\mathfrak{M}\{P5.04\},\mathfrak{M}_\rho]$

** $\nabla[\mathfrak{M}\{S_5\},\mathfrak{M}\{A3.03\}]:\mathfrak{M}\{P5.23\}$

P5.23 $\mathfrak{M}\{C5.11\}:\nabla[\mathfrak{M}\{C5.111\},\mathfrak{M}_\mu]$

Thus, C5.11 implies C5.111.

5.8.9. Inclusion from Intersection

S_{11} $\nabla[\nabla[\mathfrak{M}\{C5.50\},\mathfrak{M}\{C5.21\}],\mathfrak{M}\{P5.05\}]:\mathfrak{M}\{S_a\}$

S_a $(\mathbf{C}\{a\}\cap\mathbf{C}\{b\})\equiv((\mathbf{C}\{b\}\cup\mathbf{C}\{u\})\cap\mathbf{C}\{b\})$

S_{12} $\nabla[\mathfrak{M}\{S_a\},\mathfrak{M}\{C5.58\}]:\mathfrak{M}\{S_b\}$

S_b $(\mathbf{C}\{a\}\cap\mathbf{C}\{b\})\equiv(\mathbf{C}\{b\}\cap(\mathbf{C}\{b\}\cup\mathbf{C}\{u\}))$

S_{13} $\nabla[\mathfrak{M}\{S_b\},\mathfrak{M}\{P5.06\}]:\mathfrak{M}\{S_c\}$

S_c $(\mathbf{C}\{a\}\cap\mathbf{C}\{b\})\equiv((\mathbf{C}\{b\}\cap\mathbf{C}\{b\})\cup(\mathbf{C}\{b\}\cap\mathbf{C}\{u\}))$

S_{14} $\nabla[\mathfrak{M}\{S_c\},\mathfrak{M}\{C5.62\}]:\mathfrak{M}\{S_d\}$

S_d $(\mathbf{C}\{a\}\cap\mathbf{C}\{b\})\equiv(\mathbf{C}\{b\}\cup(\mathbf{C}\{b\}\cap\mathbf{C}\{u\}))$

As in P3.08 we shall specify C5.93 as a condition on $\mathbf{C}\{b\}$ and $\mathbf{C}\{u\}$, as asserted in S_f.

S_f $(\mathbf{C}\{b\}\cap\mathbf{C}\{u\})\equiv\mathbf{O}$

S_{15} $\nabla[\mathfrak{M}\{S_d\},\mathfrak{M}\{S_f\}]:\mathfrak{M}\{S_e\}$

S_e $(\mathbf{C}\{a\}\cap\mathbf{C}\{b\})\equiv(\mathbf{C}\{b\}\cup\mathbf{O})$

S_{16} $\nabla[\mathfrak{M}\{S_e\},\mathfrak{M}\{C5.66\}]:\mathfrak{M}\{C5.112\}$

C5.112 $(\mathbf{C}\{a\}\cap\mathbf{C}\{b\})\equiv\mathbf{C}\{b\}$

** $\nabla[\mathfrak{M}\{S_{16}\},\mathfrak{M}\{S_{15}\}]:\mathfrak{M}\{S_{17}\}$

S_{17} $\nabla[\nabla[\mathfrak{M}\{S_d\},\mathfrak{M}\{S_f\}],\mathfrak{M}\{C5.66\}]:\mathfrak{M}\{C5.112\}$

** $\nabla[\mathfrak{M}\{S_{17}\},\mathfrak{M}\{A3.05\}]:\mathfrak{M}\{S_{18}\}$

S_{18} $\nabla[\mathfrak{M}\{S_d\},\mathfrak{M}_{18a}]:\mathfrak{M}\{C5.112\}$

where

** $\mathfrak{M}_{18a}{:}\nabla[\mathfrak{M}\{S_f\},\mathfrak{M}\{C5.66\}]$

** $\nabla[\mathfrak{M}\{S_{18}\},\mathfrak{M}\{S_{14}\}]{:}\mathfrak{M}\{S_{19}\}$

S_{19} $\nabla[\nabla[\mathfrak{M}\{S_c\},\mathfrak{M}\{C5.62\}],\mathfrak{M}_{18a}]{:}\mathfrak{M}\{C5.112\}$

** $\nabla[\mathfrak{M}\{S_{19}\},\mathfrak{M}\{A3.05\}]{:}\mathfrak{M}\{S_{20}\}$

S_{20} $\nabla[\mathfrak{M}\{S_c\},\mathfrak{M}_{20a}]{:}\mathfrak{M}\{C5.112\}$

where

** $\mathfrak{M}_{20a}{:}\nabla[\mathfrak{M}\{C5.62\},\mathfrak{M}_{18a}]$

** $\nabla[\mathfrak{M}\{S_{20}\},\mathfrak{M}\{S_{13}\}]{:}\mathfrak{M}\{S_{21}\}$

S_{21} $\nabla[\nabla[\mathfrak{M}\{S_b\},\mathfrak{M}\{P5.06\}],\mathfrak{M}_{20a}]{:}\mathfrak{M}\{C5.112\}$

** $\nabla[\mathfrak{M}\{S_{21}\},\mathfrak{M}\{A3.05\}]{:}\mathfrak{M}\{S_{22}\}$

S_{22} $\nabla[\mathfrak{M}\{S_b\},\mathfrak{M}_{22a}]{:}\mathfrak{M}\{C5.112\}$

where

** $\mathfrak{M}_{22a}{:}\nabla[\mathfrak{M}\{P5.06\},\mathfrak{M}_{20a}]$

** $\nabla[\mathfrak{M}\{S_{22}\},\mathfrak{M}\{S_{12}\}]{:}\mathfrak{M}\{S_{23}\}$

S_{23} $\nabla[\nabla[\mathfrak{M}\{S_a\},\mathfrak{M}\{C5.58\}],\mathfrak{M}_{22a}]{:}\mathfrak{M}\{C5.112\}$

** $\nabla[\mathfrak{M}\{S_{23}\},\mathfrak{M}\{A3.05\}]{:}\mathfrak{M}\{S_{24}\}$

S_{24} $\nabla[\mathfrak{M}\{S_a\},\mathfrak{M}_{24a}]{:}\mathfrak{M}\{C5.112\}$

where

** $\mathfrak{M}_{24a}{:}\nabla[\mathfrak{M}\{C5.58\},\mathfrak{M}_{22a}]$

** $\nabla[\mathfrak{M}\{S_{24}\},\mathfrak{M}\{S_{11}\}]{:}\mathfrak{M}\{S_{25}\}$

S_{25} $\nabla[\nabla[\nabla[\mathfrak{M}\{C5.50\},\mathfrak{M}\{C5.21\}],\mathfrak{M}\{P5.05\}],\mathfrak{M}_{24a}]{:}\mathfrak{M}\{C5.112\}$

** $\nabla[\mathfrak{M}\{S_{25}\},\mathfrak{M}\{A3.05\}]{:}\mathfrak{M}\{S_{26}\}$

S_{26} $\nabla[\mathfrak{M}\{C5.50\},\mathfrak{M}_\rho]{:}\mathfrak{M}\{C5.112\}$

where

** $\mathfrak{M}_\rho{:}\nabla[\mathfrak{M}\{C5.21\},\nabla[\mathfrak{M}\{P5.05\},\mathfrak{M}_{24a}]]$

** $\nabla[\mathfrak{M}\{S_{26}\},\mathfrak{M}\{A3.03\}]{:}\mathfrak{M}\{P5.24\}$

P5.24 $\mathfrak{M}\{C5.112\}{:}\nabla[\mathfrak{M}\{C5.50\},\mathfrak{M}_\rho]$

Thus, C5.112 implies C5.50.

** $\nabla[\mathfrak{M}\{P5.24\},\mathfrak{M}\{C5.51\}]{:}\mathfrak{M}\{P5.25\}$

P5.25 $\mathfrak{M}\{C5.112\}{:}\nabla[\mathfrak{M}\{C5.49\},\mathfrak{M}_\rho]$

5.8.10. A Theorem about Exclusion

** $\nabla[\mathfrak{M}\{C5.67\},\mathfrak{M}\{C5.11\}]{:}\mathfrak{M}\{S_1\}$

S_1 $\mathbf{C}\{a\}\equiv((\mathbf{C}\{a\}\mathbf{w}\mathbf{C}\{a\})\cup(\mathbf{C}\{a\}\cap\mathbf{C}\{a\}))$

** $\nabla[\mathfrak{M}\{S_1\},\mathfrak{M}\{C5.62\}]{:}\mathfrak{M}\{S_2\}$

S_2 $\mathbf{C}\{a\}\equiv((\mathbf{C}\{a\}\mathbf{w}\mathbf{C}\{a\})\cup\mathbf{C}\{a\})$

** $\nabla[\mathfrak{M}\{S_2\},\mathfrak{M}\{P5.02\}]{:}\mathfrak{M}\{S_3\}$

S_3 $((\mathbf{C}\{a\}\mathbf{w}\mathbf{C}\{a\})\cup\mathbf{C}\{a\})\equiv\mathbf{C}\{a\}$

** $\nabla[\mathfrak{M}\{S_3\},\mathfrak{M}\{C5.40\}]{:}\mathfrak{M}\{S_4\}$

S_4 $(\mathbf{C}\{a\}\cup(\mathbf{C}\{a\}\mathbf{w}\mathbf{C}\{a\}))\equiv\mathbf{C}\{a\}$

** $\nabla[\mathfrak{M}\{S_4\},\mathfrak{M}\{C5.66\}]{:}\mathfrak{M}\{P5.26\}$

P5.26 $(\mathbf{C}\{a\}\mathbf{w}\mathbf{C}\{a\})\equiv\mathbf{O}$

5.8.11. Identity and Inclusion

S_1	$\nabla[\mathfrak{M}\{C5.50\},\mathfrak{M}\{C5.54\}]:\mathfrak{M}\{S_a\}$
S_a	$\mathbf{C}\{a\}\equiv((\mathbf{C}\{a\}\cup\mathbf{C}\{v\})\cup\mathbf{C}\{u\})$
S_2	$\nabla[\mathfrak{M}\{S_a\},\mathfrak{M}\{C5.44\}]:\mathfrak{M}\{S_b\}$
S_b	$\mathbf{C}\{a\}\equiv(\mathbf{C}\{a\}\cup(\mathbf{C}\{v\}\cup\mathbf{C}\{u\}))$
S_3	$\nabla[\mathfrak{M}\{S_b\},\mathfrak{M}\{P5.02\}]:\mathfrak{M}\{S_c\}$
S_c	$(\mathbf{C}\{a\}\cup(\mathbf{C}\{v\}\cup\mathbf{C}\{u\}))\equiv\mathbf{C}\{a\}$
S_4	$\nabla[\mathfrak{M}\{S_c\},\mathfrak{M}\{C5.66\}]:\mathfrak{M}\{S_d\}$
S_d	$(\mathbf{C}\{v\}\cup\mathbf{C}\{u\})\equiv\mathbf{O}$
S_5	$\nabla[\mathfrak{M}\{S_d\},\mathfrak{M}\{P5.14\}]:\mathfrak{M}\{S_e\}$
S_e	$\mathbf{C}\{u\}\equiv\mathbf{O}$
S_6	$\nabla[\mathfrak{M}\{C5.50\},\mathfrak{M}\{S_e\}]:\mathfrak{M}\{S_f\}$
S_f	$\mathbf{C}\{a\}\equiv(\mathbf{C}\{b\}\cup\mathbf{O})$
S_7	$\nabla[\mathfrak{M}\{S_f\},\mathfrak{M}\{C5.66\}]:\mathfrak{M}\{C5.11\}$
**	$\nabla[\mathfrak{M}\{S_5\},\mathfrak{M}\{S_4\}]:\mathfrak{M}\{S_8\}$
S_8	$\nabla[\nabla[\mathfrak{M}\{S_c\},\mathfrak{M}\{C5.66\}],\mathfrak{M}\{P5.14\}]:\mathfrak{M}\{S_e\}$
**	$\nabla[\mathfrak{M}\{S_8\},\mathfrak{M}\{A3.05\}]:\mathfrak{M}\{S_9\}$
S_9	$\nabla[\mathfrak{M}\{S_c\},\mathfrak{M}_{9a}]:\mathfrak{M}\{S_e\}$
where	
**	$\mathfrak{M}_{9a}:\nabla[\mathfrak{M}\{C5.66\},\mathfrak{M}\{P5.14\}]$
**	$\nabla[\mathfrak{M}\{S_9\},\mathfrak{M}\{S_3\}]:\mathfrak{M}\{S_{10}\}$
S_{10}	$\nabla[\nabla[\mathfrak{M}\{S_b\},\mathfrak{M}\{P5.02\}],\mathfrak{M}_{9a}]:\mathfrak{M}\{S_e\}$
**	$\nabla[\mathfrak{M}\{S_{10}\},\mathfrak{M}\{A3.05\}]:\mathfrak{M}\{S_{11}\}$
S_{11}	$\nabla[\mathfrak{M}\{S_b\},\mathfrak{M}_{11a}]:\mathfrak{M}\{S_e\}$
where	
**	$\mathfrak{M}_{11a}:\nabla[\mathfrak{M}\{P5.02\},\mathfrak{M}_{9a}]$
**	$\nabla[\mathfrak{M}\{S_{11}\},\mathfrak{M}\{S_2\}]:\mathfrak{M}\{S_{12}\}$
S_{12}	$\nabla[\nabla[\mathfrak{M}\{S_a\},\mathfrak{M}\{C5.44\}],\mathfrak{M}_{11a}]:\mathfrak{M}\{S_e\}$
**	$\nabla[\mathfrak{M}\{S_{12}\},\mathfrak{M}\{A3.05\}]:\mathfrak{M}\{S_{13}\}$
S_{13}	$\nabla[\mathfrak{M}\{S_a\},\mathfrak{M}_{13a}]:\mathfrak{M}\{S_e\}$
where	
**	$\mathfrak{M}_{13a}:\nabla[\mathfrak{M}\{C5.44\},\mathfrak{M}_{11a}]$
**	$\nabla[\mathfrak{M}\{S_{13}\},\mathfrak{M}\{S_1\}]:\mathfrak{M}\{S_{14}\}$
S_{14}	$\nabla[\nabla[\mathfrak{M}\{C5.50\},\mathfrak{M}\{C5.54\}],\mathfrak{M}_{13a}]:\mathfrak{M}\{S_e\}$
**	$\nabla[\mathfrak{M}\{S_6\},\mathfrak{M}\{S_7\}]:\mathfrak{M}\{S_{15}\}$
S_{15}	$\nabla[\nabla[\mathfrak{M}\{C5.50\},\mathfrak{M}\{S_e\}],\mathfrak{M}\{C5.66\}]:\mathfrak{M}\{C5.11\}$
**	$\nabla[\mathfrak{M}\{S_{15}\},\mathfrak{M}\{S_{14}\}]:\mathfrak{M}\{S_{16}\}$
S_{16}	$\nabla[\nabla[\mathfrak{M}\{C5.50\},\nabla[\nabla[\mathfrak{M}\{C5.50\},\mathfrak{M}\{C5.54\}],\mathfrak{M}_{13a}]],\mathfrak{M}\{C5.66\}]:$ $\mathfrak{M}\{C5.11\}$
**	$\nabla[\mathfrak{M}\{S_{16}\},\mathfrak{M}\{A3.05\}]:\mathfrak{M}\{S_{17}\}$
S_{17}	$\nabla[\nabla[\mathfrak{M}\{C5.50\},\mathfrak{M}\{C5.50\}],\nabla[\mathfrak{M}\{C5.54\},\mathfrak{M}_\rho]]:\mathfrak{M}\{C5.11\}$
where	
**	$\mathfrak{M}_\rho:\nabla[\mathfrak{M}_{13a},\mathfrak{M}\{C5.66\}]$

** $\nabla[\mathfrak{M}\{S_{17}\},\mathfrak{M}\{A3.07\}]:\mathfrak{M}\{S_{18}\}$

S_{18} $\nabla[\mathfrak{M}\{C5.50\},\nabla[\mathfrak{M}\{C5.54\},\mathfrak{M}_{\rho}]]:\mathfrak{M}\{C5.11\}$

** $\nabla[\mathfrak{M}\{S_{18}\},\mathfrak{M}\{A3.05\}]:\mathfrak{M}\{S_{19}\}$

S_{19} $\nabla[\nabla[\mathfrak{M}\{C5.50\},\mathfrak{M}\{C5.54\}],\mathfrak{M}_{\rho}]:\mathfrak{M}\{C5.11\}$

** $\nabla[\mathfrak{M}\{S_{19}\},\mathfrak{M}\{A3.03\}]:\mathfrak{M}\{P5.27\}$

P5.27 $\mathfrak{M}\{C5.11\}:\nabla[\nabla[\mathfrak{M}\{C5.50\},\mathfrak{M}\{C5.54\}],\mathfrak{M}_{\rho}]$

This might be restated in more conventional form by the use of the following:

** $\nabla[\mathfrak{M}\{P5.27\},\nabla[\mathfrak{M}\{C5.51\},\mathfrak{M}\{C5.55\}]]:\mathfrak{M}\{P5.28\}$

P5.28 $\mathfrak{M}\{C5.11\}:\nabla[\nabla[\mathfrak{M}\{C5.49\},\mathfrak{M}\{C5.53\}],\mathfrak{M}_{\rho}]$

Thus, identity implies the dual inclusion.

From P5.28 it is possible to derive that

P5.29 $\mathbf{C}\{a\}\supset\mathbf{C}\{a\}$

and thus state that

E5.28 $\mathfrak{M}\{\text{copula }\supset\}\in\mathbf{C}\{\text{reflexive relationships}\}$

5.8.12. Extensionality

C5.113 $\mathbf{C}\{v\}\equiv\mathbf{C}\{r\}$

S_1 $\nabla[\mathfrak{M}\{C5.106\},\mathfrak{M}\{C5.113\}]:\mathfrak{M}\{S_a\}$

S_a $\mathbf{C}\{b\}\equiv(\mathbf{C}\{c\}\cup\mathbf{C}\{r\})$

S_2 $\nabla[\mathfrak{M}\{S_a\},\nabla[\mathfrak{M}\{C5.107\},\mathfrak{M}\{P5.03\}]]:\mathfrak{M}\{C5.11\}$

** $\nabla[\mathfrak{M}\{S_1\},\mathfrak{M}\{S_2\}]:\mathfrak{M}\{S_3\}$

S_3 $\nabla[\nabla[\mathfrak{M}\{C5.106\},\mathfrak{M}\{C5.113\}],\nabla[\mathfrak{M}\{C5.107\},\mathfrak{M}\{P5.03\}]]:$
$\mathfrak{M}\{C5.11\}$

** $\nabla[\mathfrak{M}\{S_3\},\nabla[\mathfrak{M}\{C5.44\},\mathfrak{M}\{P5.02\}]]:\mathfrak{M}\{P5.30\}$

P5.30 $\nabla[\nabla[\mathfrak{M}\{C5.106\},\mathfrak{M}\{C5.107\}],\mathfrak{M}_{\mu}]:\mathfrak{M}\{C5.11\}$

where

** $\mathfrak{M}_{\mu}:\nabla[\mathfrak{M}\{C5.113\},\mathfrak{M}\{P5.03\}]$

This merely states that, under condition C5.113, $\mathbf{C}\{a\}$ and $\mathbf{C}\{b\}$ have the same composition without regard for the cardinality of $\mathbf{C}\{c\}$.

** $\nabla[\mathfrak{M}\{C5.51\},\mathfrak{M}\{P5.03\}]:\mathfrak{M}\{S_4\}$

S_4 $\mathfrak{M}\{C5.108\}:\mathfrak{M}\{C5.106\}$

** $\nabla[\mathfrak{M}\{C5.51\},\mathfrak{M}\{P5.03\}]:\mathfrak{M}\{S_5\}$

S_5 $\mathfrak{M}\{C5.109\}:\mathfrak{M}\{C5.107\}$

** $\nabla[\mathfrak{M}\{P5.30\},\nabla[\mathfrak{M}\{S_4\},\mathfrak{M}\{S_5\}]]:\mathfrak{M}\{P5.31\}$

P5.31 $\nabla[\nabla[\mathfrak{M}\{C5.108\},\mathfrak{M}\{C5.109\}],\mathfrak{M}_{\mu}]:\mathfrak{M}\{C5.11\}$

We might note that this form is related to the Axiom 1 of Kunen (16,10).

6. DEDUCTION

Deduction is the process of proceeding from a specified collection of information to another collection of information in accordance with a set of rules on how it will proceed. It is, therefore, an algorithm which may have several possible paths. It starts with the more general case and becomes specific, i.e., as Hilbert has shown, the deduced result is already included in the original information, although it may not be recognized as such. Deduction is conducted from an aggregation of intensions, from an aggregation of statements about classes or from an aggregation of statements about mathematical functions. In the latter two cases, the intensions associated with the classes or the mathematical functions are present by implication. This concept is presented in Section 3.2.2.1 where logical implication (deduction) is stated by

C3.06 $\mathfrak{M}_\alpha:\nabla[\mathfrak{M}_\beta,\mathfrak{M}_\mu]$

where the resultant $\mathfrak{M}_\beta$ is included in (deduced from) collection $\mathfrak{M}_\alpha$.

Restated: deduction proceeds from any adequate collection of declarative forms to that declarative form which is desired. The procedure is usually one of substitution, although there are several methods by which substitution is accomplished. By this procedure the unwanted information is removed; no new information is added as a result of the procedure. This is in contrast to induction (see Chapter 8) where new information may be added.

Formal Logic is concerned with the manipulation of a certain class of sentences (assertions) and terms in those sentences. In other words, Logic is a "game" or procedure which is "played" or executed with a particular set of symbols and rules, that is, executed within a particular language. Some people have assumed that deduction is merely the manipulation of symbols, and they point to logical or mathematical proofs which have that appearance. The point which they neglect is that all language is symbolism and that a unique definition (assignment of intension) has been made for each symbol (or should have been made). Each symbolic statement conveys a definite intension, and thus the entire game is a manipulation of concepts as are all of our scientific studies.

Deductive logic has been touted by some as being concerned with truth, but in actuality truth is merely incidental to the functions of Logic. As many references, e.g., Cohen and Nagel (7,9), have pointed out, logical implication does not depend on the truth of our premises. In deductive processes what we are actually saying is that the "solution" is a restatement in more useable form (possibly) of the original statements. Since no new information is added or found in deduction, if our original premises were true then our deductive result is equally true; if our initial premises were reasonable approximations then our deductive result is at least an equally reasonable approximation, if not better; if our initial premises were false then we do not know how true our result is, but we do know that it is contained in those initial premises.

As an example, the equation of an elastic string is often presented as:

** $$\frac{\partial^2 y}{\partial t^2}=\omega^2\frac{\partial^2 y}{\partial x^2}$$

Here, y is defined as the displacement from the reference axis (the line, y=0). By the equation above, y is a known function of x and t, at least. In the situation where the ends are rigidly tied at x=0 and x=π,

** $y(0,t)=y(\pi,t)=0$

If an initial condition is established such that

** $y(x,0)=A\cdot(\sin(x))$

then it can be deductively shown that the "solution" to this formulation is:

** $y(x,t)=A\cdot(\sin(x)\cdot\cos(\omega t))$

However, is this an accurate or true representation of an elastic string for such initial conditions? Initially it is reasonable, but as a representation of future conditions of the string it is poor since it shows the string continuing to oscillate forever. Thus the partial differential equation above is not a true representation of an elastic string. However, it can be very useful under those conditions where it is a reasonable approximation, even though it is not true.

So deductive processes are not concerned with truth, and deductive processes can be carried out on false information as easily as with truth. Thus the rules of deductive processes are the rules of manipulation of intensions; deduction is only concerned with intension.

In normal deductive processes we have an underlying philosophy, 𝔓, which is a particular collection of assertions. If this is, for example, a philosophy of physics (such as Newtonian physics) we can then deduce results as necessary for our purposes, and these results will reflect that philosophy. However, if a new assertion or a change to an existing assertion is hypothesized (such as relativity theory) this produces a new or changed philosophy, 𝔓'. The results deduced from 𝔓' can be expected to be somewhat different from those deduced from 𝔓. However, the general deductive processes in the two situations should be analogous. The selection of which is the more desirable result (and, therefore, which philosophy is more desirable) is determined by other criteria, usually external to Logic. This will be discussed more in Chapter 8.

6.1. Types of Proofs

A "proof" is a form of deduction in which the desired result is stated as a hypothesis and then by deduction we show that we can arrive at that result. Deduction "proves" the result. "Formal proofs" must demonstrate explicitly all actions, references or conclusions at each step. A proof which does not do so may be believable for intuitive reasons, but it is lacking, and false results may creep in. The obvious disadvantage of a completely formal proof is the volume of statements.

6.1.1. Substitution

This is the type of deduction which we have emphasized thus far. Our Sections 3.4, 4.7 and 5.8 are examples of this approach of substitution followed by elimination of the unnecessary pieces. This process occurs in almost all deductions and inductions, and it is included as a part of the procedures discussed below. The process is the use of transitive relationships which are often referred to as the Rules of Substitution but might more properly be labeled syllogism. Specifically, several were presented as A3.12, P5.03 and P4.03. Others can also be developed.

In formal proofs the particular axiom of syllogism, which is being used, should be explicitly referenced, as we have done in Section 3.4. However, because they are "intuitively obvious" their use often occurs without being recorded.

6.1.2. Mathematical Induction

This form of deduction requires the derivation of a recursion formula (a relationship between successive terms) and the derivation of one term which concurs with the recursion formula. In the conventional usage of this process, the user states that since the selected term is true then all examples from the recursion formula are true. In actuality, as we discussed above, truth has no necessary relationship to this process or other deduction. Since the sample term is deduced and since the recursion formula is deduced, this process is not induction in the usual sense of the word; it is one particular method of deduction.

6.1.3. Proof of Impossibility

This procedure merely attempts to show that a hypothesis is invalid, that is, is inconsistent with the underlying system of assertions. This is often done by deducing a result from the hypothesis and the system such that the result contradicts one or more of the underlying assertions. In this situation the hypothesis must be rejected since the underlying system is structured to be, or at least assumed to be, self-consistent. By rejecting a hypothesis we have often performed a valuable service even when we are unable to construct an alternative hypothesis which is consistent with the system.

6.1.4. Proof by Contradiction

Some deductions are purported to proceed by proving alternative statements false. Here "false" must mean contradictory or inconsistent with the system, in other words, we have demonstrated a proof of impossibility for the alternatives. The users of this approach subscribe to the "rule of excluded middle", and thus if the alternatives are "false" then the desired assertion must be "true". However, great care must be used in this approach to ensure valid deduction. The desired assertion (that which is to be proved) may be true, but it is possibly not deduced from the underlying philosophy (system of assertions). The question should always be raised as to whether the desired result can be deduced from the system, that is, whether its intension was included in the original system or whether, by finding it to be "true" at the termination of the process, something has been added which was not in the original system of assertions (the philosophy). To add to the original system is induction, not deduction. See Chapter 8.

A proof by contradiction is a "non-constructive" proof in that we are not "constructing" a straightforward proof. It is often shorter than a "constructive" proof, and many theorems are currently in use which to date have not been proved by "constructive" methods. In some cases it has merely not been possible as yet, but it appears that some theorems are conceptually impossible to prove by "constructive" methods. Such a situation arises with respect to the infinite sets of Cantor.

On occasion a "proof by contradiction" is actually a proof by, for example, substitution or by mathematical induction. Euclid's proof of the existence of an infinite number of primes is cited as an example of proof by contradiction in which we assume the statement to be false and then show that another prime number can be generated, thus "showing that it is false that the theorem is false". What is actually demonstrated is that another prime number can be generated by the recursion formula which is structured as the product of all prime numbers p_α prior to the new number.

** $$p_{n+1}=(1+\prod_{\alpha=1}^{n} p_\alpha)$$

where n can be any given number. Thus there are more prime numbers than any given number (vernacular in such a situation states that n becomes infinite), and the result is attained by constructive methods.

6.2. Conditions of Deduction

The purpose of deduction is to arrive at a necessary result in an indisputable manner. In some deductions we may impose more stringent conditions than in others.

6.2.1. "if and only if"

The subject term is often met in deductive processes, and the implied concept is

C6.01 $\nabla[\mathfrak{M}_\alpha,\mathfrak{M}_\beta]:\mathfrak{M}_\gamma$

C6.02 $\nabla[\mathfrak{M}_\alpha,\mathfrak{M}_\gamma]:\mathfrak{M}_\beta$

C6.03 S_γ if and only if S_β, based on S_α

E6.01 $\nabla[\mathfrak{M}\{C6.01\},\mathfrak{M}\{C6.02\}]:\mathfrak{M}\{C6.03\}$

As usually used, and as shown here, this phrase implies that if S_β (in light of S_α)

contains S_γ then S_γ, with S_α, contains S_β. Carnap (6,3) states one form of equivalence as this phrase, but in our system equivalence would appear to be a special case, sufficient but not necessary. Several authors, such as Kunen (16), use the symbol, iff, to represent "if and only if".

6.2.2. "necessary and sufficient"

A "sufficient" condition is any condition that can produce the result by deductive methods. Thus we can say

C6.04 $\mathfrak{M}\{S_\alpha\}:\nabla[\mathfrak{M}\{S_\beta\},\mathfrak{M}_\mu]$
C6.05 S_α is a sufficient condition for S_β
E6.02 $\mathfrak{M}\{C6.04\}:\mathfrak{M}\{C6.05\}$

This can be restated as

C6.06 $\Delta[\mathfrak{M}\{S_\alpha\},\mathfrak{M}\{S_\beta\}]:\mathfrak{M}\{S_\beta\}$
E6.03 $\mathfrak{M}\{C6.06\}:\mathfrak{M}\{C6.05\}$

A "necessary" condition is one without which the deduced result could not be obtained. An example is

** It is necessary that S_1 so that S_2
S_1 I pay my admission fee
S_2 I am allowed to enter the theater

Note in this example that S_1 is a necessary condition but not the only necessary condition. For example, decent clothing is also required. Thus, S_1 is necessary but not sufficient. On this basis we can say

C6.07 $\nabla[\mathfrak{M}\{S_\alpha\},\mathfrak{M}_\mu]:\mathfrak{M}\{S_\beta\}$
C6.08 $\blacksquare[\mathfrak{M}_\mu,\mathfrak{M}\{S_\alpha\}]:\mathfrak{M}\{S_\beta\}$
C6.09 S_α is a necessary condition for S_β
E6.04 $\blacksquare[\mathfrak{M}\{C6.07\},\mathfrak{M}\{C6.08\}]:\mathfrak{M}\{C6.09\}$

This can be restated as

C6.10 $\Delta[\mathfrak{M}\{S_\alpha\},\mathfrak{M}\{S_\beta\}]:\mathfrak{M}\{S_\alpha\}$
E6.05 $\mathfrak{M}\{C6.10\}:\mathfrak{M}\{C6.09\}$

However, this does not ensure that S_α is the only necessary condition since $\mathfrak{M}\{S_\alpha\}$ is a member of a class of "solutions" which can be deduced from $\mathfrak{M}\{S_\beta\}$, and we may not know all members of the class. Thus to prove that a condition is necessary is often a much more difficult task than proving sufficiency and has not been accomplished yet in many important areas of mathematics.

The forms of necessity which are presented in modal logic are again only statements about truth-values. Carnap (6,174) in his 39-1 defines

** For any sentence S_α, $N(S_\alpha)$ is true if and only if S_α is L-true

and he defines, (6,173),

** $\mathfrak{M}\{N(S_\alpha)\}:\mathfrak{M}\{$it is logically necessary that $S_\alpha\}$

Lewis (17,161) forms a similar definition.

A definition which is viewed as the antithesis of "necessary" is

C6.11 $\Delta[\mathfrak{M}\{S_\alpha\},\mathfrak{M}\{S_\beta\}]:\mathfrak{O}$
C6.12 S_α is not a necessary condition for S_β
E6.06 $\mathfrak{M}\{C6.11\}:\mathfrak{M}\{C6.12\}$

A common statement in many languages is one of the form:
S_1 It is necessary that S_a.
where S_a is some assertion. The assertion S_1 is a contraction of an assertion S_2 which might be the answer to a question, "Why?", following S_1.
S_2 It is necessary that S_a because S_b.
Thus the person who is stating S_1 is stating a form of
S_2 $\mathfrak{M}\{S_b\}:\nabla[\mathfrak{M}\{S_a\},\mathfrak{M}_\mu]$
and we discussed this form earlier as logical implication.

6.2.3. "consistent"

The word, consistent, and its antonym, inconsistent, in normal usage are defined in some cases in terms of deduction and in other cases in terms of induction (in agreement with or not in agreement with the given data). In this Section we are only concerned with the former.

Even within the context of deduction we find that ambiguities arise. Consider the two situations,
S_1 $\Delta[\mathfrak{M}_\alpha,\mathfrak{M}_\beta]:\mathfrak{M}_\beta$
S_2 $\Delta[\mathfrak{M}_\alpha,\mathfrak{M}_\gamma]:\mathfrak{O}$
Clearly, in assertion S_1, $\mathfrak{M}_\beta$ is logically consistent with $\mathfrak{M}_\alpha$. However, in assertion S_2, $\mathfrak{M}_\gamma$ is not necessarily inconsistent with $\mathfrak{M}_\alpha$. In a sense these two assertions might be viewed by some as also defining "inconsistent" as that which is not included in these statements. However, such a definition is not explicit or "constructive", and there is the danger of such an implied definition being too broad.

7. PHILOSOPHY AND TRUTH

We have noted in the last Chapter that deduction is independent of truth. Deduction is a "game" or algorithm which is "played" or executed according to a specified set of "rules" or underlying axioms and conventions. Within these "rules" deduction is thus only concerned with the concept and symbolism and the allowable manipulations of these. Deduction rests heavily on Semantics but can be completely independent of our "real" world.

In our "real" worlds (physics, religion, sociology, etc.) we establish underlying assumptions which are from then on, at least for that subject and until revisions take place, considered to be basic truths. Such a collection of underlying assumptions or hypotheses (assertions) constitutes a philosophy for that subject. This definition can include what others might call data. Of course, a complete philosophy must incorporate the axioms and definitions upon which a Logic, with respect to that subject, is based.

The underlying assumptions which are included in a philosophy are the basic truths, and thus truth is dependent on and derived from the philosophy. Any statement derived from the philosophy is "true"; any statement in opposition to the philosophy is "false".

These are the major points which we shall discuss and elaborate upon in this Chapter.

7.1. Philosophies

Philosophy, as a field of study, usually includes a broad array of abstract investigations, so broad as to defy precise definition. In some degree the subject includes all parts of this book and much more. Philosophy, to paraphrase Hospers (10,55), is concerned with: conceptual analysis; issues and problems of the highest degree of generality; reasoning and argument; foundations and presuppositions; related and similar discussions. However, the restrictions which we assigned early on have limited the scope of our discussions so as to keep them more manageable. Here we are less concerned with Philosophy as a broad field of study than with that aspect which is called the philosophy of the individual. We are not analyzing the nature, concept or structure of knowledge beyond that which we have discussed to this point. We choose to accept the views of the individual as to what his knowledge and beliefs are. These beliefs are his personal philosophy.

Our personal philosophy usually consists of several parts. Our religion is one part. We each usually have a part of our philosophy which, beyond our religion, further defines our other relationships with our peers. In addition, a physicist, for example, has a philosophy of physics, the "laws" upon which his physical science is based. The aggregation of such parts constitute the total philosophy of the individual. That is to say, the philosophy is the aggregate conjunction of the intensions of our axioms (accepted beliefs), though in our normal discourse, other than in Logic, we do not usually refer to our accepted beliefs as axioms.

Any aggregation of assertions may constitute a philosophy, $\mathfrak{P}$. Usually in such a philosophy there is included an assertion that all statements in $\mathfrak{P}$ are true and define truth. This is our definition of a philosophy.

Knowledge is the aggregation of all concepts of which a person is aware. Thus our philosophy is a part of our total knowledge. It is that part which we believe has certainty of truth. This is a variation from the definition of knowledge as used by some, such as Hospers (10,144). We are stating that knowledge of a concept is not necessarily belief that the concept is true. I may not accept (believe) the concept of a unicorn, but I am aware of that concept. Perhaps here we are playing with the definition of the word, know. I *know* no unicorns exist; I *know* of the concept, unicorn.

A philosophy will usually have, explicitly or implicitly, a collection of assertions which define or provide a basis for reasoning. Our collection herein of A and D statements is one such a collection. On the basis of the total collection we state that we can proceed with deductive and inductive reasoning.

A philosophy may or may not be self-consistent. Generally a philosophy is defined to be self-consistent if no pair of assertions which are contained in or can be derived from that philosophy are contradictory. If a person accepts a philosophy, that person accepts it without proof since any such proof is dependent on the philosophy and thus must be circular at best.

Any two philosophies may be mutually inconsistent. Further, a concept which exists in one may be absent from the other. In that event the person following one philosophy will usually derive different conclusions from those of a person following the other philosophy. Thus, arguments between proponents of different philosophies are futile unless they can agree on a common method of evaluation. As an example of such a difference, consider the concept, sin. Some monotheists have stated that the religions of a certain modern country have no concept of sin. That particular country has two major religions, one agnostic and one polytheistic. Most citizens of that country are noted for very rigidly following the requirements of protocol and law and their own religion. However, some of the "sins" recognized by the monotheistic mind are acceptable to the citizens of this country. These two observations seem inconsistent, according to the default assumptions of the Western mind. But by definition, a sin is a violation of "God's Law", and "God's Law" is defined differently in different religions. Further, a religion which has no God can thus have no "Laws of God" and thus no sin since there is no violation of a "Law of God". A religion with multiple Gods may have other "Laws of the Gods". In such situations, arguments about sin between proponents of either of these religions and proponents of monotheistic religions are useless because the concept exists in one philosophy and not in the other.

We have said little to this point about the methods by which an individual acquires a philosophy. Parts of a total philosophy are adopted from those of our peers. This process probably accounts, for example, for that part of our philosophy called religion. Such a process is not a logical process and needs no further discussion here except to note that these parts of our philosophy seem to be reasonably invariant over time. On the other end of the spectrum is the acquisition and the augmentation or modification of, for example, our philosophy of the sciences in which these actions occur in a more rational manner but, also, where changes are accurring almost daily. Here we allow questioning of the "truth" stated by the philosophy or some part of it. We do consider alternative approaches, and we attempt to evaluate these alternatives by "rational" procedures. Eventually we may accept the alternative statements as a replacement for a part of our philosophy. For example, consider Newtonian mechanics versus relativistic mechanics and "waves" versus "particles". In such studies induction is central and essential to the logical evolution of the subject. This is an area of our concern in this study. In Chapter 8 we will discuss more details of the creation and evaluation of hypotheses which may be proposed as revisions to our scientific philosophies.

The philosophy of an individual is an embodiment of his beliefs about the environment (the "world") in which he exists. A theory which is held by an individual about, for example, physics is a part of that philosophy; those statements which he accepts as "laws" of physics are a part of that philosophy. The differences among a law, a theory and a hypothesis, from the standpoint of the individual, is in the degree of possible variation or the invariance which does or does not occur in or from the statement. We can observe that, to an engineer who designs machinery, Newton's Second Law is immutable; a physicist might view Newton's Second Law as a reasonable approximation within specified ranges of the parameters or variables.

We have equated laws, theories and hypotheses with statements or assertions. Since a compound assertion can be rewritten as an aggregation of simple assertions, we do not differentiate between the singular and plural forms of the word, assertion, in this statement. And since each equation is a complete sentence we do not need to distinguish between assertions in English and assertions in other symbollism, to the extent that each symbol (in English the symbol is a word or phrase) has been previously defined. Thus a theory, e.g., might be a lengthy treatise or a single equation or a boundary-value aggregation.

As has been discussed in Suppe (25,130 etc.), some nouns in a theory are defined by the theory, that is, until explication in the theory the concept did not exist or was not defined in precisely the same manner. From this definition (in the theory) the defined concept begins to have a reality in the mind of a person who accepts the theory. As an example, the "hidden variables" of Bohm (25,183) are perhaps related to current theories of nuclear structure and efforts to provide a unified theory of primary quantities. Most of these quantities are not directly observable; they are defined by the theory, and were created in an effort to accomplish the goals of the person who created the theory.

7.2. Truth

In the usual definitions, truth and falsehood are the opposites of a dichotomy. We, however, view the two nouns as different values of the same quantity; we shall call this quantity "truth-value". As with many other words in the English language there is an ambiguity of definition or the presence of multiple definitions of truth-value (or of the word, true, etc.). Many of the uses of "true" are substitutions for more precise words, but in the sense in which we discuss it there are two related but different approaches: truth-values based on the philosophy which we shall call "inherent truth"; truth-values based on observations which we shall call "verified truth". Another type of "truth" is sometimes discussed which, in reality (as we have stated before), is unrelated to truth-values. This type is logical implication, and we might call it "conditional truth". Thus if

** $\mathfrak{M}\{S_1\}:\nabla[\mathfrak{M}\{S_2\},\mathfrak{M}_\mu]$

and we believe that S_1 is true then we often state it as

** "If S_1 is true then S_2 is true"

However, if we initially believe that S_1 is false we instead use the subjunctive

** "If S_1 were true then S_2 would be true"

In each case we are actually discussing deduction with the use of either A7.02 or P7.03 (below). The use of the word, truth, is irrelevant to the discussion. Thus we still have only the two approaches discussed above. Both approaches are necessary and useful. However, one problem is that some people do not differentiate between truth based on the philosophy and truth based on observations. We shall now consider each.

7.2.1. Metric of an Intension

Inherent truth is that which is defined by the person's philosophy. If truth is defined by the philosophy then statements within the philosophy have a truth-value of "truth", and other statements may or may not be true, depending on their relationship to the philosophy. Indeed, if we don't know the relationship of the statement to the philosophy then we don't know its inherent truth-value. In each case truth is associated with the assertion. To be more specific, we may view the truth-value as a metric associated with the assertion. This is in accord with Hospers (10,78). But what is the nature of this metric, and how can we quantify it? This metric is not assigned to the symbolism which constitutes the sequential display of an assertion (that is, the printed sentence); it is assigned to the concept which is asserted or connoted by the sentence; it is the metric of the intension of the assertion. As a metric, truth is the existence of the intension of the assertion; for asserted actions, truth is the occurrance of the action.

As discussed by Wiggins (24,17), one view is that "... to know the meaning of (an arbitrary sentence) is to know under what conditions the sentence would count as true." This view is consistent with our view, when considered in light of or in comparison with the philosophy, which is usually implied or assumed rather than stated in these presentations.

It would be highly desirable if the metric which we use could be similar in form and definition to that used for verified truth since each will occur later in our inductive processes; our goal here is to minimize the potential problems which may arise. In the case of induction, with Jeffries (12,9) we must provide explicitly for the possibility that inferences may turn out to be wrong. Though in many situations related to induction we may use deductive methods and have certainty of the relative truth of the results, in other inductive situations we may have only a reasonable degree of confidence in the results because of the addition of new information which is not included in the philosophy. The establishment of inherent truth and verified truth as parallel concepts is consistent with prior practice, and as such each is sometimes viewed as a "probability" of truth. This leads to the ambiguities in the definition of "probability" which is discussed at length by Carnap (5).

In an assertion about the probability of occurrance of event S_1, such a statement can be restated in terms of the truth-value of S_1. Statement S_1, to be more precise, is not an event but an assertion about the occurrance of the event (or a contraction of an assertion), and the probability of that event would be presented as an assertion about $\mathfrak{t}_1$. In D7.01 et seq we define the characteristics of $\mathfrak{t}$.

As has often been pointed out, the study of probability was originally given incentive by the situations in gambling. This prompted a desire to be able to evaluate what might happen after the dice were thrown, the cards were dealt, etc. Some students contend that probability is only based on the extent of knowledge about the situation on the part of the observer, and this might well be a valid statement about the majority of applications in gambling. Consider the act of throwing a die. In our philosophy of classical physics we state that if we know the elasticity or plastic deformation characteristics and attitude of the die and each surface which the die encounters and if we know the forces and velocities and positions then we can specify what the final position of the die will be. If we know nothing about the physical parameters of the situation (which is the usual case for a player at the dice table) then we make assumptions about the physical parameters. We often assume, for example, a total lack of control, that is, unknown initial positions, velocities and forces. We also assume that the die is ideal or "honest". Note that a "loaded" die is not ideal; a "loaded" die is a form of control by someone. We further observe that, in our usual philosophy of physics, ignorance of the physical situation does not change that physical situation. As a result of these assumptions (lack of knowledge) our philosophy of physics leads us to state that the probability of any particular face coming up (the probability of selection of the final position) is one-sixth. As we will discuss later, this process is actually an example of induction. Obviously, the observed results can be quite different from the predicted results.

We must better define the two adjectives, true and false, or the two related nouns, truth and falsehood. The latter is not merely the "opposite" of truth; often there is no "opposite" but merely inconsistency. For example, the atheist states

S_1 $\mathfrak{b}\{\mathbf{C}\{gods\}\}=0$

whereas the monotheist (e.g., Christian, Muslim, Jew) states

S_2 $\mathfrak{b}\{\mathbf{C}\{gods\}\}=1$

and the polytheist (such as some ancient Greeks and others) asserts

S_3 $\mathfrak{b}\{\mathbf{C}\{gods\}\}>1$

In a sense any one of these statements contradicts the other two but is not the "opposite" of either. However, to the monotheist, $\mathfrak{M}\{S_2\}$ is true while $\mathfrak{M}\{S_1\}$ is false and $\mathfrak{M}\{S_3\}$ is false. Restated, if

S_4 $\mathfrak{b}\{\mathbf{C}\{gods\}\}\neq 1$

then the monotheist believes that $\mathfrak{M}\{S_2\}$ is true and that $\mathfrak{M}\{S_4\}$ is false. In such an approach there is no "middle ground". To this person that which is not in accordance with his philosophy is false. This statement, when combined with A7.01 below gives the person a dichotomy, and the Logic of Aristotle with its "Law of Excluded Middle" reflects such an approach. However, this is an additional axiom if it is used.

Or, restated, the dichotomy is a result of inherent truth being based on the philosophy. We shall now further define the metric. We shall adopt the following convention, unless otherwise specified in particular instances.

D7.01 $\mathfrak{M}\{\mathfrak{t}\{\mathfrak{M}_\alpha\}\}:\mathfrak{M}\{t_\alpha\}$

A truth-value is a number, and as such conforms to the following constraints.

C7.01 $t_\alpha \in \mathbf{S}\{real\text{-}number\}$

C7.02 $t_\alpha \geq 0$

C7.03 $t_\alpha \leq 1$

The equivalents in English are:

C7.04 $t_\alpha=0$

C7.05 S_α is false

E7.01 $\mathfrak{M}\{C7.04\}:\mathfrak{M}\{C7.05\}$

C7.06 $t_\alpha=1$

C7.07 S_α is true

E7.02 $\mathfrak{M}\{C7.06\}:\mathfrak{M}\{C7.07\}$

To repeat, t_α is with respect to $\mathfrak{P}$ and might more properly be shown as $t_\alpha^{\mathfrak{P}}$. However, we shall use it without the superscript and with the understanding that it is based on $\mathfrak{P}$ in each case. Further, as stated above,

A7.01 $\mathfrak{t}\{\mathfrak{M}\{\mathfrak{P}\}\}=1$

At this point we must assert another axiom.

C7.08 $t_\alpha = t_\beta$

A7.02 $\Delta[\mathfrak{M}\{C3.01\},\mathfrak{M}\{D7.01\}]:\nabla[\mathfrak{M}\{C7.08\},\mathfrak{M}_\mu]$

This states that identity of intensions implies equality of truth-values. Note here that equality of two metrics (e.g., both being true) does not necessarily mean that the assertions underlying the metrics are related or identical. In other words, the inverse of A7.02 does not necessarily hold, as is indicated by the term $\mathfrak{M}_\mu$. Thus we define truth-value as

D7.02 $\mathfrak{M}\{t_\alpha\}:\Delta[\mathfrak{M}\{A7.02\},\mathfrak{M}\{C7.01\}],\Delta[\mathfrak{M}\{C7.02\},\mathfrak{M}\{C7.03\}]]$

We earlier stated that a system of logic must be an integral part of the philosophy of the individual. Since all assertions in the system of logic are axioms or theorems and since they are each a part of the philosophy then each must be true since a basic tenet of each philosophy must be that all axioms of that philosophy are true. Further, we must compute the truth-value of each definiendum from that of the definiens (per A7.02) for each definition since no new information is being added in the process (reference Section 2.5.1). Thus all such newly defined symbols in the philosophy must be true since they are defined from existing terms in the philosophy which are true. For our own system this says that, by adopting this Logic as a part of our philosophy, the A and D assertions each have a truth-value $t_\alpha = 1$. Since the P assertions have been deduced from A and D assertions we can also deduce that each of them has the same truth-value.

The class of axioms which constitutes our philosophy will, in addition to other forms of assertions, probably contain some assertions which are each constructed with a disjunction of several alternative assertions. The disjunctive statement is thus a true statement, but the truth-value of each alternative, before selection, is usually less than certain. This will be investigated in more depth later.

A theorem is needed for the development of other theorems.

** $\Delta[\mathfrak{M}\{A7.02\},\mathfrak{M}\{A3.17\}]:\mathfrak{M}\{P7.01\}$

P7.01 $\Delta[\mathfrak{M}\{t\{\mathfrak{M}_\alpha\}\},\mathfrak{M}\{C3.01\}]:\mathfrak{M}\{t\{\mathfrak{M}_\beta\}\}$

Note that this also is classified.

E7.03 $\mathfrak{M}\{P7.01\}\epsilon\mathbf{C}\{\text{Rules of Substitution}\}$

7.2.1.1. Complement of Truth-Value

We shall define the complement of a truth-value as

D7.03 $t^c_\alpha = (1 - t_\alpha)$

E7.04 $\mathfrak{M}\{t^c_\alpha\}:\mathfrak{M}\{\text{the complement of truth-value } t_\alpha\}$

If t_α is the measure of the extent that $\mathfrak{M}_\alpha$ is true then t^c_α is the measure of the extent that $\mathfrak{M}_\alpha$ (as presented by S_α) is false. On this basis and on the assumption of Law of Excluded Middle, t^c_α has been called not-S_α. Further, by assuming that deduction proceeds on the basis of truth-values, some people have viewed the complement as the value of truth of concepts external to $\mathfrak{M}_\alpha$. This view can lead to erroneous results since, in general, we have not defined all concepts external to $\mathfrak{M}_\alpha$.

7.2.1.2. Truth-Value of Conjunctions

The conjunctions which we have discussed for intensions have been the coincident conjunction, the aggregate conjunction and the exclusion. Following a form of Johnson (13) we state that the probability of truth of the aggregate conjunction of two independent assertions is the product of the truth-values of the two assertions, or

C7.09 $t\{\nabla[\mathfrak{M}_\alpha,\mathfrak{M}_\beta]\}=(t\{\mathfrak{M}_\alpha\}\bullet t\{\mathfrak{M}_\beta\})$

A7.03 $\mathfrak{M}\{C5.88\}:\nabla[\mathfrak{M}\{C7.09\},\mathfrak{M}_\mu]$

In the more general situation, the two assertions are not necessarily independent; to demonstrate this situation we may consider two new assertions, S_γ and S_δ, which we shall define in the following manner. In C7.09 we shall define $\mathfrak{M}_\alpha$ and $\mathfrak{M}_\beta$ such that

C7.10 $\mathfrak{M}_\beta:\blacksquare[\mathfrak{M}_\delta,\mathfrak{M}_\gamma]$

C7.11 $\mathfrak{M}_\alpha:\mathfrak{M}_\gamma$

then

** $\Delta[\Delta[\mathfrak{M}\{C7.09\},\mathfrak{M}\{C7.11\}],\Delta[\mathfrak{M}\{A3.13\},\mathfrak{M}\{P7.01\}]]:\mathfrak{M}\{S_1\}$

S_1 $t\{\nabla[\mathfrak{M}_\gamma,\mathfrak{M}_\beta]\}=(t\{\mathfrak{M}_\gamma\}\bullet t\{\mathfrak{M}_\beta\})$

** $\Delta[\Delta[\mathfrak{M}\{S_1\},\mathfrak{M}\{C7.10\}],\Delta[\mathfrak{M}\{A3.13\},\mathfrak{M}\{P7.01\}]]:\mathfrak{M}\{S_2\}$

S_2 $t\{\nabla[\mathfrak{M}_\gamma,\blacksquare[\mathfrak{M}_\delta,\mathfrak{M}_\gamma]]\}=(t\{\mathfrak{M}_\gamma\}\bullet t\{\blacksquare[\mathfrak{M}_\delta,\mathfrak{M}_\gamma]\})$

** $\nabla[\mathfrak{M}\{S_2\},\nabla[\mathfrak{M}\{P3.06\},\mathfrak{M}\{P7.01\}]]:\mathfrak{M}\{P7.02\}$

P7.02 $t\{\nabla[\mathfrak{M}_\gamma,\mathfrak{M}_\delta]\}=(t\{\mathfrak{M}_\gamma\}\bullet t\{\blacksquare[\mathfrak{M}_\delta,\mathfrak{M}_\gamma]\})$

E7.05 $\mathfrak{M}\{P7.02\}:\mathfrak{M}\{\text{compound probability}\}$

We might note that P7.02 is also sometimes called "conditional probability" and is stated in the form

** $P(p\&q)=(P(p)\bullet P(q\text{ given }p))$

which is closer to the form of Johnson. However, we must remember that $\nabla[\mathfrak{M}_\alpha,\mathfrak{M}_\beta]$ represents the aggregate conjunction of intension, not necessarily the truth of simultaneous occurrance of $\mathfrak{M}_\alpha$ and $\mathfrak{M}_\beta$. Johnson's rule is concerned with occurrance. $t\{\nabla[\mathfrak{M}_\alpha,\mathfrak{M}_\beta]\}$ is the truth-value of the aggregate conjunction of two assertions; we can not necessarily assume that either assertion is concerned with occurrance.

Another result which can be important in induction can also be developed.

S_1 $\nabla[\mathfrak{M}\{C3.06\},\nabla[\mathfrak{M}\{A7.02\},\mathfrak{M}\{A3.12\}]]:\mathfrak{M}\{S_a\}$

S_a $t\{\mathfrak{M}_\alpha\}=t\{\nabla[\mathfrak{M}_\beta,\mathfrak{M}_\mu]\}$

S_2 $\nabla[\mathfrak{M}\{S_a\},\nabla[\mathfrak{M}\{P7.02\},\mathfrak{M}\{A3.12\}]]:\mathfrak{M}\{S_b\}$

S_b $t\{\mathfrak{M}_\alpha\}=(t\{\mathfrak{M}_\beta\}\bullet t\{\blacksquare[\mathfrak{M}_\mu,\mathfrak{M}_\beta]\})$

** $\mathfrak{M}\{C7.03\}:\nabla[\mathfrak{M}\{S_c\},\mathfrak{M}_\rho]$

S_c $t\{\blacksquare[\mathfrak{M}_\mu,\mathfrak{M}_\beta]\}\leq 1$

S_4 $\nabla[\mathfrak{M}\{S_c\},\mathfrak{M}\{P3.06\}]:\mathfrak{M}\{S_d\}$

S_d $(t\{\mathfrak{M}_\beta\}\bullet t\{\blacksquare[\mathfrak{M}_\mu,\mathfrak{M}_\beta]\})\leq(t\{\mathfrak{M}_\beta\}\bullet 1)$

S_5 $\nabla[\mathfrak{M}\{S_d\},\nabla[\mathfrak{M}\{C4.15\},\mathfrak{M}\{P4.03\}]]:\mathfrak{M}\{S_e\}$

S_e $(\mathfrak{t}\{\mathfrak{M}_\beta\}\bullet\mathfrak{t}\{\blacksquare[\mathfrak{M}_\mu,\mathfrak{M}_\beta]\})\leq\mathfrak{t}\{\mathfrak{M}_\beta\}$

S_6 $\nabla[\nabla[\mathfrak{M}\{S_b\},\mathfrak{M}\{S_e\}],\mathfrak{M}\{P4.03\}]:\mathfrak{M}\{C7.12\}$

C7.12 $\mathfrak{t}\{\mathfrak{M}_\alpha\}\leq\mathfrak{t}\{\mathfrak{M}_\beta\}$

** $\nabla[\mathfrak{M}\{S_2\},\nabla[\mathfrak{M}\{S_6\},\mathfrak{M}\{A3.12\}]]:\mathfrak{M}\{S_7\}$

S_7 $\nabla[\mathfrak{M}\{S_a\},\mathfrak{M}_f]:\mathfrak{M}\{C7.12\}$

where

** $\mathfrak{M}_f:\nabla[\nabla[\mathfrak{M}\{P7.02\},\mathfrak{M}\{A3.12\}],\nabla[\mathfrak{M}\{S_e\},\mathfrak{M}\{P4.03\}]]$

** $\nabla[\mathfrak{M}\{S_1\},\nabla[\mathfrak{M}\{S_7\},\mathfrak{M}\{A3.12\}]]:\mathfrak{M}\{P7.03\}$

P7.03 $\nabla[\mathfrak{M}\{C3.06\},\mathfrak{M}_\nu]:\mathfrak{M}\{C7.12\}$

in which

** $\mathfrak{M}_\nu:\nabla[\nabla[\mathfrak{M}\{A7.02\},\mathfrak{M}\{A3.12\}],\mathfrak{M}_f]$

In deduction and induction this is in accord with conventional thought in that, in logically deducing $\mathfrak{M}_\beta$ from $\mathfrak{M}_\alpha$, the equality between the truth-values holds if $\mathfrak{M}_\alpha$ is true, but if $\mathfrak{M}_\alpha$ is false there are situations where true results can accidently be deduced from false hypotheses. Also, we may observe that S_3 above, and this result P7.03, are in accord with statement T57-1h of Carnap (5,306).

A variation on the above derivation (P7.03) is the following.

** $\mathfrak{M}\{C7.03\}:\nabla[\mathfrak{M}\{S_1\},\mathfrak{M}_\rho]$

S_1 $\mathfrak{t}\{\blacksquare[\mathfrak{M}_\delta,\mathfrak{M}_\gamma]\}\leq 1$

** $\nabla[\mathfrak{M}\{S_1\},\mathfrak{M}\{A4.07\}]:\mathfrak{M}\{S_2\}$

S_2 $(\mathfrak{t}\{\mathfrak{M}_\gamma\}\bullet\mathfrak{t}\{\blacksquare[\mathfrak{M}_\delta,\mathfrak{M}_\gamma]\})\leq(\mathfrak{t}\{\mathfrak{M}_\gamma\}\bullet 1)$

** $\nabla[\mathfrak{M}\{S_2\},\mathfrak{M}\{C4.15\}]:\mathfrak{M}\{S_3\}$

S_3 $(\mathfrak{t}\{\mathfrak{M}_\gamma\}\bullet\mathfrak{t}\{\blacksquare[\mathfrak{M}_\delta,\mathfrak{M}_\gamma]\})\leq\mathfrak{t}\{\mathfrak{M}_\gamma\}$

** $\nabla[\mathfrak{M}\{S_3\},\nabla[\mathfrak{M}\{P7.02\},\mathfrak{M}\{A3.12\}]]:\mathfrak{M}\{P7.04\}$

P7.04 $\mathfrak{t}\{\nabla[\mathfrak{M}_\gamma,\mathfrak{M}_\delta]\}\leq\mathfrak{t}\{\mathfrak{M}_\gamma\}$

Thus, in a compound concept, the assertions P7.03 and P7.04 state the obvious that though part of the aggregation is true, the aggregation itself may have a lower truth-value or be false.

Theorem P7.03 may also be used in the discussion about the truth-value of an augmented system. As we have stated before, a philosophy $\mathfrak{P}$ is a specific collection of assertions, one of which is

S_0 $\mathfrak{t}\{\mathfrak{M}\{\mathfrak{P}\}\}=1$

However, our philosophy is often inadequate for all situations which arise, and we often must act on the basis of additional assertions, some of which may be suspect. Consider the situation of an assertion S_1 which is used in conjunction with $\mathfrak{P}$ and for which, by our current belief,

S_2 $\mathfrak{t}\{\mathfrak{M}_1\}<1$

We shall define the augmented system as S_3.

S_4 $\mathfrak{M}_3:\nabla[\mathfrak{M}\{\mathfrak{P}\},\mathfrak{M}_1]$

Two situations can exist in that either S_1 is independent of $\mathfrak{P}$ or it is not. However, we can show that, in the latter case, S_1 is then composed of a conjunction of terms, one part being included in $\mathfrak{P}$ and one part being independent. Thus we shall consider only the former situation.

** $\nabla[\mathfrak{M}\{P7.03\},\mathfrak{M}\{S_4\}]:\mathfrak{M}\{S_5\}$

S_5 $\mathfrak{t}\{\mathfrak{M}_3\}\leq\mathfrak{t}\{\mathfrak{M}_1\}$

It can easily be established that, in the case where one part of the aggregation is $\mathfrak{P}$, the equality holds in S_5. In any event, this shows that the truth-value of an augmented system can not exceed the lowest truth-value of any member of the system.

7.2.1.3. Truth-Value of Null Intension

In conventional philosophies we usually assume that the existence of a truth-value (a metric), whether it be truth or falsehood, presupposes meaningfulness of the associated assertion. A statement is often made which is equivalent to: "A null intension should have no metric since nonsense is neither true nor false". However, as we demonstrate below, this is in opposition to the content of the assertions which we have developed prior to this point.

** $\nabla[\mathfrak{M}\{C3.13\},\nabla[\mathfrak{M}\{A3.04\},\mathfrak{M}\{A3.12\}]]:\mathfrak{M}\{S_1\}$

S_1 $\nabla[\mathfrak{O},\mathfrak{M}_\alpha]:\mathfrak{M}_\alpha$

** $\nabla[\mathfrak{M}\{S_1\},\nabla[\mathfrak{M}\{A7.02\},\mathfrak{M}\{A3.12\}]]:\mathfrak{M}\{S_2\}$

S_2 $\mathfrak{t}\{\nabla[\mathfrak{O},\mathfrak{M}_\alpha]\}=\mathfrak{t}\{\mathfrak{M}_\alpha\}$

** $\nabla[\mathfrak{M}\{S_2\},\nabla[\mathfrak{M}\{P7.02\},\mathfrak{M}\{A3.12\}]]:\mathfrak{M}\{S_3\}$

S_3 $(\mathfrak{t}\{\mathfrak{O}\}\cdot\mathfrak{t}\{\blacksquare[\mathfrak{M}_\alpha,\mathfrak{O}]\})=\mathfrak{t}\{\mathfrak{M}_\alpha\}$

** $\nabla[\mathfrak{M}\{S_3\},\nabla[\mathfrak{M}\{P3.02\},\mathfrak{M}\{A3.12\}]]:\mathfrak{M}\{S_4\}$

S_4 $(\mathfrak{t}\{\mathfrak{O}\}\cdot\mathfrak{t}\mathfrak{M}_\alpha\})=\mathfrak{t}\{\mathfrak{M}_\alpha\}$

** $\nabla[\mathfrak{M}\{S_4\},\nabla[\mathfrak{M}\{C4.15\},\mathfrak{M}\{P4.03\}]]:\mathfrak{M}\{S_5\}$

S_5 $(\mathfrak{t}\{\mathfrak{O}\}\cdot\mathfrak{t}\{M_\alpha\})=(1\cdot\mathfrak{t}\{\mathfrak{M}_\alpha\})$

** $\nabla[\mathfrak{M}\{S_5\},\mathfrak{M}\{A4.07\}]:\mathfrak{M}\{P7.05\}$

P7.05 $\mathfrak{t}\{\mathfrak{O}\}=1$

Thus, by this, nonsense is true. This result is of rather trivial importance, but it again demonstrates the point that the implications of our axioms and definitions are often unexpected. And to say that $\mathfrak{t}\{\mathfrak{O}\}=0$ is to refute A7.03 or C3.13, and so we must proceed on this basis.

7.2.1.4. Truth-Value of Disjunction

A question might legitimately be raised about how exclusive disjunction could appear in our philosophy $\mathfrak{P}$ since all statements in $\mathfrak{P}$ are true and no alternative is allowed. In various parts of $\mathfrak{P}$ we must make what appears to be an exception; some statements must be included in the philosophy as members of a class of statements from which only one can be chosen and applicable. This is especially true in our philosophy of physics, and the statements about the faces of a die are a common simple example. The six possible statements are mutually exclusive. Another common example is the "spin" of an electron in atomic theory. Thus we do use exclusive disjunction in $\mathfrak{P}$ in cases where we have an exhaustive collection of the options. The disjunctive statement includes the options and thus the disjunctive statement is always true, though the truth-value of any one alternative may exist anywhere in the range from certainly false to certainly true. In the case of the die, where we know nothing about initial conditions we assume that the truth-value of each of the six alternatives before selection (before the "throw") is 1⁄6. After selection one of the alternatives is true and the other five are each false.

The truth-value of disjunction is important in another sense alluded to in the last paragraph: it is a basis of the "frequency" version of probability, since it is, in the "random" case (see below), determined from the ratio of cardinalities of the classes of options. Further, in most cases it implies the acceptance of the physical quantity, time, by a comparison of the situation before an event with the situation after that event. The possible options in that disjunction are assertions which are the members of a class. The rules by which selection is made from that class may or may not be a part of the philosophy. The definition of the situation and these rules of selection (which are a part, implied or stated, of the definition) determine the truth-value of each member before selection. That truth-value may, thus, be unknown to us, and on the basis of this ignorance we assume, as a convenience, the probabilities of selection based on a non-existent random situation.

Throwing the die, selecting balls from an urn, drawing a card and playing roulette are all examples of selection (supposedly by random methods) of an assertion from a class of allowable options. Thus these are examples of disjunction, and these particular physical situations are each exclusive disjunction. By the assumption of a probability of being selected, prior to the actual selection, we are assigning that probability as the truth-value of the assertion.

Though we often refer to examples of gambling, very important applications exist in many other areas. For example, the Schrodinger equation has been used to predict the amplitude (probability) and wavelength of lines in the spectrum of the hydrogen atom. This equation was developed from the Principle of Uncertainty.

In the above examples we are referring to physical events, changes in spatial configurations with respect to time. Are truth-values of disjunction related to the physical concept, time, by definition? No, but many of the important applications seem to be with respect to time, being selections or changes of state or condition. But until we postulate a philosophy of physics which includes the variable, time, our discussions about disjunction must, of necessity, omit changes of state.

For the example of disjunction we shall define

** $\mathfrak{M}\{t\{\mathfrak{M}_{\mu}\}\}$:$\mathfrak{M}$\{truth-value of the selection\}

** $\mathfrak{M}\{\mathfrak{M}_{\alpha}\}$:$\mathfrak{M}$\{$\alpha$'th member of the class from which we select\}

** $\mathfrak{M}\{t\{\mathfrak{M}_{\alpha}\}\}$:$\mathfrak{M}$\{the truth-value of $\mathfrak{M}_{\alpha}$\}

The Theorem of Total Probability (A7.05 below) is a result of having a class of options $\mathbf{C}\{S_{\alpha}\}$ and of selection in exclusive disjunction.

A7.04 $\mathfrak{M}_{\gamma} \epsilon \mathbf{C}\{S_{\alpha}\}$

C7.13 $\mathfrak{h}\{\mathbf{C}\{S_{\alpha}\}\}=N$

C7.14 $t\{\mathfrak{M}_\mu\}=\sum_{\alpha=1}^{N} t\{\mathfrak{M}_\alpha\}$

A7.05 $\Delta[\mathfrak{M}\{C7.12\},\mathfrak{M}\{C7.13\}]:\mathfrak{M}\{C7.14\}$

E7.06 $\mathfrak{M}\{A7.05\}:\mathfrak{M}\{\text{Theorem of Total Probability}\}$

If the class of options is exhaustive then we are stating with certainty that one of the options will be selected.

C7.15 $t\{\mathfrak{M}_\mu\}=1$

C7.16 The collection $\mathbf{C}\{S_\alpha\}$ is exhaustive

E7.07 $\Delta[\mathfrak{M}\{A7.05\},\mathfrak{M}\{C7.15\}]:\mathfrak{M}\{C7.16\}$

We might notice that, in A7.05, if there is no reason to select one member of $\mathbf{C}\{\mathfrak{M}_\alpha\}$ in preference to another (all t_α are equal) and if the collection is exhaustive then we can say

** $N{\bullet}t\{\mathfrak{M}_\alpha\}=1$

In cases where a bias exists t_α must be determined on the basis of other information, such as in the examples below.

In our earlier discussion of inclusive disjunction (Section 5.6.2) we viewed the class $\mathbf{C}_\gamma$ which has two members as a new class $\mathbf{C}_\delta$ which has three members with exclusive disjunction. The selection in this case was shown as

** $\mathfrak{M}_\mu \in \mathbf{C}_\delta$

and by the Theorem of Total Probability the truth-value of this selection is

** $t_\mu=t\{\mathfrak{M}_\alpha\}+t\{\mathfrak{M}_\beta\}+t\{\nabla[\mathfrak{M}_\alpha,\mathfrak{M}_\beta]\}$

We must also note that this is an exhaustive collection or class and so

** $t_\mu=1$

Since $\mathfrak{M}_\alpha$ appears in both the first and third terms of this last statement, the truth-value of $\mathfrak{M}_\alpha$ in any form is

** $t_\alpha=t\{\mathfrak{M}_\alpha\}+t\{\nabla[\mathfrak{M}_\alpha,\mathfrak{M}_\beta]\}$

and, in like manner, the truth-value of $\mathfrak{M}_\beta$ in any form is

** $t_\beta=t\{\mathfrak{M}_\beta\}+t\{\nabla[\mathfrak{M}_\alpha,\mathfrak{M}_\beta]\}$

The truth-value of only the term of conjunction is $t\{\nabla[\mathfrak{M}_\alpha,\mathfrak{M}_\beta]\}$ By substitution among these last equations we can show that

P7.06 $t_\mu=(t_\alpha+t_\beta-t\{\nabla[\mathfrak{M}_\alpha,\mathfrak{M}_\beta]\})$

We may note from P7.02 below that if $\mathfrak{M}_\alpha$ and $\mathfrak{M}_\beta$ are independent then the last term becomes a product.

** $t_\mu=t_\alpha+t_\beta-(t_\alpha{\bullet}t_\beta)$

which is a commonly used form. In this instance, by regrouping we arrive at deMorgan's Theorem.

P7.07 $t_\mu=(1-(1-t_\alpha){\bullet}(1-t_\beta))$

7.2.1.5. Random Selection

To review what we discussed above, consider the situation where

** $\sum_{\alpha=1}^{N} t\{\mathfrak{M}_\alpha\}=1$

** $\flat\{\mathbf{C}\{\mathfrak{M}_\alpha\}\}=N$

** $(N{\bullet}t\{\mathfrak{M}_\alpha\})=1$

This is a collection in which there is no bias toward any member, and a selection from such a collection is defined as a random selection. Kendall (14,187) defines "random selection" as any selection which lacks aim or purpose, but such a statement is not a precise definition. He then (14,190) states conditions similar to those stated above. A "random sample" is a sample in which each member has been chosen by a truly random selection, but, as his examples show, the attainment of an actual random sample is difficult. His footnote (14,191) seems to refer again to the principle of indifference. In many applications the use of "random selection" is also an example of this principle, as if the mental attitude of the person making the selection were the determining factor in randomness. Lack of knowledge about the situation does not make the selection random, but, in the absence of precise information about prior events, we often assume that such is the case as a convenience. This assumption can, of course, bias our observations.

Again, consider the act of throwing a die, as discussed above. Our classical physics states that randomness is not inherent in the performance of the die. Rather, classical physics states that the situation should be determinate. When we assume a random distribution of the selected face (final position) we are admitting that we do not know the relevant physical parameters. In actuality the die, or its initial conditions, might have a built-in bias of some type.

Now consider weather prediction. By stating the predictions as probability figures, the weather people have attained a reasonable degree of success. The weather system of the earth is a tremendous aggregation of local conditions, so large that we can not devise and compute a world-wide and complete model. Yet each small segment can be described by our theory of gas dynamics. Thus our limited capabilities force us to assume a probability model, an example of randomness, rather than apply gas dynamics on such a grand scale.

Quantum mechanics is also formulated as a probability model because of the Heisenberg Principle of Uncertainty which asserts that we can not measure both position and momentum below a specified degree of inaccuracy. Thus, here again we are ignorant of the actual status of the "particle". Our attempted observation of the particle will produce unpredictable results, except that our results seem to fall in a specified pattern in the aggregate or statistical sense.

Is randomness based on inherent characteristics or on observed characterists? Merely because we are ignorant of the situation and have no control over that situation, there is no reason to believe that the results are selected in a random manner. Randomness is one possible state of inherent truth-values, without regard for the observer or his knowledge. Our assumption of randomness for purposes of calculation from our position of ignorance is merely a "prudent" basis for our inductive reasoning in that situation.

7.2.2. Verified Truth

A more natural form of "truth" but one which is intellectually more difficult is that of the assertion which is true because it has been verified by a preponderance of the observations. If a person states, "I am cold", and if he is shivering and if his surface temperature is low then we would agree that his assertion is true. If his surface temperature is 37°C and there is no shivering then we would tend to view such a statement as false. Of course, "cold" is a descriptive adjective, relative to the situation. "Cold weather" is air in which the temperature is lower than what the speaker considers to be normal. For example, air at 13°C in a Washington, D.C. summer is "cold"; air at 13°C in Wisconsin in the winter is "warm" or "hot".

We shall define verified truth to be the arithmetic mean of the truth-values of individual observations. This statement, obviously, contains concepts (terms) which must be more precisely defined, and we shall do so in the ensuing Sections.

Observations are measurements, by highly accurate devices or by other less accurate systems such as our senses. Observations are the basis for the descriptive adjectives, but observations can be with respect to limiting adjectives. For example, the assertion, "My height is 1.78 meters", contains the limiting adjective, 1.78. The accuracy of this adjective can be determined (within specified tolerances) by measurements. Such verification by observations is stated by some in the form, "Truth is correspondence with fact". This statement, of course, disregards inherent truth. Further, the statement contains some ambiguous terms, and it might be more completely stated in the form

** A true statement is one which agrees with the preponderance of prior observations.

The word, preponderance, here reflects our experience (prior observations also) that slight variations are expected to be found when we make observations. This preponderance of experience then becomes a formally stated hypothesis or an informal hypothesis and then eventually, if further confirmed, can become a part of our philosophy. We should also note that this discussion states a sequence of activities over time and is thus implying a dependence on a philosophy of physics.

Another view of this is that truth is determined by our philosophy and an aggregation of supplementary hypotheses which are verified or refuted by our observations. The hypotheses are, to some extent, extensions of observations (as determined by inductive methods) and are necessary for those situations where observations are not available as a basis for our actions.

These remarks would indicate that in most philosophies we have included a statement (an assumption) that our observations are "facts" and are not open to much dispute. However, illusion or misinterpretation have often produced "facts" which have later been disproved. Since we are aware that observations are our only source of new information and the source of our knowledge and the basis of induction, our only admonishment is that care be used at each stage of verfied truth and induction.

The results of observations are usually "data". Data are abbreviated forms of assertions, abbreviated only for our efficiency and convenience. For example, a tabulation of the form

t	σ
32	3.4
41	4.3
54	5.7

represents three assertions of the form

** "At measured time t the measured angle was σ."

Thus observations, abbreviated as data, form a set $\mathbf{S}_\alpha$ of ordered n-tuples; these are ordered pairs in the above example of the form $(t_\beta,\sigma(t_\beta))$. In such sets we must allow multiple observations at the same values of the independent variables (such as t), and we must allow different observed values of the function (such as σ) at such value of t; though variations in observed values are expected, precise duplicates may also occur. This fact gives these sets a different character than some sets which we have considered earlier, such as **N**.

The truth of the common statement

S_1 The time is 08:32

might be viewed in two ways. The truth-value of S_1 is near zero, as stated. What is usually implied by such a statement is that it is a contraction of one of the following:

S_2 The time is approximately 08:32

S_3 The time is 08:32$\pm$30seconds

Though S_2 is the more common statement (outside of the sciences) it actually also implies a statement of the form of S_3.

Once we have determined a standard for comparison (in the case of a descriptive adjective or measurement) and a range of values (within which we will accept the measurement as verifying the statement) then we define the "truth" or "falsehood" of our assertion with respect to the observations. The assertion is true or verified if the observation is within the allowable range of values and is false or refuted if the observation is outside that range. We should admit, however, that such an approach to truth is usually implicit in our philosophies since it is the natural approach and the only verification of the majority of our experiences. However, many philosophies do not explicitly include this approach; in disregarding this type of truth such philosophies perpetuate the confusion between the two types.

As opposed to the truth-value of selection which is often concerned with the future, observations are in the present or past. "Experience" is an aggregation and synthesis of observations. Thus, as inherent truth is measured with respect to a philosophy so verified truth is measured with respect to this experience. We immediately see that there is a statistical aspect to verified truth. We also see parallels between our two types of truth and the $probability_1$ and $probability_2$ of Carnap (5,25). We have defined a basis of evaluation for inherent truth; we must now define a method of evaluation for verified truth. An example might be in order here.

We discussed previously that a complete ignorance of the physical parameters, initial position and velocity and force, of a die can lead us to view the "throw" of the die as a probability situation. The die is assumed to be a perfect cube in a Euclidian space; the center of gravity (first moment of mass) is at the geometrical center of the cube. Thus when "throwing" we are certain that the cube will rest eventually on one face if unconstrained; the opposite face is "up". In our ignorance of actual circumstances, we must rely on "ideal" physical theory and on the truth-value of disjunction in Section 7.2.1.4. Observe that our assumed theory would show that each of the six faces has an equal chance of being up. It also says that, for physical reasons, these six possible occurances are mutually exclusive situations. Certainty is the sum of the assigned probabilities, and some might say that each probability is an "expected" truth-value for that event. Thus the assumed probability, before the throw, of a specified face being up after the throw is 1/6.

The observation of the behavior of an actual die will provide us with the observed frequency of occurance. For a large number of observations we might find that the ratio approaches a figure slightly different from 1/6 for a specified face. Of course, even for an "honest" die there is no reason to believe that any one face will appear in precisely one-sixth of the observations. But when the number of observations becomes large and we still find a variation, we tend to rationalize and argue that the die is not perfect. Thus our expectation is that the observed frequency of occurance should have the assumed probability as a limit if our hypothesis is reasonable but that a variation from that assumed probability indicates an imperfection in the hypothesis.

These remarks lead us to the question of the relationship of inherent to verified truth. The conventional view often has been that verified truth "flowed" or was developed from inherent truth. In such a view the verified truth is merely a representation or observed approximation to the inherent truth. However, we can see that in inductive changes to a philosophy the situation is reversed; the part of the philosophy under discussion (the hypothesis) is being accepted or rejected based on its correspondence (degree of confirmation) with observations. In the sciences it seems to be generally accepted that the philosophy is a currently "best" reflection of observations. Once we have such a philosophy we then proceed to promulgate the axioms of that philosophy as inherent truth, though they were developed by induction.

From these remarks it is apparent that verified truth is the applied side of the "frequency" theory of probability, and it is determined by the methods of statistical analysis. By such methods we determine estimates of truth rather than finding certainties, and these estimates of truth may be any value in the range (0,1). The maximization of verified truth is the intent of induction, and we discuss this further in Section 8.

7.3. Traditional Logic

Traditional Logic is based on the demonstration of truth. Usually the presentations of Traditional Logic are not concerned with determinations of what the basis of truth is or what the reference philosophy is. Traditional Logic proceeds as if there is an absolute truth, a standard with which no person can take exception. In this sense it could be developed from any philosophy which includes it. Thus, it can be consistent with our Inherent Truth. However, many of the examples given in various texts are examples of Verified Truth, as if there were no difference between the two concepts. Further, the interpretations of the notation used often vacillates among intension, truth as a concept and truth as a number. These criticisms are one reason for the development of this text. We might add that these and related criticisms have been prevalent for some time. For example, Lewis and Langford (17,49) point out that "A logic which is adequate for all propositions must ... cover both intension and extension. The traditional logic is unsatisfactory on this point.".

The formulas which are presented below are based on Traditional Logic and a dichotomy of truth-values. This might lead us to say that Traditional Logic is a logic of verified truth. But such a statement is too strong. There are a number of points which we should discuss that appear in Traditional Logic and bear on our overall subject.

In the event that an assertion is composed of some relationship of one or more assertions then that function or relationship can often be evaluated in terms of the truth-values of the individual assertions. Earlier in this Chapter we established some formulas for inherent truth, and those formulas may be used as a guide. We shall also develop some additional formulas, all based on the dichotomy of affirmation or denial of observation. From these formulas we could develop a table of truth-values (as is often done) for the dichotomy of each relationship versus its components. Such dichotomous functions will then be the individual terms in the summation by which we determine the arithmetic mean which will be our estimate of the verified truth-value. Where we have several possible functions of assertions we may not know which would be in agreement with the observations; we wish to select that which seems to conform, and the estimate of the verified truth-value is our determinant criterion.

7.3.1. Quantification

In Section 9.3.3.2.1 and elsewhere we mention propositional functions and one use of the verb, to exist. The three forms mentioned in those Sections were

1. Qx
2. (x)Qx
3. $(\exists x)Qx$

These notations (or close relatives of them) are now well established. The first represents a propositional function, but it is not a proposition since x has not been specified yet. The second is a proposition since it states that for all x the form Qx holds; this is an implicit reference to truth-values. The third is a proposition which states that at least one x exists for which Qx. The forms, (x) and $(\exists x)$, have been labeled "quantifiers", universal and existential.

Relationships between these have been established with the use of a negation symbol, ~. Some of these are:

** $\mathfrak{M}\{(\exists x)Qx\}:\mathfrak{M}\{\sim(x)\sim Qx\}$

** $\mathfrak{M}\{\sim(\exists x)Qx\}:\mathfrak{M}\{(x)\sim Qx\}$

** $\mathfrak{M}\{(\exists x)\sim Qx\}:\mathfrak{M}\{\sim(x)Qx\}$

** $\mathfrak{M}\{\sim(\exists x)\sim Qx\}:\mathfrak{M}\{(x)Qx\}$

Referring to Section 9.3.3.2.1 and others, we state there some seemingly equivalent assertions in terms of classes. However, we frequently point to our avoidance of the negation (as opposed to exclusion) of intensional and extensional statements. Yet here we have negation. What is demonstrated is that our equivalence was of extensional statements, while the statements above might more properly be viewed as statements about truth-values. The word, not, here refers only to the opposite truth-value; if Qx is true then ~Qx is false. In other words, it appears that some make use of the forms above for two purposes while we take a more restricted position.

7.3.2. Structure and Use

A better comparison of the Logics can be made by review of some of the features of the Traditional Logic.

7.3.2.1. Law of Excluded Middle

This so-called law is stated as, "Every proposition is either true or false". Lewis and Langford (17,123) imply this rule of Aristotle in their primitives, especially numbers 2 and 11.01. It is explicitly stated in their earlier developments, although in their Chapter VII they discuss the Three-valued Calculus which was developed by Lukasiewicz and Tarski. This "law" has been central to much of the work in Traditional Logic, and it is used in a Proof by Contradiction, as we discussed in Section 6.1.4.

7.3.2.2. Implication

Two types of implication (sometimes referred to as deduction) are usually presented: strict implication and material implication. As stated, (17,137), strict implication is a narrower relation and stronger statement than material implication. On the other hand, each is a statement about truth.

C7.17 p strictly implies q
C7.18 It is false that it is possible that p be true and q false
E7.08 $\mathfrak{M}${C7.17}:$\mathfrak{M}${C7.18}

"Possible" is discussed in Section 9.3.3.1.1.

C7.19 p materially implies q
C7.20 ~(p•~q)
E7.09 $\mathfrak{M}${C7.19}:$\mathfrak{M}${C7.20}

Thus a question can arise as to whether it is valid to assume that merely because q is true when p is true then q can be deduced from p. Such an approach is used in statistical studies to show a correlation, but it is not necessarily a proof of deduction. Some other relationship might exist instead of deduction of one from the other. We also note, in the case of material implication, that though q must be true if p is true, there is no requirement placed on q if p is false; q may be true or false. This is similar to our truth-values for logical implication, Theorem P7.03, in the event that q has been deduced from p.

Since these types of implication are defined in terms of truth, they would seem to exclude deduction from false premises. This is the process use in a Proof of Impossibility, Section 6.1.3. Alternatively, some form of "temporary truth" would need to be assigned to a false premise before proceeding with deduction. Such a situation is at odds with our normal processes of deduction.

7.3.2.3. Material Equivalence

Material equivalence of two assertions is defined as the situation where the two are either both true or both false, (p•q)V(~p•~q).

7.3.2.4. Identities

The following identities are frequently used in discussions of Traditional Logic.

1.	p	~~p
2.	p	pVp
3.	p	p•p
4.	pVq	qVp
5.	p•q	q•p
6.	pV(qVr)	(pVq)Vr
7.	p•(q•r)	(p•q)•r
8.	p•(qVr)	(p•q)V(p•r)
9.	pV(q•r)	(pVq)•(pVr)

10.	~(p•~q)	~pVq
11.	~(p•q)	~pV~q
12.	~(pVq)	~p•~q
13.	p=q	(p•q)V(~p•~q)
14.	p=q	(~(p•~q))•(~(q•~p))

Among these statements a degree of redundancy can be noticed, and other related statements can be developed from these. Their importance is primarily in their ease of use.

7.3.2.5. Forms of Valid Arguments

Those arguments which are valid in the traditional sense can be reduced to combinations of one or more of the following forms. Each form has been given a descriptive name or abbreviation which is then referenced when demonstrating validity. Note that in the tabulation, preceeding each result, we use the symbol ∴ as a contraction of the actual deductive process which wouldproduce that result. The symbol ∴ represents the adverb, therefore.

Modus Ponens

~(p•~q)
p
∴ q

Modus Tollens

~(p•~q)
~q
∴ ~p

Absorption

~(p•~q)
∴ ~(p•~(p•q))

Conjunction

p
q
∴ p•q

Disjunction

p
∴ pVq

Simplification

p•q
∴ p

Hypothetical Syllogism

~(p•~q)
~(q•~r)
∴ ~(p•~r)

Disjunctive Syllogism

$p \vee q$

$\sim p$

$\therefore q$

Constructive Dilemma

$(\sim(p \bullet \sim q)) \bullet (\sim(r \bullet \sim s))$

$p \vee r$

$\therefore q \vee s$

7.3.2.6. "contradictory"

Two propositions are contradictory if one is the denial of the other; if one is true then the other is false. Consider

S_1 All halides are gases at standard T/P.

S_2 Some halides are not gases at standard T/P.

We would assert that S_2 is true on the basis of experience. Since S_1 is in opposition then it must be false. Thus S_1 and S_2 are contradictory.

7.3.2.7. "invalid argument"

An argument in Logic is the sequence of deductive assertions which lead from the premises to the conclusion. In Traditional Logic an invalid argument is that in which the premises are true and the conclusion is, or can be, false. An example is

** If p then r

** If q then r

therefore

** If p then q

Note that in this Logic the conditional is always true when its consequent is true; the conditional is false only when its antecedent is true and the consequent is false. Above, in the situation where r is true and p is true, if q is false then the third statement is false since we have a true premise and a false consequent. Thus that sequence is an invalid argument.

7.3.3. Bayes Theorem

Bayes Theorem is often postulated as based on the physical quantity, time, at least in the sense of past/present versus future. As Kendall (14,176) has presented it, the probability of q_r after it has happened varies as the probability before it happened, multiplied by the probability that it happens on data q_r and the data known before the event. A simple presentation is that for two statements, p and q, although more complete presentations allow N statements. A conventional approach might be of the following form.

S_1 $P(p) \bullet P(q \text{ given } p) = P(p\&q)$

but

** $p = (p\&q) \vee (p\&\sim q)$

since $q \vee \sim q$ is a tautology. Thus, with this, S_1 becomes S_2.

S_2 $\quad [P(p\&q)+P(p\&\sim q)]\bullet P(q \text{ given } p)=P(p\&q)$

The inverse forms of S_1 are equally valid, and those are S_3 and S_4.

S_3 $\quad P(q)\bullet P(p \text{ given } q)=P(p\&q)$

S_4 $\quad P(\sim q)\bullet P(p \text{ given } \sim q)=P(p\&\sim q)$

Substitution of S_1, S_3 and S_4 into S_2 produces S_5.

S_5 $\quad [P(q)\bullet P(p \text{ given } q)+P(\sim q)\bullet P(p \text{ given } \sim q)]\bullet P(q \text{ given } p)=P(q)\bullet P(p \text{ given } q)$

This formula, S_5, when restated as P(q given p) equal to a ratio, is used to compute (as stated above and in Kendall) the "posterior" probability from the "prior" probability and the "likelihood".

However, though the above form is the traditional approach, there seems to be a difficulty when we attempt to develop an analogous form in our system. Statements analogous to S_1, S_2 and S_3 can be written in our notation, but we have (intentionally) not established a form parallel to $\sim q$ where q is an assertion. Our definition D7.03 is still stated in terms of the intension itself rather than in terms of the negation of an intension; S_4 here is written about the negation of an intension.

7.3.4. Modal Logic

A modality has been defined as a proposition in which the predicate is affirmed or denied of the subject with any kind of qualification. Another definition is as the class which includes possibility, impossibility, necessity and contingency. These are related but not identical definitions. Our discussion will be more in line with the latter definition.

In Section 6.2 we discussed (with respect to deduction) necessary conditions, sufficient conditions and impossible statements. In some common usages the adjectives, necessary, sufficient, impossible, are treated as descriptive adjectives by the addition of the adverbs, more or most. However, these are in our usage limiting adjectives. On the other hand, the adjective, possible, is a descriptive adjective if it is viewed as a measure, that is, as related to the probability of occurance. By this we mean that an event which is possible has a probability of occurance greater than zero whereas an event which is impossible will with certainty not occur; the probability of occurance is zero. The probability of a possible event is, in our view, the truth-value of the assertion of that event. In Section 9.3.3.1.1 we also discuss "possible" and "impossible" further.

7.3.5. Resolution

"Resolution" is a process which attempts to prove that a hypothesis is consistent with or inconsistent with a prescribed collection of statements. This is an application of proof by contradiction and proof of impossibility. The basis is that all statements in the prescribed collection are true and the hypothesis is then negated.

If substitution and other combinations with the collection produce a contradiction then the negation must be false and the original hypothesis must be true.

This process has achieved a reputation for success where other processes of Logic have not been fruitful. However it is usually recognized that if the hypothesis is false at the outset then the possibility exists that the process might in some circumstances be endless. The process is also realistically limited by the number of statements in the prescribed collection. At some level the number of substitutions and comparisons becomes too large to process in a reasonable amount of time.

8. INDUCTION

Whereas deduction proceeds from a specified collection of information to a specific statement which was logically contained in that collection, induction proceeds from a specified collection to a statement which is related to the collection but not necessarily contained in it in entirety. This raises the question of how to proceed; what criteria can be used to determine validity? Deduction is the formal manipulation of intensions; induction is essentially an extrapolation, an extrapolation of intensions. As with any extrapolation, there is a lack of certainty as to which of the possible results should be chosen. A measure must be applied, and any two results having equal measure might then be considered to be equally valid. Further, as with any extrapolation there is no unique method by which to conduct induction; there are possibly an infinity of methods. In any extrapolation or interpolation we must assume some uniformity. In the interpolation of data, for example, we may assume a linear or a quadratic approximation to that uniformity, and frequently our assumption produces disastrous results (such as in Newton-Raphson methods of solution of non-linear systems which suddenly diverge). In a similar manner we must expect that induction may, on occasion, lead to improper results.

The result of the extrapolation mentioned in the last paragraph is a hypothesis; the process of extrapolation is creativity, which is discussed briefly below.

Many applications of induction are viewed as "divination" or foretelling of the future, but this is a superficial attitude. Carnap (3,451) states that inductive logic may be viewed as the theory of degree of confirmation. It would seem that this is a very major part of induction, but, by our statements above, we view induction as a somewhat broader concept.

Deduction and induction are more than a game in that they constitute the basis for our conscious actions. Some of our actions are the result of determinations which are made in a deductive manner from our philosophy. However, many of our actions are not related directly to our philosophy, and the philosophy must be augmented by some "rational" approach for these cases. Probably "rational" decisions are more frequently made by inductive methods than by deductive methods because of incomplete or inadequate information, because of a deficiency in our philosophy or (occasionally) because of the lengthy process which some deductions would require. For example, induction underlies the decisions to buy or sell in the markets; therefore, induction is one basis of the study of econometrics.

Thus the question of defining that which is "rational" arises. We might note that

** $\mathfrak{M}\{\text{rational decision}\} \in \mathbf{C}\{\text{possible decisions}\}$

but beyond this all definitions become subjective. In situations where the results can be measured (such as in economics and physics) we might define

** $\mathfrak{M}\{\text{rational decision}\} : \mathfrak{M}\{\text{that decision which produces a maximum value of verified truth}\}$

Here, of course, we have traded an unknown symbol, rational, for a term which we have defined as a number. This number is, of course, determined from observations which are dependent on or determined by our particular viewpoint. But this number is the goal of induction. Thus we might say that rational decisions are the goal of induction.

We all recognize that many decisions in our lives are made on a basis other than money or physical quantity, and some economists have defined this basis as "utility". They then proceed to discuss utility as if it could be measured. Of course, utility is defined or described by the philosophy of the individual, and that result which may have a maximum utility for one person might not be near the maximum utility for another. Whatever our basis, we state that the purpose of the process of induction is to allow rational decisions on imperfect or incomplete information. This then raises the further question of the determination of suffieiency of information for any such evaluation.

Our normal approach is to base our actions on experience; if some action seems to have a reasonably good success ratio (number of successful attempts compared to the total number of attempts) we tend to continue that pattern, at least until we find an even more successful approach. This type of pattern is based on a belief of continued or recurring uniformity; "uniformity" means a low value of the standard deviation of observations. This is the more or less "conservative" form of extrapolation, and examples can be found in the behavior of all animals. The selection of an action based on such experience is not the only approach, and some people seem to be inclined to take a more erratic method where a higher risk of failure seems inherent but which might result in improved patterns of action. The "conservative" approach is sometimes referred to as "common sense" or "adhering to the tried and true". This "common sense" approach and the "rational" approach are specific forms of induction. They may be completely opposed to each other or may, in some cases, determine the same results.

Experience is an aggregation of observations over a period of time. Implied in this and our previous statements is another assumption. We have assumed a "continuity of existence", that the physical system is capable of being observed even when it is not being observed and, thus, will continue to be capable of being observed in the future. This is a form of "uniformity of nature", and it is implicit, for example, in our assertions about the conservation of mass and energy.

The "uniformity of nature" is a continuity of the present with the future and past. The "uniformity of nature" is a possible hypothesis or an axiom of a philosophy of physics. From the "common sense" view, its major justification has been that those who assume it have been able to build a more complete and consistent philosophy than could those who postulate that "Mother Nature is a bitch". This justification is another example of the "common sense" maxim, "To be successful, emulate the successful". However, in studies other than physics (might psychology be an example?) such a continuity over time perhaps should not be assumed. The "grue" and "bleen" of Goodman (3,512) might well the types of situations occurring in these studies.

Experience, as discussed above, is directly applicable experience, such as a series of measurements of a variable in a new hypothesis in physics. However, much of our experience, upon which we often base our inductive processes and decisions, is only related or parallel experience rather than directly applicable experience. In this type of application we choose the approach which had a reasonable success in the parallel situation and attempt to apply a similar technique in the existing situation. An example might be the application of the concept of entropy (a thermodynamic concept) to sociological situations. A problem which is immediately apparent is that of numerically evaluating the expected success; with direct experience this might be possible, but in the parallel situation evaluation beyond all reasonable doubt is difficult.

The changes to a pattern of actions and the changes to a philosophy are analogous, if not identical, concepts since rational actions are based on an augmented philosophy. Thus we should only treat changes to a philosophy henceforth.

8.1. Truth and Induction

As opposed to deduction, induction is based on "truth" since "truth" is the desired end result. "Truth", as displayed by our observations, is the beginning. Then we synthesize a hypothesis which seems to have a high correlation with our observations so that when it is added to the corpus of our philosophy the resulting deductions will produce "truth". To repeat, truth is the desired result, the goal, though truth-values are not used in the deductions which support the induction. Therefore, as with the traditional logic of deduction, the traditional logic of induction has been performed with truth-values.

To review, in deduction our task is to derive a specific intension, $\mathfrak{M}_\gamma$, from a given group of intensions, $\mathfrak{M}_\alpha$; $\mathfrak{M}_\gamma$ is our goal. In this case t_γ is incidental and can be determined from t_α by the assertions in Section 7.2. In induction, on the other hand, $\mathfrak{M}_\gamma$ is a hypothesis, and $\mathfrak{M}_\alpha$ comprises the assertions believed to be relevant; the task is to evaluate an estimate of t_γ on the basis of $\mathfrak{M}_\alpha$ and to take actions which maximize that estimate of t_γ. For this is the purpose of induction: to develop and choose that approach which has the most true result. The hypothesis, then, may be used for the problem at hand or may become a part of our philosophy. There is little difference in the logical aspects of the procedure, regardless of how $\mathfrak{M}_\gamma$ is used.

8.2. Changes to a Philosophy

To change a piece of a philosophy, such as some aspect of a philosophy of physics, requires perhaps three major, not necessarily exclusive actions: creation of a hypothesis; validation of that hypothesis; acceptance of the hypothesis. Of course, creativity and validation, at least in the early stages of a new hypothesis, may be intertwined as an iterative process while minor changes are being made in the hypothesis to obtain a better "fit". A more complete procedure is that of "nonmonotonic logic".

This approach recognizes a condition which is common in all practical situations: reasoning is conducted on the basis of our philosophy as augmented by an additional set of hypotheses, some of which must be discarded or replaced during the process of evaluation. The name of this process was chosen to be in contrast to the "monotonic" processes of deduction in which we maintain or build up the existing structure of definitions, axioms and theorems, but we never destroy them. In a sense, the purpose of all induction is nonmonotonic in practical situations, but we have not always recognized the fact.

Wald (28) recognized a need for such a process and formalized the revision of experimentation during the process and the selection of decisions as a result of the process. More recently, several logicians have studied the implications of nonmonotonic approaches such as the use of default assumptions. The use of default assumptions is a common situation in our normal lives. For example, a normal default assumption is

** All railroad engineers are men.

We can (at least in our modern society) find examples where this statement is false. But in our observations, nearly 100% of the sample will conform to this statement; by its use the speaker is correct nearly all the time. A default assumption, such as this generalization, is a rule or assertion which we add to our philosophy and use as a part of that philosophy, except in those instances where it is explicitly found to be incorrect. Theorems which may have been derived by the use of a default assumption must, for the incorrect instance, be replaced. Default assumptions are usually based on experience and thus the name, generalizations; they seem to work for most situations which arise.

The term, found to be incorrect, as used above can have at least two possible interpretations: the default assumption might be found to be logically inconsistent with the philosophy and some other collection of augmenting hypotheses; it might be found to be inconsistent with the data being used for evaluation. Logical inconsistency was discussed in Section 6. Inconsistency with the data becomes evident if the evaluation of the verified truth (Section 7.2.2) is near zero. Either result forces us to modify our collection of hypotheses.

In review, this process consists of deduction conducted in the normal manner until we find an erroneous result (with respect to observations) or inconsistency (with the basic philosophy). At that point we must determine which default assumptions are causing the problem, replace them and redo the deduction. This has been a usual process in the development of scientific theorems. Some recent presentations have been concerned with the mechanics of this process in an effort to reduce the possibility of bad default assumptions, their replacement and the necessity of replacement of the resultant deductive work.

On the third aspect of the establishment of a change to a philosophy, the acceptance of a hypothesis by an individual can be a completely rational occurrance (though not necessarily), but the acceptance of a hypothesis by the community at large, even with strong supporting data, has historically been an emotional issue for most of the major changes because philosophies must be accepted; they can not be "proved". As someone once remarked, hypotheses are fallible interpretations based on imperfect data. This is, then, the basis for rejection by those who hold opposing or differing views.

There is often an early form of acceptance, or quasi-acceptance, necessary when the creator or theoretician is a party separate from the party who can or will do the verification. This situation arises, for example, in theoretical physics. In such an instance the creator must present a justification of his new hypothesis so that the other party will perform experiments for verification. We can observe that some of the most useful hypotheses were created (or "discovered") with incorrect justifications (the wrong "reasons") for those hypotheses, yet the intuition of the creator was later supported during the validation. This seemed to be, in several instances, the situation in the early development of quantum mechanics. Reference Reichenbach (20,66). There sometimes seems to be more groping for a justification of the hypothesis than for the hypothesis itself.

Acceptance will not be discussed further here.

8.2.1. Creativity

Creativity requires, first, a recognition that a need exists, even though others may not be aware that the need exists. Next is an equally crucial phase, the development of an answer to that need. Creativity has been discussed for centuries, and efforts have been made to codify or mechanize it to some degree. Creativity is not a part of Logic, but it has some aspects which are related to facets of Logic.

The word, creativity, is poorly defined, and its definition is often subjective. It may be the combination of previously unrelated concepts, such as the application of "entropy" (from thermodynamics) to sociological situations. Or it may appear to be a newly invented concept. Whatever the result (such as "carryover" of concept or newly invented concept), some students of the subject seem to contend that creativity is a result of "fantasizing" about the need and about its solutions.

We previously stated that creativity consists of two steps: recognition of a need; development of an answer to that need. Either of these steps can be the result of previously unrelated concepts or a new concept. A completely new concept which is unrelated to any in our existing aggregation would seem to be the result of some random process in a field of infinite or unbounded variation. Thus, the determination of a completely new need or the discovery of a completely new answer which has reasonable utility in the given situation would seem to have a very low probability of occurance. This leaves us with the majority of creative efforts being the conjunction (aggregate and/or disjunctive) of existing (though perhaps previously unrelated) concepts. Again, the field has tremendous variation (even if bounded), and in "genius" there must be some learned or inherent capability for "filtering out" fruitless conjunctions of concepts.

Are there other processes by which new concepts are generated? This is a subject of great discussion with few solid answers yet.

The hypothesis of Kepler of elliptical orbits and the adjustment of such equations to the data of Brahe might be viewed as merely a random curve-fitting process. In the final steps perhaps such was the case, but this occurred at a time when many still believed that the earth was the center of the universe. Thus, the hypothesis of a heliocentric system with elliptical orbits was a major innovation, an example of creativity, and it explained the "anomolies" of the observations by means of a simple model.

Bohm (25,188) states that a law or a theory affords correct knowledge that goes beyond the experimental facts which helped lead to the proposal of that law or theory. Thus a properly constructed philosophy should be the basis from which inductive reasoning proceeds. The example of Kepler introduces one other action which might be considered to be a part of creativity or it might be viewed as a separate prior step. This action is that of synthesizing the data or information into useful forms. We prefer to view this as a part of the creativity phase since the manner in which the observations (e.g., those of Brahe) are processed is completely dependent on the form of the hypothesis (Kepler's elliptical paths, e.g.). This is in agreement with Hanson (25,154) who states, in our terms, that the manner in which observations are interpreted is biased by the philosophy held by the observer. A different form of hypothesis would require different processing. This step in the process leads us into the extensive fields of Estimation, Curve-Fitting, Correlation, Regression, Significance Tests and contingent areas.

The "amount" of creativity can not be measured. Some view popular works as "highly" creative, whereas they view unpopular works as "lacking" creativity, as if creativity could be measured. What is actually measured is the public response to each work.

By creativity a person may devise a new postulate. By creativity a person may devise a new logical process. Deduction can not demonstrate its own methodology. Thus the method of determining a "solution" to a boundary value problem might be a result of creativity, but the method itself must be purely deductive in its demonstration.

8.2.2. Validation

Once a new hypothesis has been devised by creative processes, it then becomes necessary to substantiate that hypothesis in some manner. Substantiation becomes a process of evaluation of the hypothesis or of subsidiary assertions deductively developed from the hypothesis and the existing philosophy. This evaluation is our preliminary validation of the hypothesis. The procedure of deducing results from the philosophy as augmented by the hypothesis and of comparing these deduced results with observed results has been termed the "hypothetico-deductive" model of confirmation (3,376). Hanson (3,626) analyzes this process in more detail.

Evaluation is a comparison between the theory and observations. One type of example (such as that referenced above) is the comparison of observed data and computed data. Several potential problems can be found, even in this simple situation.

We commonly state our theories in the notation of mathematics, such as algebraic equations or partial differential equations. Thus we have, in this approach, stated the quantities which can be measured, either as constants or variables (either as specified or unspecified numbers). In the theory we have defined the intension of each such quantity. Note that there may be variables in the theory which, by their definition, can not be directly observed, that is, only their effect on other observable quantities can be measured and compared. Such variables are sometimes referred to as "hidden" variables. Present quantum theory (nuclear theory) is an elaborate situation of this type, and other common examples can also be demonstrated. We then assume that the data derived from the theory are accurate, unless we have intentionally entered approximations into the process for ease of computation or unless the theory itself is a probability statement.

The observed data is not necessarily neutral. As Suppe (3,191) points out, what is observed is dependent on the philosophy and the postulates which the observer is attempting to validate. Further, the observed values must be recognized as containing some degree of error, even with respect to the system which is being validated, because of human fallacy and equipment inaccuracy. When we recognize that we have possible errors in measurement then we realize that the differences between computed and observed values must themselves be evaluated as to their significance. Significance in itself is a major area of study.

Significance can not be evaluated only by statistical methods, however, in the earlier stages of validation of a hypothesis. Differences between computed and observed values can also be an actual "anomoly" with respect to the hypothesis or a preliminary form of the hypothesis. Anomolies can be the basis of important changes to that hypothesis, as well as being a reason for rejection of the hypothesis.

We shall now define some formulas by which observations on individual assertions can be used to evaluate proposed relationships between the assertions. Here we have only used two assertions in the functions, but in a parallel manner more elaborate relationships can be devised.

As suggested by Boole (2,70), to test the validity of an assertion a useful approach is to record a 1 each time the assertion is observed to be true and to record a 0 each time the assertion is observed to be false. Observations which agree with values deduced from the hypothesis are "true"; those observations which do not agree are "false". Actually it is the deduced value which is true or false, but in a procedural sense we often view it in an inverse manner.

As the number of observations becomes large we might expect the ratio of the sum of the observations divided by the number of observations to begin to converge on some value. By "converge" we mean that, with increasing number of observations, the ratio varies about some value; the variation becomes smaller with increasing number. However, there is no logical requirement for such convergence other than "uniformity of nature" or some similar assumption and the fact that, with increasing number of observations, the next observation has less effect on the sum than the last observation.

This ratio is the arithmetic mean of the observed values, and some consider this ratio to be the observed probability of truth of the assertion. For binary members the arithmetic mean provides a more meaningful measure than some of the others, and it has had extensive application by practioners.

This is only one of the possible approaches. Other approaches are also available and have been studied extensively, but this approach provides us with a basic structure for discussion.

Thus, our philosophy as augmented by a hypothesis (for example, a function) is observed across the range of the hypothesis. Values deduced from the augmented philosophy are compared with the equivalent observed values. In the case of functions which can only display certain prespecified values (such as the die) the comparison between the "computed" and the observed values can be made directly. In the case of functions which are continuous, our philosophy or hypothesis must allow for an acceptable range or "tolerance" around the "computed" value; the observed value is then compared as a value within this range. In either event we have a dichotomy as discussed above. In the continuous case a value which falls at the precise end of the range may be a nuisance, but it is an arbitrary decision since the range is somewhat arbitrary. Thus, to record the results of the comparisons of our observations with "computed" values, we shall use $\delta\{\Delta[\mathfrak{M}_\beta(x_\alpha),\mathfrak{M}_\gamma(x_\alpha)]\}$ as the truth-value of observation S_γ for value x_α compared to the analogous result of hypothesis and philosophy S_β for value x_α. Note that here we are again stating that observed data are abbreviated forms of statements, and S_γ is the aggregation of these statements and any applicable statements about "tolerances". A more usual presentation would be in terms of the recorded numbers for each observation compared to the allowable range of numbers, as defined by the hypothesis and underlying philosophy.

This form for δ is directly analogous to our definition of $\mathfrak{t}\{\mathfrak{M}_\alpha\}$ since, as we mentioned in Section 7.2.1, inherent truth is determined with respect to the philosophy $\mathfrak{P}$, and a more complete notation for that truth-value would be $\mathfrak{t}\{\Delta[\mathfrak{M}_\alpha,\mathfrak{M}\{\mathfrak{P}\}]\}$. Moreover, this form for the specification of δ is such that

D8.01 $\delta\{\mathfrak{O}\}=0$

which is restated below, though it would not seem to be in accord with P7.05. The justification is that in this method we are counting only supportive observations; observations which are not supportive are not counted. This is at variance with the definition of truth-value which we have established, unless the axiom ("Law") of Excluded Middle is also included.

As a restatement,

D8.02 $\delta\{\Delta[\mathfrak{M}_\beta,\mathfrak{M}_\gamma]\}\in\mathbf{S}\{0,1\}$

E8.01 $\mathfrak{M}\{\delta\{\Delta[\mathfrak{M}_\beta(x_\alpha),\mathfrak{M}_\gamma(x_\alpha)]\}\}:\mathfrak{M}\{$the value (0 or 1) of the comparison made at x_α between $\mathfrak{M}_\beta$ and $\mathfrak{M}_\gamma\}$

In addition to the definition D8.02 some further statements of definition are needed. These are:

D8.03 $\mathfrak{M}\{\Delta[\mathfrak{M}_\beta(x_\alpha),\mathfrak{M}_\gamma(x_\alpha)]:\mathfrak{M}_\beta\}:\nabla[\mathfrak{M}\{\delta\{\Delta[\mathfrak{M}_\beta,\mathfrak{M}_\gamma]\}=1\},\mathfrak{M}_\mu]$

D8.04 $\mathfrak{M}\{\blacksquare[\mathfrak{M}_\beta(x_\alpha),\mathfrak{M}_\gamma(x_\alpha)]:\mathfrak{M}_\beta\}:\nabla[\mathfrak{M}\{\delta\{\Delta[\mathfrak{M}_\beta,\mathfrak{M}_\gamma]\}=0\},\mathfrak{M}_\mu]$

Of course, these truth-values of observation δ can be viewed as the elements or members of a set $\mathbf{S}\{\delta\}$. The number of observations on S_β is

D8.05 $N=\mathfrak{b}\{\mathbf{S}\{\delta\{\mathfrak{M}_\beta,\mathfrak{M}_\gamma\}\}\}$

We now define an arithmetic mean $\mathfrak{r}\{\mathfrak{M}_\beta,\mathfrak{M}_\gamma\}$ by

D8.06 $N\cdot\mathfrak{r}\{\mathfrak{M}_\beta,\mathfrak{M}_\gamma\}=\sum_{\alpha=1}^{N}\delta\{\Delta[\mathfrak{M}_\beta(\alpha),\mathfrak{M}_\gamma(\alpha)]\}$

E8.02 $\mathfrak{M}\{\mathfrak{r}\{\mathfrak{M}_\beta,\mathfrak{M}_\gamma\}\}:\mathfrak{M}\{$ratio of occurrance of S_β on evidence $S_\gamma\}$

It has been customary to synthesize or develop special forms of observed values for each allowable form of hypothesis. Note the forms in the subsections below. However, if we define (as we have) that the value of the ratio of occurrance is developed from a summation then very few forms can factored from that summation. Further, the term δ is hardly a factorable element even when the conditions which define it are. Thus, our definition D8.06 is the form which we must use in all applications.

In our usual use of probabilities, a computed value of 1 or 0 indicates certainty, true or false. A value of the ratio $\mathfrak{c}$ which is 1 or 0 does not give us that assurance. A value of 1 merely indicates that all observations confirmed our hypothesis, but it does not indicate that all other observations will also confirm. A value of 0 indicates that no observations confirmed, with the same proviso. However, on occasion we may use a value of 0 as part of our evidence for a hypothesis of exclusion. In a conventional view, the ratio of occurrance is the probability of truth of the assertion of hypothesis (i.e., "Truth is correspondence with fact"), and if the degree of confirmation is near unity for some restricted region of discussion, then we often, by extrapolation of the concept, use it for all applications. Later we may notice the error of our ways. Newton's Second Law was, perhaps, an example of this when effects at large distances or high velocities were studied (i.e., where relativistic effects were involved).

In the formulas below we shall use δ_ρ for the recorded value, with δ_α and δ_β the two observed values for the respective referenced assertions.

As in D7.03 we define the observation of the complement of observed truth-value as

D8.07	$\delta_\alpha^c=(1-\delta_\alpha)$
C8.01	$\delta_{n\alpha}^c$ is the observed complement of δ_α
E8.03	$\mathfrak{M}$\{D8.07\}:$\mathfrak{M}$\{C8.01\}

If we can assume independence of the two assertions then by P7.06 the observation of the aggregate conjunction would be

D8.08	$\delta_\rho=(\delta_\alpha\cdot\delta_\beta)$
C8.02	δ_ρ is the observation of aggregate conjunction for independence
E8.04	$\mathfrak{M}$\{D8.08\}:$\mathfrak{M}$\{C8.02\}

In E6.05 we defined the term, necessary condition, as it is usually used in deduction. With observations, if δ_α is present whenever δ_β is present then some would claim that S_α is a necessary condition for S_β. From the standpoint of deduction such a claim can be demonstrated to be too broad; from the standpoint of induction such a situation could be a very useful indication. To test this hypothesis we would test a conjunction (or product) of the two observations $\delta_\alpha\cdot\delta_\beta$, and if the arithmetic mean of these products of the observations is unity we might suspect that one is a necessary condition for the other.

In E6.02 we defined the term, sufficient condition. With observations we might again say that if when δ_β is absent and we find that δ_α is absent then S_α appears to be a sufficient condition for S_β. This statement uses the product of the complements $(1-\delta_\alpha)\cdot(1-\delta_\beta)$.

The measurement of exclusive disjunction for two assertions is true only if one is present and the other is not. If neither or both are present then the measurement has failed for this particular postulate. This condition is, therefore, represented by the product of the observation of one assertion and the complement of the observation of the other. As a concise statement,

D8.09 $\delta_\rho=(\delta_\alpha\bullet(1-\delta_\beta)+\delta_\beta\bullet(1-\delta_\alpha))$

We might restructure this as

** $\delta_\rho=(\delta_\alpha+\delta_\beta-(010\bullet\delta_\alpha\bullet\delta_\beta))$

C8.03 δ_ρ is the observation of exclusive disjunction

E8.05 $\mathfrak{M}$\{D8.09\}:$\mathfrak{M}$\{C8.03\}

We may note that since δ_α can only assume one of the dichotomy of values, 0 or 1, then we may restate D8.09 as

D8.09 $\delta_\rho=(\delta_\alpha-\delta_\beta)^2$

In certain instances this may aid computation.

Inclusive disjunction is the exclusive disjunction of three quantities, where two are as in exclusive disjunction of two assertions (above) and the third is the simultaneous occurrance of both.

D8.10 $\delta_\rho=(\delta_\alpha\bullet(1-\delta_\beta)+\delta_\beta\bullet(1-\delta_\alpha)+(\delta_\alpha\bullet\delta_\beta))$

This also can be restructured.

** $\delta_\rho=(\delta_\alpha+\delta_\beta-(\delta_\alpha\bullet\delta_\beta))$

C8.04 δ_ρ is the observation of inclusive disjunction

E8.06 $\mathfrak{M}$\{D8.10\}:$\mathfrak{M}$\{C8.04\}

If, by our observations, we attempt to confirm identity of two assertions then the two observed truth-values are equal or the supposition of identity is false. Refer to A7.02.

D8.11 $\delta_\rho=(\delta_\alpha\bullet\delta_\beta+(1-\delta_\alpha)\bullet(1-\delta_\beta))$

C8.05 δ_ρ is the observation of identity

E8.07 $\mathfrak{M}$\{D8.11\}:$\mathfrak{M}$\{C8.05\}

Assertion P7.07 provides the conditions by which we might accept the indication of material implication.

D8.12 $\delta_\rho=(1-(1-\delta_\beta)\bullet\delta_\alpha)$

C8.06 δ_ρ is the observation of material implication

E8.08 $\mathfrak{M}$\{D8.12\}:$\mathfrak{M}$\{C8.06\}

9. LANGUAGE

"Language" is a vague term; it usually consists of a collection of allowable symbolism in allowable sequences or patterns. In most cases the allowable symbols are interrelated through definitions in some form of dictionary or handbook which has the concurrance or acceptance of the user group. Since, to a large extent, all spoken or written patterns (which are variations along a single axis) are equivalent to the printed pattern, only the printed pattern will be discussed herein. Also, since the English language has many of the bad features (as well as many good features) found in other languages and is often more difficult for the foreigner to learn, most of our discussion of an object language will be concerned with English or the symbolic forms which we shall develop.

What are the uses of language? Communication is the single answer, but what are we communicating? The scientist and engineer must formulate and communicate precise information, and the various languages perform this function reasonably well. But the major uses of communication are external to the sciences. Literature and poetry are types of communication which are attempting to convey emotions rather than precise statements. Directives from a supervisor to employees may convey precise information, but the purpose is to evoke a response which achieves a result. Thus the several types of sentences, which will be discussed shortly, have evolved to meet these many needs. As noted at several points elsewhere herein, we shall only concern ourselves with the languages of science. By doing so we may achieve more in this limited area than if we attempted a universal discussion.

The purpose of most texts which are concerned with the English language is to teach the reader how to write or speak more correctly and more interestingly. Our purpose herein is to be correct but consistent from the standpoint of Logic, eliminating all forms which are not actually necessary in a discussion of Logic. This means that we shall, in line with the historical approach to Logic, attempt to be completely explicit and only use assertions in our symbolic work. These two conditions place a heavy load on the writer, and, though it removes ambiguity in the communication between the writer and the reader, it makes the presentation dull and repititious for the reader. Here we are willing to pay that price so as to achieve our purpose, but this is not a recommended approach for normal communications.

So what is the advantage of English as it is presently formulated? Why should we live with an unnecessarily elaborate language which has a very low level of uniformity (compared to other existing languages)? One obvious answer is the history of the language. But another answer is the broad utility of English. It is used in all types of subjects and all types of writing. We shall restrict ourselves to completely rational expositions, and in doing so many of the "tools" of conventional English usage become unnecessary. This is because many of these "tools" are needed only for conveying emotion or for adapting to the emotions of the reader.

Concerning another aspect of our native language, we sometimes find that we need more precision in our formulations and methods of solution to avoid the traps in our language which may ensnare us. Each "paradox" which has been clarified serves to illustrate this point. In the large bulk of our day-to-day logical work such paradoxes do not arise, and what we do here should have no effect on that work. But if we can achieve a precision of exposition which effectively avoids (or clarifies) the few paradoxes which do arise then our efforts have been useful.

Thus, here we attempt to reduce our language to a small number of standard forms, and we shall attempt to retain complete precision in our statements. In this Chapter we discuss the English language and the possibilities for conversion to precise standard forms. Such standard forms might be useful in the translation from one language to another. For further elaboration on the forms and classifications of the English language, reference should be made to any of a number of texts on English, such as Curme (9).

9.1. Semiotics

Before discussing English some general comments are in order. We postulate that the whole purpose of language in science and the other "exact" arts is communication. Communication is an attempt to convey information; information is a collection of concepts or data. With Alston (1,59) we state that the language used in the communication is a symbolic representation of the concepts which are being presented. The normal representations are adapted to our physical capabilities of sight, hearing, touch and speech and are used so continuously that the average person ceases to view these as representations. But, for example, when an unimpaired person views Braille he does treat those characters as codes even though to the blind person Braille can become as natural as the printed Roman alphabet is to that unimpaired person. The point here is that the printed words and the Braille words are used as symbols for concepts; they are not the concepts themselves. These same statements can be applied to the spoken language and the sign language of hearing-impaired people. Each is merely a symbolic representation of concepts. See Carnap (4,4). This approach is ancient; for example, Boole (2,25) and his predecessors recognized that a language consists of signs or symbols.

In the written form of English a "word" is a sequence of non-space characters (also excluding certain punctuation) which is preceded and followed by spaces or in some cases followed by punctuation. In the last paragraph we discussed words as though they were entities, and in languages of Indo-European derivation such is the case. However, languages exist where the sentence is a single utterance, and that sentence cannot be subdivided into discrete "words". For example, see polysynthetic languages (such as certain American Indian languages), Hughes (11,76). Tozzer (27,9) cites Mayan as also being a polysynthetic language. One-word sentences have some advantages and are used daily in our scientific world. An advantage of one-word sentences is that the need for some punctuation is removed. We have this situation in mathematics, chemistry and other sciences where each equation is actually a complete sentence, and that sentence is preceded and followed by spaces. There are those who do not consider an equation to be a sentence, but each equation has a subject and a predicate. Each symbol in the equation has been previously defined much as each English word has been previously defined in a dictionary. The equation of such symbols is thus merely a compact method of stating a concept which is often very elaborate.

Herein, the structures we developed were one-word sentences, but for ease of communication with the reader we have interjected discussions in English. Also, we have referred primarily to the English language for examples, but the general concepts should be applicable in many languages.

In the written English language, in printed form or in Braille, each elementary symbol or "word" consists of even more elementary codes, "letters". These elementary codes actually include more than what we usually mean by "letters"; they include the numbers, punctuation and a special character called a "space". That a "space" is a character becomes obvious when a person works with representations of English, for example, in a computer. A space is perhaps the most prevalent character used in English writing, even more prevalent than the letter, e. It is an important form of punctuation or demarcation.

There are several written languages in which words are not composed of letters; in many of these languages the most elementary symbol is the word. Other languages are intermediate to this. For example, Modern Standard Chinese, the official language of one-fourth of the world's population, uses essentially one symbol for each morpheme, and often that morpheme might be viewed in the European sense as a word. In English the alphabetic symbols supposedly give an indication of pronunciation, that is, most English uses an approximation to a phonemic script. On the other hand, numbers in English are not phonemic; a number, like many Chinese symbols, represents a concept but not a phoneme. For example, the symbol, 2, gives no phonemic indication; it represents a concept which is the same in English, Spanish, German and many other languages, regardless of pronunciation. Again, these differences in the reference symbolisms do not affect our discussions.

Spoken and written languages are also classified according to whether they are inflected, agglutinating or analytic. See Hughes (11). The Chinese languages are a reasonable approximation to an analytic language. In an analytic language all structural information is conveyed by syntax. Mathematical symbolism constitutes a limited, written, analytic language. In mathematical notation, all statements about time and location are separate, explicit statements. There are no tenses to the verbs; form does not change with plurality. In contrast, English is somewhat of an inflected language, but it is slowly becoming more analytic. Our language which we constructed herein was analytic, though synthetic. This language led to and included a part of the language, the algebra of number, which is a part of mathematics. We might note that the analytic language of mathematics, as devised by the European mind, includes explicit verbs and descriptors which are distinct from each other, as opposed to a frequent situation in Chinese. Reference Kratochvil (15,109).

Thus, in our attempt to communicate we must abide by certain pre-established protocols so that the recipient can comprehend (decipher) that which he is receiving (hearing, reading, etc.). The English language with its rules and dictionary is one such protocol. When using these protocols we must also realize that, although both parties in the communication process know and properly use the language (the protocol) the recipient can only build the complete concept in a sequential manner from the aggregation of concepts, each of which is presented in an assertion or statement. Each word and each sentence present only a small piece of the total which the speaker or writer is attempting to define. A technical communication, the aggregate, attempts to build a new, large concept in the recipient's mind.

Semiotics is the study of what we have been discussing in the last few paragraphs. Semiotics is composed of syntactics, semantics and pragmatics. Syntactics is the formal relationship between symbols or expressions (ordered collections of symbols) as properties of the language or calculus, without regard for the signification or interpretation of the symbols. Semantics is the study of meanings or connotative meanings associated with symbols. We will, herein, be more concerned with these two aspects of semiotics than with pragmatics which is the relationship between the symbols and the users.

From the standpoint of syntax the elementary structures of English are the word and the sentence and related punctuation; we shall now discuss each. We must, however, recognize from the outset that consistency is not a universal characteristic of the syntax of the English language. With this in mind, as we have stated, the structure, sentence, is composed of words and certain other "control" symbols. In the traditional view, each of these words has been classified by function as one of the parts of speech. These parts of speech are: noun, pronoun, adjective, verb, adverb, conjunction, preposition, interjection. For each word, its part of speech is specified with its definition in the dictionary. In a sense (as will be shown) these parts of speech provide overlapping functions. These functions will be discussed further in this section, following the discussion of sentences.

We might interject here that the parts of speech in English and related languages are not fundamental to all languages. These parts of speech are a part of the formulation of English but do not necessarily have counterparts in, for example, Chinese. See Kratochvil (15,106).

9.2. Sentences

Our early lessons in English have taught us that "a sentence is a group of words which express a complete thought". This definition is inadequate since it uses poorly defined or undefined terms. However, one reason for this type of definition is that the instructors of English are attempting to allow for a great diversity of sentence structure. On one hand they attempt to avoid specifying syntactical form, and then on the other hand they start specifying form. We shall use a definition with respect to syntax: a sentence is a structure which meets prescribed rules of construction, regardless of content. As to whether a sentence expresses a "complete thought", some sentences express pure nonsense (e.g., see Lewis Carroll); however, if a structure meets the rules of construction, it is a sentence. Custom does allow the occasional use of structures which are incomplete, yet which are called sentences. Context and custom usually implicitly provide the needed missing pieces.

A sentence in English is composed of words and, perhaps, terms enclosed in parentheses or quotation marks. These terms, including their enclosures, must meet the same rules as words. Note here that some style manuals require a resequencing of the final quotation mark and certain terminal punctuation; such practice is not logical but is prevalent. The first word or term of a sentence must be preceded by a space. The last word (or term) of a sentence is followed by semicolon, period, question mark or exclamation mark. Except for a sentence following a semicolon, the first letter of the first word of the sentence is upper case.

We can define five types of structures which are recognized as sentences. As we will point out in the related definition of each, the last four can be restated in terms of the first. Why are these four structures needed and used? For purposes of Logic they are not needed and might not be used. However, to retain the interest of many of the readers all five types are used in normal writing. The five types are: assertions, exclamations, interjections, commands, questions.

9.2.1. Assertions

In English an assertion should be composed of a subject and a predicate, in that sequence. The predicate describes some aspect of the subject. Thus, in a sense the predicate is performing somewhat the function of an adjective which is modifying or defining the subject. In this view, the subject of the assertion is the important element, the nucleus of the sentence.

A simple assertion has a period as the character immediately following the last character of the last word, and a space follows that period. Two assertions may be joined for continuity of thought; the first is followed by a comma, a space, a conjunction and the second assertion. Two related assertions may be joined by having the first followed by a semicolon, a space and the second assertion. These are compound sentences.

Therefore, for purposes of Logic compound sentences can be written as two or more simple assertions. Though we will not go into the discussion now, complex sentences can also be rewritten as two or more simple assertions in like manner. This leads us to the fact that, for a discussion of Logic, we need only to concern ourselves with simple assertions.

The subject of an assertion is a descriptor which is discussed in Section 9.3. The predicate can take any one of several forms; in each the key element is the verb. Again, as will be discussed in Section 9.4, it appears that one syntactical structure could suffice for all. That structure in English is: descriptor, copula, descriptor.

9.2.2. Exclamations

An exclamation is a special form of an assertion or of a group of assertions. It is an attempt to convey emotion or stress in the voice of the speaker via the written form. It may contain an interjection. Such forms are unnecessary for purposes of Logic, because descriptive assertions (even if they are dull writing) can explicitly state surprise, fear and other emotions.

9.2.3. Interjections

An interjection is a completely truncated form of an exclamation with almost the entire connotation being implicit. It should not occur in scientific writing. Its form is that of an exclamation, with some parts omitted completely.

9.2.4. Commands

A command seems to have a different structure from an assertion in that a verb form appears as the first word in most instances, and this verb is in the imperative mood. Actually there is an implicit subject; it is the audience of the speaker and can be represented by the second person pronoun. In this structure the verb can then be viewed as a version of the future indicative tense. But even this form is a contraction of a simple assertion in which the speaker is the subject and a subordinated clause is the object.

** Hit the ball!

becomes

** You shall hit the ball!

which is a contraction of

** I demand that you shall hit the ball.

This then refers to the use of subordinating conjunctions in Section 9.6.2.2. It seems also that commands are concerned only with potential physical actions and thus can only occur subsequent to the application of a physical theory or philosophy. For example, to issue the command, Think, is futile. "Think" is an excellent recommendation, but it can not be monitored or measured. Thus, even the person who gives the command is aware that his truncated statement is actually a request which might be more properly stated in another manner. When we ask a person to think, we are actually asking for a written or spoken output or an action. However, we have no way of knowing if that output is the result of thought or a result of coercion.

Programming of computers is done in the same manner as programming of people. A detailed sequence of unambiguous instructions (commands) is provided to the programmed device or personnel. Descriptive assertions can completely define a situation, but nothing will be accomplished until the designee, device or personnel, is commanded to perform the particular function (sequence of actions). A command, as discussed above, is a contraction of one or more assertions, but it also contains an implied concept of subordination of the designee.

9.2.5. Questions

When writing English a question is usually indicated by an interrogative word, an inverted structure and a terminal question mark in place of the terminal period. As opposed to the command, a question is usually a request for information. Usually such a question can be restated as the conjunction of three or more assertions. See, e.g., Jeffreys (12,378). However, another type of question must also be recognized, the rhetorical question. No response is actually being solicited in the rhetorical question; rather, the stated question is merely an introduction to the material which follows and which ostensibly answers the question. This type of question is frequently used, but its purpose is primarily to involve the reader or listener and to hold his attention.

9.3. Descriptors

A descriptor is a symbol (or ordered group of symbols) which represents, for example, a physical object or a concept or an action. A descriptor can also represent properties, relations, attributes and functions. A descriptor is used as the subject of a sentence or, when using a copula of equality, the term of equivalence is also a descriptor. With a transitive verb the direct object is a descriptor.

The descriptor is a noun or some structure which acts as a noun. It may contain pronouns, adjectives, adverbs which modify an adjective, conjunctions, prepositions and associated phrases. The following sentence contains two descriptors:

** The class, biped, includes the member, Sir Walter Raleigh.

The two descriptors are: "the class, biped", "the member, Sir Walter Raleigh". In conventional writing this would more probably be stated as:

** Sir Walter Raleigh is a biped.

Here we must observe that the latter form is as much a statement about classes as the former is, but it is an implicit version of that situation. This is discussed more extensively in other Sections.

In form, a descriptor is a group of words which ends with a noun, pronoun or gerund. It may contain adjectives and adverbs as a part of the description, and each of these may be constructed terms.

9.3.1. Nouns

A noun is a symbol, often called a name, of anything. A noun represents or is the label for an assertion, that assertion being (in some instances) the definition of that noun. Since English is yet at least partially an inflected language we find that different words may be used to represent the same concept in different circumstances. For example, an analytic language might say, "one child" and "five child", but our inflected language uses a different word in the latter case. We have been taught that "child" and "children" are the same word, but our computers do not accept them as the same word because, obviously, the symbols are different. From the standpoint of Logic such inflected forms are unnecessary. Auxiliary statements, position within the sequence and other parts of speech can replace such inflections and can convey precise meaning.

9.3.2. Pronouns

A pronoun is a word which is used instead of a noun. Its great useage is a result of its convenience, but such useage often produces ambiguity because of uncertainty about the antecedent. An antecedent is always required, directly or implicitly. In all cases a pronoun can be replaced by an explicit descriptor. In doing so we shall find cases where a dependent clause becomes an independent sentence; such a conversion increases the bulk of the converted document.

9.3.3. Adjectives

An adjective is a word which describes or limits a noun or pronoun or composite noun. We usually consider adjectives to consist of two classes, descriptive and limiting.

9.3.3.1. Descriptive Adjectives

In normal usage descriptive adjectives are classified into three degrees: positive, comparative, superlative. Actually there is only one form of the descriptive adjective in the logical sense, and that is the comparative degree. The other two are merely variations on the comparative based on what quantities are being compared. This is obvious when we admit that a small house is much larger than a large dog.

In other words, by using the positive degree of an adjective we are comparing the modified noun to our own estimate of some arithmetic mean of the class or some standard for the class named by that noun. A "small" house is smaller than the average house for our economic class; a large dog is larger than the average dog that we are accustomed to seeing. Use of the superlative degree is a similar comparison, but here the comparison is with all other members of the class. "The largest dog at the kennel" is the one which is larger than all other members of the class of dogs defined as being in that kennel. Thus, descriptive adjectives are comparative adjectives, and each can be defined in terms of descriptors and the concept of "greater than". The term, greater than, is defined in Chapter 4.

To repeat, the positive degree compares the modified noun to the arithmetic mean of its class; the comparative degree explicitly compares two nouns; the superlative degree compares a noun to all other members in its class.

Consider the adjectives in the form,

S_1 He is a strong man.

As discussed elsewhere, this is equivalent to conjunction of

S_2 $\mathfrak{M}\{\text{he}\}\in\mathbf{C}\{\text{strong-men}\}$

S_3 $\mathbf{C}\{\text{strong-men}\}\subset\mathbf{C}\{\text{men}\}$

In the definition of the class strong-men obviously more than one measure of strength can be used, but a common definition is concerned with lifting force (such as being able to press 200 kilograms). For purposes of comparison, force can be measured in kilodynes and thus be stated as a number. Since we do not consider someone of average strength to be strong, we can say

S_4 The strength of a member of the class strong-men is greater than the arithmetic mean of the strength of all men of our knowledge.

Symbolically, S_1 might be stated as

** $F_{he}>A$

where A is the arithmetic mean value of strength.

Another statement that is often viewed as equivalent to S_1 is

S_5 He is a man of great physical strength.

Note that this has the form of the genitive as does S_4, but whereas S_4 speaks about strength S_5 speaks about a man. The form S_5 is quite common and may occur as a definition of the adjective, strong. Such a definition is then dependent on the definition of the word, strength, and this reverts back to form S_4.

9.3.3.1.1. "possible"

Lewis and Langford (17,160) define the adjective, possible, as meaning self-consistent or without self-contradiction. Whereas we have defined "possible" as a descriptive adjective (thus allowing varying degrees of possibility) their definition makes it a limiting adjective. As they have pointed out, for material implication the statements "p is true" and "p is possible" are indistinguishable. For strict implication they seem to avoid stating anything about the truth of p, discussing only its consistency or lack thereof. Carnap (6,175) takes a similar position where he defines "possible" as $\Diamond p$. He further defines "impossible" as $\sim\Diamond p$.

That which is possible is that S_β which may or can be the situation under the prevailing conditions S_α. Note that S_β is not necessarily the existing situation. As such, S_β could not occur in deduction except in connection with disjunction where each of the alternatives may be selected. Thus for some assertion to be possible we have

C9.01 $\mathfrak{t}\{\mathfrak{M}\{S_\beta\}\}>0$

If this possibility results from the specified conditions S_α then

C9.02 $\mathfrak{M}\{S_\alpha\}:\nabla[\mathfrak{M}\{C9.01\},\mathfrak{M}_\mu]$

Restated, this then appears as

** $\mathfrak{M}\{C9.02\}:\mathfrak{M}\{S_\beta$ is possible under $S_\alpha\}$

Frequently we hear the statement that

S_1 S_β is possible but not probable

We would state this approximately as

** $\mathfrak{M}\{S_1\}:\mathfrak{M}\{0.1>\mathfrak{t}_\beta>0\}$

since a probable condition is one for which $\mathfrak{t}_\beta$ is greater than one-half (0.1), or some value even greater than one-half.

An example of such a statement could be

S_2 It may rain tomorrow

This is a conjecture about the future and can be restated approximately as

** $\mathfrak{M}\{S_2\}:\nabla[\nabla[\mathfrak{M}\{S_3\},\mathfrak{M}\{S_4\}],\mathfrak{M}\{S_5\}]$

S_3 Rain occurs

S_4 $t=(t_0+1)$

S_5 $\mathfrak{t}\{\mathfrak{M}\{S_2\}\}=0.01$

If S_2 were, instead,

** It will probably rain tomorrow

then the value of $\mathfrak{t}_2$ in S_5 would be more on the order of 0.11. These values are, of course, only approximate.

That which is impossible is that S_β which, in light of the prevalent conditions S_α can not be the situation. Here we have

C9.03 $\mathfrak{t}\{\mathfrak{M}\{S_\beta\}\}=0$

based on conditions S_α

C9.04 $\mathfrak{M}\{S_\alpha\}:\nabla[\mathfrak{M}\{C9.03\},\mathfrak{M}_\mu]$

and this appears as

** $\mathfrak{M}\{C9.04\}:\mathfrak{M}\{S_\beta$ is impossible because of $S_\alpha\}$

9.3.3.1.2. "necessary"

In E6.05 we defined "necessary", and in E6.06 we defined "not necessary". These may be contrasted with those of Traditional Logic where "necessary" is defined as $\sim\Diamond\sim p$ and "not-necessary" is defined as $\Diamond\sim p$.

9.3.3.1.3. "contingent"

A contingency is dependent on fulfillment of some related condition. Thus a contingent condition is neither a necessary condition nor an impossible condition. It is a possible condition. However, Carnap (6,175) defines "contingent" as $\Diamond\sim p\bullet\Diamond p$. Non-contingent is defined as $\sim\Diamond\sim p\vee\sim\Diamond p$.

9.3.3.2. Limiting Adjectives

The limiting adjectives include: numeric (definite and indefinite); demonstrative; relative; possessive; participles, phrases and nouns used as adjectives; interrogative; intensifying; articles. As discussed herein, limiting adjectives (sometimes called absolute adjectives) can in each case be replaced by nouns after a suitable rearrangement of the sentence. The principal purpose of these adjectives is convenience and ease of writing. The major disadvantage is an occasional loss of specificity (such as an indefinite antecedent).

Since limiting adjectives are not comparisons, the "degrees" referenced above for descriptive adjectives have no applicability here.

9.3.3.2.1. Numeric Adjectives

The definite numeric adjectives are perhaps the most common of the limiting adjectives; there are two classes of them, cardinal and ordinal. That these words are adjectives is apparent from their use. The cardinal adjectives include the words: one, two, three, dozen. They also frequently include the words "a" (used in place of "one") and "no" (used in place of "zero"). We notice that the former words are also used as nouns to represent numbers: 1», 010», 011», etc. The ordinal adjectives include the words: first, second, third.

"Counting" is the basis of the numeric adjectives and of numeric nouns other than the numbers themselves. Four of these numeric nouns are "none", "one", "pair" and "triplet". A cardinal adjective is derived from the set of non-negative integers, and in English the word used (except in some cases of 0 and 1) is the same as the noun from the set, natural number. An ordinal adjective is derived from the same set, with a suffix added for numbers above 011». "First", "second" and "third" are unique forms.

A short tabulation of the first few words of cardinal and ordinal adjectives might be useful.

noun	cardinal adjective	ordinal adjective
0	no	
01»	one (or an)	first
010»	two	second
011»	three	third
0100»	four	fourth
0101»	five	fifth
0110»	six	sixth
0111»	seven	seventh
01000»	eight	eighth
01001»	nine	ninth
01010»	ten	tenth
etc.	etc.	etc.

Both cardinal and ordinal adjectives are often used as nouns in common practice. However, since such usage is actually an abbreviated form, an antecedant must have been clearly specified or the resulting ambiguity will possibly destroy the intent of the communication. For example,

S_1 "There is a row of ducks in the shooting gallery"
S_2 "One is brown, two are white, one is ..."
S_3 "The first is white, the second is brown, the third is ..."

The antecedant here is "ducks" and is understood because of S_1. A more complete version of S_2 and S_3 would be

S_2 "One duck is brown, two ducks are white, one duck is ..."
S_3 "The first duck is white, the second duck is brown, the third duck is ..."

The cardinal adjective states the measure or the metric of the referenced class or subclass. For example

S_4 There are 5 people in the group

becomes

S_5 $\mathbf{C}\{\text{the-group}\}\subset\mathbf{C}\{\text{people}\}$
S_6 $\mathfrak{b}\{\mathbf{C}\{\text{the-group}\}\}=0101»$
** $\mathfrak{M}\{S_4\}:\nabla[\mathfrak{M}\{S_5\},\mathfrak{M}\{S_6\}]$

"No" is a similar adjective.

S_10 No x_α is y_β
S_{11} $(\mathbf{C}\{x_\alpha\}\cap\mathbf{C}\{y_\beta\})\equiv\mathbf{C}_0$
S_{12} $\mathfrak{b}\{\mathbf{C}_0\}=0$
** $\mathfrak{M}\{S_10\}:\nabla[\mathfrak{M}\{S_{11}\},\mathfrak{M}\{S_{12}\}]$

Of course, S_{11} and S_{12} could also be restated as

** $(\mathbf{C}\{x_\alpha\}\cap\mathbf{C}\{y_\beta\})\equiv\mathbf{O}$

On occasion "an" is also a numeric adjective (meaning "one") as opposed to being merely the indefinite article.

S_7 An x_α is y_β

S_8 $(\mathbf{C}\{x_\alpha\}\cap\mathbf{C}\{y_\beta\})\equiv\mathbf{C}_1$

S_9 ƀ$\{\mathbf{C}_1\}=1$

** $\mathfrak{M}\{S_7\}:\nabla[\mathfrak{M}\{S_8\},\mathfrak{M}\{S_9\}]$

We could now look at another example. If we say, "The Apostles are pious", we would write it as

** $\mathbf{C}\{\text{Apostles}\}\subset\mathbf{C}\{\text{pious-men}\}$

and with other assertions of intension and extension we would define the term, pious-men. However, when we say, "There are 12 Apostles", we would write this as

** ƀ$\{\mathbf{C}\{\text{Apostles}\}\}=01100$»

Here "12" is an adjective as was "pious", and here "12" is not a class or member of a class of numbers which are nouns. The adjective 12 is a limiting or absolute adjective whereas the adjective pious is a descriptive adjective.

The ordinal adjective refers back to our subclasses in Section 5.5. Cardinal adjectives are related to counting, and as such the sequence of objects being counted is unimportant. Ordinal adjectives refer to sequence, though the determination of sequence (such as a temporal sequence) is external to our discussion here. When a sequence has been determined we may represent it by the assignment of new names or labels for each member, each label specifically referring to a member of **N**, as in Section 5.5. As a result, we say that

E9.01 $\mathfrak{M}\{\mathfrak{M}\{d_n\}\}:\mathfrak{M}\{\text{the n'th member}\}$

For example, $\mathfrak{M}\{d_{010}\}$ is the second member.

The indefinite numeric adjectives include the words: some, several, all, many, few, little, much and others. In some instances these are also used as comparative or descriptive adjectives.

The limiting adjective, all, in discrete populations, indicates that its modified noun is a subclass of the other class which is presented in the assertion. An example is

** All transistors operate at low voltages.

As discussed in Section 9.3.3.2.1, this assertion may be viewed as a description by classes, such as

** $\mathfrak{M}\{\text{transistors}\}\in\mathbf{C}\{\text{low-voltage-devices}\}$

In the continuous case this adjective modifies a mass noun or an abstract noun. However, in such instance it is denoting a subinterval instead of a subclass.

As a variation on this, Kunen (16,3) and others have defined "all v are ψ" as equivalent to the assertion

** There does not exist a v which is not ψ

In this statement, ψ is a symbolic assertion and v is a noun. If v is a number and ψ is an assertion about numbers (such as an algebraic equation) then in our notation it would appear as

** $\mathbf{C}\{v\}\subset\mathbf{C}\{\text{roots-of-}\psi\}$

** $\mathfrak{M}\{\text{roots-of-}\psi\}:\mathfrak{M}\{\text{those values of v for which the two terms of } \psi \text{ are equal}\}$

Note that ψ may exist for which there are no proper roots. The theorem P4.01 is such a case.

This word refers to the aggregate of a class or the range of a continuum. For discrete entities it is a "flag" denoting a class statement. Thus the statement

** All men are mortal

becomes

** $\mathbf{C}\{\text{men}\}\subset\mathbf{C}\{\text{mortal-beings}\}$

where "mortal-beings" must have been previously defined. This, of course, is a specific example of

C9.05 $\mathbf{C}\{x_\alpha\}\subset\mathbf{C}\{y_\beta\}$

C9.06 All x_α are y_β

E9.02 $\mathfrak{M}\{C9.06\}:\mathfrak{M}\{C9.05\}$

In another form of notation, propositional functions (propositions for which the subject is a variable) are represented by, e.g., Hx. Then, as one type of quantification (where H represents the property, human) the definition is made that

C9.07 All x are human

C9.08 (x)Hx

** $\mathfrak{M}\{C9.07\}:\mathfrak{M}\{C9.08\}$

The form C9.08 is directly parallel to the form C9.05 above where x_α there is (x) here and y_β represents human beings. Other related forms of the propositional function and quantification will be discussed in later Sections.

The adjective, many, is much the same in its definition as "some" which is discussed below, but it includes the additional factor, greater than. In the assertion

** Many x_α are x_β

we see that the adjective implies that x_α is a subclass of x_β and also implies that the measure of the class, x_α, is greater than our average expectation for that class.

As an adjective the word, no, is a limiting adjective which specifies a count of zero. Many of its uses as an adverb are related to "not".

For discrete entities the word, some, also denotes a class statement.

** $\mathfrak{M}\{\text{some men are brown}\}:\mathfrak{M}\{\mathbf{C}\{\text{brown men}\}\subset\mathbf{C}\{\text{men}\}\}$

C9.09 $\mathfrak{b}\{\mathbf{C}\{x_\alpha\}\}>\mathfrak{b}\{\mathbf{C}_\gamma\}>1$

E9.03 $\mathfrak{M}\{\text{some } x_\alpha \text{ are } y_\beta\}:\nabla[\mathfrak{M}\{C9.05\},\mathfrak{M}\{C9.09\}]$

It should be noted that numeric adjectives are related to the class, number. The members of that class are nouns, and they are discussed in Chapter 4. Thus numeric adjectives are statements about classes.

9.3.3.2.2. Demonstrative Adjectives

This group includes the words: these, those, this, that, the and others. This group is normally used to refer to a member of a class or to a subclass. As such they can be replaced by the proper name.

9.3.3.2.3. Relative Adjectives

Here we include: which, what and similar structures. These are used in clauses which refer to another part of the sentence. As such the clauses can be replaced with independent clauses with specific subjects and predicates.

9.3.3.2.4. Possessive Adjectives

Such words as my, your, his, her, their and our are included here. These forms are logically equivalent to the genitive form using the preposition, of. See Section 9.6.1 where we discuss the prepositional phrase as an adjective.

9.3.3.2.5. Participles, Phrases and Nouns Used as Adjectives

Another characteristic of the English language is that other types of words (for example, nouns) are often used as adjectives. Thus we have composite terms such as "printer paper" to denote the paper which is used in a printer. In English the last noun of such a sequence is the "dominant" noun, the word which is being modified. As shown above, this sequence of nouns is a contraction of a proper phrase or clause and can be replaced by that phrase or clause. Thus, these structures are defining subclasses of the "dominant" noun.

9.3.3.2.6. Interrogative Adjectives

These are closely related to the interrogative pronouns. As we discussed in Section 9.2.5, questions can be replaced by assertions, thereby removing the need for interrogative adjectives.

9.3.3.2.7. Intensifying Adjectives

It is doubtful that intensifying adjectives have a rightful place in scientific writing.

9.3.3.2.8. Pseudo-Descriptive Adjectives

A notable group of adjectives appear to be descriptive adjectives but in reality are limiting adjectives. Colors as adjectives, for example, fall in this group. To say that "this object is more red than that object" is an ambiguous phrase since each color (once a name has been assigned) is a mixture of certain visible frequencies at specified amplitudes (that is, a particular spectrum of visible light). Thus, differences in color are differences in spectra (amplitude and frequency distribution). Consider, for example, the adjectives: brown, tan, beige, taupe. In the dictionary the last three all reference the word, brown, with variations. But to define a color in terms of a definite spectrum is to make that color a limiting adjective rather than a descriptive adjective.

The sentence

** "Bring me the black coat from the closet"

is a class statement. The object of the sentence is an intersection of the class, coats in the closet, and the class, black objects. Black, of course, is defined as a zero amplitude across the visible spectrum.

9.3.3.2.9. Articles

The articles are "the", "a" and "an". "The" is called the definite article; the other two are variant forms of the indefinite article. Proper use of articles is important, not only because of their prevalence, but also because of the type of concept that each implies. Usage now puts articles in the role of syntactical indicators, rather than assigning properties as other adjectives do. If an article is used, it must be the first term in the descriptor.

The indefinite article is a contraction of the adjective, one, in an etymological sense. If used with the subject of a copula it states that the subject is a member of a class. For example,

S_1 A cat is a mammal

** $\mathfrak{M}\{S_1\}:\mathfrak{M}\{S_2\}$

S_2 $\mathfrak{M}\{cats\}\epsilon\mathbf{C}\{mammals\}$

An alternative presentation of this same statement uses the plural of each noun.

** Cats are mammals

When used with verbs other than a copula, the indefinite article is usually a replacement for the adjective, one.

A descriptor which begins with the definite article must have an antecedent, stated or implied. In its singular form such a descriptor then specifies a particular object or concept as uniquely as a proper noun would. If the plural form of a common noun is the last word of a descriptor then it is a collective form which usually refers to all members of the previously defined class. Plural forms without the definite article are also class statements. In Spanish the definite article is sometimes used in place of demonstrative or possessive adjectives. This can occur in English to a limited degree.

9.4. Verbs

That English is yet an inflected language is evidenced in its verbs. The inflections are changes in form which may or may not be related to other parts of the sentence. The form of the verb with respect to number must be in agreement with that of the subject, whereas tense can often be indicated solely by the verb. Inflected changes of form occur for voice, mode, tense, number, person and use. Whether or not these forms are needed from a logical standpoint is a valid question.

Verbs have been more or less divided into four classes: transitive, intransitive, linking, auxiliary. To some extent certain words may appear in more than one of these classes, depending on useage. For transitive and intransitive verbs, the verb is the important member of the predicate, and the predicate establishes the purpose of the sentence in that it tells something about the subject. In a sense, the predicate acts as an adjective in that it modifies the subject.

Though verb forms in English are gradually becoming more simple and uniform, they are probably the most elaborate part of the language. As an example, the Simple conjugation of a transitive verb takes more than three pages in one text on English, and the Progressive conjugation would probably be as lengthy. Here is an example where English is more elaborate than several other languages. In many languages the two types are represented by one conjugation, context being necessary to distinguish which is intended. As a generalization, the various conjugations of a verb in an Indo-European language each have purpose. Those of English do provide great flexibility of expression. But an equivalent of these conjugations can be constructed by other means; in some cases it is accomplished by other verb forms, forms which can appear in English but which are not common. The regular use of such forms might classify them as auxiliary verbs. For example, in Mayan (ref. (27, 30)) completed action is denoted by using the verb, to finish or complete, with the verb which denotes the action. Apparently that language did not have past participles but yet found that expression of the concept of completed action was necessary.

For a regular verb the basic parts are: the present root, the past root, the present participle, the past participle. These are the usual indicators of the structure of the verb. Irregular verbs will display variations in these and in the use of these parts. From these parts are constructed the present infinitive, the perfect infinitive, the perfect participle, the verbal noun, the gerund and the conjugations in each tense, mood and voice. Auxiliary forms are used in several of these structures.

In a truly analytic language the various forms of the verb can be handled by other parallel methods. Consider the tense of a verb. Sowa (23,174) points out that tense is accomplished by many other methods in languages outside of the Indo-European group. Tense is largely concerned with time and completion of the action. Time is a part of the physical world as is distance; this is the realm of the physicist, not the logician. In physical descriptions the specification of time or of relative time can eliminate the need for that aspect of tense. Completion, or lack thereof, can be specified by an adverbial phrase. The type of subject does not need to be reflected in the verb form for purposes of Logic. By these methods we can show that for use in Logic the conjugation of a verb can be unnecessary.

When a sentence in the active voice is restated in the passive voice (a past participle preceded by the copula, to be) it becomes obvious that the sentence is a class statement.

** I see John.

becomes

** John is seen by me.

which is equivalent to

** John is included in the class, `seen by me´.

Similar reformulations across the universe of verbs can bring each of them into a standard structure for manipulations in symbolic Logic. By these means we bring all verbs to the classical forms of Logic. Note that the active voice and passive voice of a verb are used interchangeably in equations by reversing the sequence of the equation. An example is:

** A includes B

** B is included in A

As class statements these would be written:

** $A \supset B$

** $B \subset A$

In definitions of symbollism these pairs of statements are treated as identical definitions. We are thus postulating that the differentiation between active and passive voices is not necessary, and as an example Tozzer (27,35) notes that the distinction made in Spanish between active and passive voices is not found in Mayan.

In the above example a reformulation of "A includes B" would also be

** Class A is the union of class B and class U

where class U is external to our discussion. Here we have defined A with a linking verb and a descriptor. However the descriptor is a contraction, and the sentence would be stated more completely by

** Class A is a union. The union is an aggregation of the members of class B and class U.

Translation of various verb forms will be discussed more completely in Section 9.4.4, including some discussion of conjugations and their significance.

9.4.1. Linking and Auxiliary Verbs

A number of verbs have progressed to the point where they denote very little; their only purpose is as a part of the formation of a predicate which defines some aspect of the subject. The most common linking verb in many languages is the verb, to be. Other examples are: become, feel, smell, taste, sound, get, look. Linking verbs are the copulas. Copulas also appear as auxiliary verbs. The auxiliary verb is used in the formation of the various inflected forms of other verbs. Included are: has, had, have, do, must, will, would, shall, should, may, might, can, could, and the linking verbs. Copulas have extensive useage in modern languages. However, they are a special type, an abstraction. They do not in themselves predicate; they link or establish equivalence or inclusion. The need is sometimes questioned, even by well-established linguists; they are often omitted in Russian and occasionally in English. Copulas provide tense; they provide a "key" to the reader in the determination of sentence structure. The copula displays most of the characteristics of most verbs, but it does not have a passive voice. However, it is used in the construction of the passive voice of other verbs.

9.4.1.1. The Verb, to be

The verb, to be, is among the most frequently used verbs in modern inflected languages. It is used to express identity and inclusion in symbolic, intensional and extensional statements. If the usage is not defined explicitly, logical ambiguities may then be expected.

It has been noted that this verb, at least in the present tense, is not actually necessary in a logical sense except for reasons of custom or demarcation. It is merely equating two descriptors, such as two nouns, and its absence in certain circumstances in English is not noted. Thus, its function is largely syntactical, though time is also indicated by the tense of the verb. For this reason this copula can also be classified as a morpheme.

In Russian the omission of the forms of the present tense of this verb is normal. For example,

** Книга и газета там.

** (The) book and newspaper (are) there.

One of the axioms asserted in Section 3 is that identity of symbols conveys identity of concept. However, identity of concept can be conveyed by different patterns; for example, we often define one descriptor in terms of others. Thus the statement

** Elizabeth is the Queen

establishes an identity of concept between the two descriptors, and the relationship is symmetric. Thus this statement can be written as

** $\mathfrak{M}$\{Elizabeth\}:$\mathfrak{M}$\{the Queen\}

This verb is frequently used in statements about classes, statements about kind or attribute.

** A cat is a mammal.

** The water is boiling

These two statements are class statements. Therefore they become:

** $\mathbf{C}$\{cats\}$\subset\mathbf{C}$\{mammals\}

** $\mathbf{C}$\{the water\}$\subset\mathbf{C}$\{boiling liquids\}

A signal to the reader of these sentences is given by the indefinite articles in the first, the adjective in the second and the definite article in the second.

The form, be, must be preceded by one of: must; will; would; shall; should; may; might; can; could; to. The form, been, must be preceded by one of: have; has; had. The form, have been, if not used alone must be preceded by one of: must; will; would; shall; should; could; may; might; to. The form, being, must be preceded by some conjugated form of the verb, to be.

9.4.1.2. The Verb, to exist

Much has been written about existence, physical, spiritual, supernatural and others. That is to say that the verb, to exist, has had extensive use. The verb is an intransitive verb; the verb is a restatement about the noun, existence. But what is $\mathfrak{M}$\{existence\}? One definition which is related to our usage appears in our dictionary as, "to exist is to have being". Thus such a definition merely equates this verb with the copula, to be.

Existence can perhaps be treated in four parallel manners:

(a) existence of a number.

Whitehead and Russell (29) use $\exists$ xS(x) to state the existenceof a number, x. This is an assertion that "There exists an x such that S(x)", where S(x) is an assertion (an equation) which is "satisfied" by that x. Quine (19,102) presents the use of a double negative as a definition of existence.

** $\mathfrak{M}\{(\exists\ \alpha)\phi\}:\mathfrak{M}\{\sim(\alpha)\sim\phi\}$

In either case, such an assertion of existence beforehand is either redundant with the result or in error.

(b) existence of a class.

A class is defined on the basis of the properties of its members (the requirements of membership). Hospers (10,429) states that "to say something exsits is to say that there is something that has the properties". Thus, the assertion of existence of a class is redundant with the definition of properties and assertions about cardinality of the class. Consider the statement

S_1 There are two roots for a quadratic equation

This may be viewed as a restatement of

S_2 Two roots exist for any quadratic equation

Assertion S_1 has an implied antecedent, the definition of the term, quadratic equation. This is of the form

S_3 $\mathfrak{M}\{S_4\}:\mathfrak{M}\{S_5\}$

S_4 $a \bullet x^2 + b \bullet x + c = 0$

S_5 $x \in \mathbf{S}\{d\}$

where $\mathbf{S}\{d\}$ is a set of numbers, each of which is a root. Thus the statement

** at least one root exists for S_4

is equivalent to the assertion

** $\mathfrak{b}\{\mathbf{S}\{d\}\} \geq 1$

(c) existence of an intension.

A symbol and its intension exist merely by being devised. The intension of the symbol, unicorn, is known and comprehended without benefit of a physical mammal to measure. And so here, also, the statement of existence is not necessary.

(d) existence of a physical entity.

This is the usual sense of the verb, to exist. However, our knowledge of a physical entity is the result of measurements by our sight, hearing, touch, etc., as augmented by measuring instruments. Such knowledge (observations) are intensions. Thus this is another example of the cases presented above.

For these reasons we would assert that the verb, to exist, and its noun form are unnecessary for purposes of Logic.

9.4.2. Transitive Verbs

A transitive verb requires a direct object. A transitive verb is the conventional manner of stating action; however, it is not the only method. Incorporation of the object of a transitive verb into the verb form creates a new intransitive verb. This has been observed in Mayan (27,35) with respect to verbs which denote habitual actions.

9.4.3. Intransitive Verbs

An intransitive verb denotes, in itself, a condition, and it has no direct object. We may notice that an intransitive verb does not have a passive form and that the passive form of a transitive verb is intransitive. Further, the subject of a transitive verb is stated by an explicit adverbial term when the sentence is restructured in passive form.

An intransitive form is a class statement about the subject.

** The liquid boils

** $\mathfrak{M}\{\text{the-liquid}\} \in \mathbf{C}\{\text{boiling-liquids}\}$

Thus, and assertion which is constructed with an intransitive verb is a descriptive assertion.

9.4.4. Conjugation of a Verb

In the usual conjugation of a verb the change of the verb form for each person is a result of the etymology of the word, but it has no logical purpose except redundancy with the subject. Thus a synopsis of the verb is often used to show the other variations in form which result from tense, mood, aspect and voice. In the active voice the indicative mode often has a somewhat ambiguous meaning, at least from the view of the reader. In many languages no distinction is made between the active indicative and the progressive conjugation. Compare the forms for an intransitive verb:

** I run

** I am running

for a transitive verb:

** I accuse the man

** I am accusing the man

A transitive verb can also have a passive voice.

** The man is accused by me

** The man is being accused by me

We can begin to notice that the active indicative (which probably is used more extensively than other forms) is used to attempt to convey a variety of slightly different intensions and is therefore less easily translated into notation which has precision. Perhaps with intransitive verbs there is less difference between the indicative and the progressive forms because the intransitive verbs in general denote continuing actions. But with transitive verbs we may attempt to denote that the action was a single event which (with respect to the present time t_0) by tense of the verb states that the time t of the occurrance is

present	$t=t_0$
past	$t<t_0$
future	$t>t_0$

On the other hand we may attempt to denote continuing actions (where $a<t<b$) by stating

present	$a<t<t_0<b$
past	$a<t<b\leq t_0$
future	$t_0<a<t<b$

A vague difference exists between the past tense in either of these statements above and the present perfect. The connotation of any of the perfect tenses is that the action has been completed prior to the point in time under discussion. The past tense is more vague about completion (value b above). If we define a reference point t_1 in the past and another t_2 in the future then $t_1<t_0<t_2$ and the forms for the perfect tenses are

present perfect	$a<t<b<t_0$
past perfect	$a<t<b<t_1$
future perfect	$a<t<b<t_2$

Thus tenses become unnecessary if we provide the additional statements about time-intervals. Use of either the progressive or the passive structure creates the form, descriptor-copula-descriptor. This feature has been more noticeable in our discussions of, e.g., number and class. The two forms

** $\mathbf{C}_\alpha \supset \mathbf{C}_\beta$

** $\mathbf{C}_\beta \subset \mathbf{C}_\alpha$

can be stated in English as

** $\mathbf{C}_\alpha$ includes $\mathbf{C}_\beta$

** $\mathbf{C}_\beta$ is included in $\mathbf{C}_\alpha$

The form, includes, is termed the active voice of the verb; the form, is included, is termed the passive voice. Yet from the standpoint of Logic $\supset$ and $\subset$ are equivalent verbs except for sequence, and in this view the word, includes, and the term, is included in, are equivalent verbs except for sequence. Similarly

** $\mathfrak{M}\{x=y\}:\mathfrak{M}\{x \text{ equals } y\}$

** $\mathfrak{M}\{y=x\}:\mathfrak{M}\{y \text{ is equal to } x\}$

The indicative mood is usually concerned with reality, whereas the subjunctive mood discusses that which is, e.g., false or unknown or desired. An example was discussed in Section 7.2 as a situation concerned with a truth-value being zero.

The imperative mood was reviewed in Section 9.2.4, Commands.

Since a verb or a predicate expresses a concept and since concepts are denoted by descriptors then some equivalence must exist between verbs and descriptors. An example of our view is shown below.

S_1 He is buying a watch now

d_1 purchasor of a watch

d_2 purchasor

d_3 watch

S_2 $t=t_0$

S_3 $\mathfrak{M}\{\text{He}\}\epsilon\mathbf{C}\{d_1\}$

At this level our formulation would be

S_4 $\mathfrak{M}\{S_1\}:\nabla[\mathfrak{M}\{S_2\},\mathfrak{M}\{S_3\}]$

We also state that

S_5 $\mathfrak{M}\{d_1\}:\Gamma[\mathfrak{M}\{d_3\},\mathfrak{M}\{d_2\}]$

so that our formulation would be the aggregation of S_4 and S_5.

9.5. Adverbs

An adverb is a word which modifies a verb, an adjective, another adverb or a sentence. In addition, adverbial phrases can perform similar functions. Adverbs have been segregated into classes by form, by function and meaning.

9.5.1. Simple Adverbs

At this point the form of greatest interest to us is the adverb of negation. The word, not, has major useage in normal writing and in Logic. Here we must be very careful with the concepts which we feel may be implied by a statement. For example,

S_1 "The boy is running"

S_2 "The man is not running"

The structure S_1 describes a condition of the boy, but the structure S_2 tells us nothing except that the man is not running. In other words, in S_2 we have defined nothing; we have only shown a concept from which the man is excluded. A "running boy" is a concept; a "not-running man" is an exclusion from a concept (running vs. standing, sitting, lying down) and is not a defined concept.

The adverb, not, is used in two senses: exclusion, which is the manner we have used it; opposition. As we discussed earlier, only in the case of a actual dichotomy can we use the word, not, in the denotation of an opposite situation. For example, in Euclidian geometry the normal to a plane has precisely two directions, e.g., A and B. If we choose to exclude A we have thereby selected B. Thus, B is "not-A". However, where the measure of the class of alternatives is greater than 010 we have no opposite as such.

The negation of a statement S_α is sometimes treated as if there were an opposite concept to $\mathfrak{M}\{S_\alpha\}$ and is denoted S_α; the negation of a class $\mathbf{C}\{A\}$ is sometimes treated as if there were only two classes and is denoted by A. We have avoided such usages herein because of the absence of a dichotomy of intension or class in the general case.

To divide the universe of intensions or classes into dichotomies requires the use of "universal" intensions or classes. These are discussed briefly in Sections 3.2.2.4 and 5.4.3. Exclusions of intension or class are discussed in Sections 3.3.2 and 5.4.2.

Adverbs of degree include: once, twice, thrice, 4 times, 5 times, etc. These are actually adverbial forms of cardinal adjectives, as is to some extent acknowledged in the higher numbers. Each can be replaced by a (perhaps more awkward) prepositional phrase which uses a cardinal adjective; this cardinal adjective can then be restated in terms of the metric of a class.

9.5.2. Adverbial Clauses and Phrases

These clauses and phrases provide great flexibility of useage and expression and can be used in place of other types of adverbs.

9.6. Morphemes

A morpheme is a unit of language which can not be subdivided; in English, morphemes and punctuation act as syntactic "flags" which denote function and type of structure. Morphemes include prefixes, suffixes, prepositions, articles, conjunctions, certain adverbs, copulas and certain other auxiliary verbs. Important morphemes in Logic have traditionally been the conjunctions and negation. Negation was discussed above in Section 9.5.1. These particular morphemes have allowed the great achievements that have been attained in Logic. But conjunctions, nouns and simple verbs are inadequate for a complete representation of the logical aspects of English, even if we disregard the requirements of our philosophy of physics. A few prepositions would appear to be of importance also, notably the preposition, of, in its use as the genitive. Further, certain logical ambiguities exist between the definitions of prepositions and those of conjunctions; for that reason we classify them together.

Does a morpheme have intension or is it only a syntactic device? The answer is varied, depending on which morpheme we study. For example, it often appears that the various definitions of the conjunction, and, are only syntactic in function. However, for the same pairs of nouns each different morpheme, and, (where applicable) is used to construct a different intension; this might be construed as intension being imparted by the morpheme.

As examples, consider our claims that each of the following was a use of the word, and: $\nabla[\mathfrak{M}_\alpha,\mathfrak{M}_\beta]$; $\Delta[\mathfrak{M}_\alpha,\mathfrak{M}_\beta]$; $(\mathbf{C}_\alpha \cup \mathbf{C}_\beta)$; $(\mathbf{C}_\alpha \cap \mathbf{C}_\beta)$; $(x+y)$; $(x \cdot y)$.

9.6.1. Prepositions

A preposition establishes a relationship between the descriptor which is its object and some other word. It usually precedes its object, but in interrogative form its object may be the first or last word of the question.

A prepositional phrase acts as an adjective or an adverb in most cases, as discussed above. The dative and genitive cases in English are usually prepositional phrases with either an explicit or an implicit preposition. In addition, idiomatic useage has created new transitive verbs from an intransitive verb plus a preposition. The verb, "look up", is one of these, as in "I will look up the formula in the reference book". Transitive verbs are, in some cases, modified in this same manner. For example,

S_1 He shot her twice

S_2 He shot at her twice

The form, S_2, might be viewed as an intransitive form with an adverbial phrase, or "shot at" can be viewed as a transitive verb. In normal useage, "shot at" is treated as a transitive verb form, as we can recognize in the passive form, "to be shot at".

9.6.2. Conjunctions

A conjunction is a word which joins together words, phrases or sentences. It can be used to show the intersection of concepts or classes; it may provide a union of two concepts or classes.

There are two general classes of conjunctions, coordinating and subordinating. Both classes have been used extensively in classical Logic, sometimes with inadequate explication.

9.6.2.1. Coordinating Conjunctions

The copulative conjunctions have been an important class in Logic, especially the word, and (including "both ... and"). This word is used to denote union, aggregation, coincidence and parallel constructions. There are even cases where two sentences are joined by "and" but where the two sentences are not related. Because of these multiple uses we will differentiate carefully when we establish our symbolism.

"Neither ... nor" is used to exclude explicit concepts or explicit members of a class.

We might note here that ambiguities of grammatical classification often arise in the vernacular of, e.g., arithmetic. Usually the word, and, is a conjunction while the word, plus, is a preposition. Consider the examples:

** The sum of x and y equals z.
** The sum of x plus y equals z.
** x with the addition of y equals z.

In symbolism each of these would be stated in the same manner. Thus there is a logical equivalence of function among "and", "plus" and "with the addition of". A similar situation can be found in multiplication. In each case we are attempting to verbalize a logical structure which is quite simple:

** $(x+y)=z$

Thus for the sake of uniformity we shall view the symbol, +, and other parallel symbols as conjunctions, though they can be presented as prepositions, etc.

9.6.2.2. Subordinating Conjunctions

"That; Whether; If; How; Which; What; Who"

With the following transitive verbs these words add in a subordinate clause:

** hope, believe, demand, ask, assume, understand, know,
** tell, hear, say, state, demonstrate, point out, show,
** indicate, fear, dream

These are all personal actions relating to concepts. Each of these verbs can be replaced by a descriptor and a copula such that

S_1 I hope that S_2

can be replaced by

S_3 My hope is that S_2

The assertion S_3 can be replaced by

S_4 The concept of S_2 is my hope

Another type of statement is:

S_5 What you say is true

This may be restated as three assertions, one of the above form.

S_6 You say that S_9

S_7 I say that S_8

S_8 S_9 is true

In Logic the conditional form is used extensively.

** If a>0 then y=sin(ax)

This is actually a representation of logical implication when all preceeding statements are known. Logical implication will be discussed later. However, the mood of the verb is important here. For example, the present indicative form can be used to represent fact while the subjunctive mood is used in the representation of something unreal such as a wish or an unfulfilled desire. The use of this conditional form with the subjunctive is still logical implication in that unreal situation.

** If I were rich then I would buy that car

Quine (19,16) points out that the subjunctive is used when the antecedent is false; this is a possible definition of "unreal".

"Since; Because"

These terms are related to the conditional.

S_1 I am sick

S_2 I can't go

The form here is:

S_3 S_2 because S_1

This can be restated as

S_4 The concept of S_1 implies the concept of S_2 to me

9.6.2.3. Disjunctions

Sometimes called disjunctive conjunctions, these words denote a selection of descriptors, phrases or clauses. The most common terms used are "either A or B" and "A or B". The difference between the forms can be (in precise writing) in the selection of one or the selection of one or more alternatives. Consider the example,

** Either Carl or Joe did it

Here we are selecting one person from the pair. Often, however, the word, either, is dropped, and the reader is not sure whether the selection is uniquely one or if a selection of both is allowed. There is no such ambiguity in

** Carl and/or Joe did it

Some people do not consider this to be a proper form, however.

Another useage of the preposition, of, is as an alternative for a stated disjunction and has no relationship to possession. The sentence

** One of the three men (A, B or C) will go

can be restated as

** Either A or B or C will go

This last form is the usual form of exclusive disjunction which is selection of a member from a class. Disjunctions are discussed more thoroughly in Section 5.6.

9.6.3. Punctuation

Punctuation serves many purposes in English. It is used to group, to separate, to synthesize, to denote function, to denote emotion, to denote omission and other important syntactic operations. Some punctuation symbols, such as comma, have a large variety of uses; some, such as parentheses, have more easily defined functions. Punctuation usage is not common to all languages. Even within the European languages there are major variations. For example, Spanish uses the symbols ¿ and ¡. The uses of periods and commas in numbers varies in some European countries from the usage in the United States. Even greater differences can be found between these and the non-European languages such as Chinese. Thus our discussion will be limited to scientific English in the United States. As we have mentioned above, with this severe limitation some punctuation, such as ? and !, are almost unnecessary in their usual functions.

9.6.3.1. Space

Earlier we stated that a space is a character, and as such it is used to separate words from each other. It is not unique in this function; other characters also perform this function in certain instances. It is used in conjunction with other characters to denote end of a clause, such as: parenthesis-space or semicolon-space or colon-space or comma-space or period-space. A space is not allowed within a word, by definition of the word, word.

9.6.3.2. Parentheses

Parentheses must always come in pairs, a left parenthesis immediately followed by the first letter of the first word of the term and then, later, a right parenthesis immediately following the last character of the last word or structure of the term. Braces and brackets are infrequently used in the same manner for special effects.

9.6.3.3. Period

A period is used, with a following space, to denote the end of a sentence. It immediately follows the last character of the sentence. A period may occur within a number as a decimal point (or, e.g., binary point, etc.), and in this usage no space occurs with it; it is a part of the word.

9.6.3.4. Colon

This symbol is used to denote an itemization or tabulation or explanation of a preceding descriptor or implied descriptor. In itemizations the individual terms may be separated by semicolon or comma, depending on custom and degree of clarity needed.

9.6.3.5. Semicolon

The definition of the use of semicolon is more vague. A somewhat prevalent usage is as a separator for two related sentences. The first sentence is terminated by semicolon-space which is followed immediately by the next sentence. The first word of the succeeding sentence is not capitalized if it is not a proper noun.

Following a colon, semicolon may be used to separate items in a listing. In legal documents it is also often used where a comma would normally be used in essay-style of writing. However, in scientific writing its use is limited.

9.6.3.6. Ellipsis

An ellipsis is usually indicated by three periods in sequence. Normally such a symbol occurs within a quotation, and within that structure the symbol is treated in the same manner as a word. The symbol indicates the omission of an undefined number of words. Ellipsis, without being denoted by the symbol, also occurs frequently in common discourse. Such omissions are discussed elsewhere herein.

9.6.3.7. Comma

A comma is usually followed by a space. The comma is often used to set out a parenthetical phrase, and in such usage, like the parentheses, it should occur in pairs, with some exceptions. Where other punctuation ends a sentence or a clause (period, question mark, exclamation point or comma) the closing or second comma, incontrast to a closing parenthesis, is omitted.

A comma is used to represent omitted words (a form of ellipsis), most frequently the word, and. Thus,

** She bought apples and oranges and peaches

becomes, with the substitution of a comma,

** She bought apples, oranges and peaches

A comma is used to set out a phrase merely for emphasis or improved clarity, even though the comma would not be needed for other reasons.

A comma is sometimes used in place of a colon in an itemization.

A comma is often used in large numbers to group digits to the left of the decimal point into multiples of one thousand; it is a part of the word. In such usage no space follows the comma.

9.6.3.8. Hyphen

The hyphen is used at the end of a line within the normal sequence of a word to indicate that the remainder of the word continues at the beginning of the next line. As such it is a convenience given to the composing device or person for maintenance of appearance of the text.

The hyphen is sometimes used in synthesized words such as the term, air-to-ground. This synthesized word is used as an adjective. However, many synthesized nouns in English do not use the hyphen. Often we follow Germanic construction of juxtaposition without intervening space or hyphen; in other instances such as "computer paper" we use juxtaposition with an intervening space.

A hyphen is occasionally used in place of a colon.

9.6.3.9. Quotation Mark

These symbols must be used in pairs, opening and closing. The use of such a pair is to indicate an exact quotation which was made by someone else. As a variation on this usage a pair of quotation marks are used to denote a term within context that someone else has defined outside of the text. The opening mark is preceded by a space or parenthesis; the closing mark is followed by a space or other closing mark.

9.6.3.10. Apostrophe

The apostrophe has two uses: the contraction of two words into one; the possessive form of a noun. Examples of the former are: it is, it's; do not, don't. An example of the latter (to erroneously convert an idiom) is: the cat's pajamas, the pajamas of the cat. To be completely correct, the possessive form is also a contraction of a longer form.

10. SUMMARY OF STATEMENTS

This Chapter contains an aggregation of the A, D, E, and P assertions which were developed in earlier Chapters.

10.1. Summary of Statements, Intension

To repeat our early statements, we may note that in the specification of terms about intension there has been a degree of circularity or simultaneity. This is a result of an absence of a language, the language which we are starting to develop.

10.1.1. Auxiliary Assertions, Intension

This Section contains a collection of assertions which are used in several deductions, definitions and axioms. In itself each C assertion is usually meaningless since it is out of context here. To repeat, these are presented only as referenced forms which appear in the A, D and P assertions.

C3.01 $\mathfrak{M}\{\mathfrak{M}_\alpha\}:\mathfrak{M}\{\mathfrak{M}_\beta\}$

C3.02 Intension $\mathfrak{M}_\alpha$ is identical to intension $\mathfrak{M}_\beta$

C3.03 $\mathfrak{M}\{\mathfrak{M}_\beta\}:\mathfrak{M}\{\mathfrak{M}_\alpha\}$

C3.04 $\mathfrak{M}\{\nabla[\mathfrak{M}_\alpha,\mathfrak{M}_\beta]\}:\nabla[\mathfrak{M}_\alpha,\mathfrak{M}_\beta]$

C3.05 $\mathfrak{M}\{\Delta[\mathfrak{M}_\alpha,\mathfrak{M}_\beta]\}:\Delta[\mathfrak{M}_\alpha,\mathfrak{M}_\beta]$

C3.06 $\mathfrak{M}_\alpha:\nabla[\mathfrak{M}_\beta,\mathfrak{M}_\mu]$

C3.07 $\mathfrak{M}\{\nabla[\mathfrak{M}_\alpha,\mathfrak{M}_\gamma]\}:\mathfrak{M}\{\nabla[\mathfrak{M}_\beta,\mathfrak{M}_\gamma]\}$

C3.08 $\mathfrak{M}\{\Delta[\mathfrak{M}_\alpha,\mathfrak{M}_\gamma]\}:\mathfrak{M}\{\Delta[\mathfrak{M}_\beta,\mathfrak{M}_\gamma]$

C3.09 $\mathfrak{M}\{\mathfrak{M}_\beta\}:\mathfrak{M}\{\mathfrak{M}_\gamma\}$

C3.10 $\mathfrak{M}\{\mathfrak{M}_\alpha\}:\mathfrak{M}\{\mathfrak{M}_\gamma\}$

C3.11 $\mathfrak{M}\{\mathfrak{M}_\alpha\}:\mathfrak{M}\{\nabla[\Delta[\mathfrak{M}_\alpha,\mathfrak{M}_\beta],\blacksquare[\mathfrak{M}_\alpha,\mathfrak{M}_\beta]]\}$

C3.12 $\Delta[\Delta[\mathfrak{M}_\alpha,\mathfrak{M}_\beta],\blacksquare[\mathfrak{M}_\alpha,\mathfrak{M}_\beta]]:\Phi$

C3.13 $\mathfrak{M}\{\nabla[\mathfrak{M}_\alpha,\Phi]\}:\mathfrak{M}\{\mathfrak{M}_\alpha\}$

C3.14 $\mathfrak{M}_\beta:\nabla[\mathfrak{M}_\gamma,\mathfrak{M}_\nu]$

C3.15 $\mathfrak{M}_\alpha:\nabla[\mathfrak{M}_\gamma,\mathfrak{M}_\rho]$

C3.16 $\nabla[\mathfrak{M}_\alpha,\mathfrak{M}_\gamma]:\nabla[\nabla[\mathfrak{M}_\beta,\mathfrak{M}_\gamma],\mathfrak{M}_\mu]$

C3.17 $\blacksquare[\mathfrak{M}_\alpha,\mathfrak{M}_\gamma]:\blacksquare[\mathfrak{M}_\beta,\mathfrak{M}_\gamma]$

C3.18 $\Delta[\mathfrak{M}_\alpha,\mathfrak{M}_\beta]:\mathfrak{M}_\beta$

C3.19 $\mathfrak{M}_\alpha:\Phi$

C3.20 $\mathfrak{M}_\beta:\Phi$

C3.21 $\nabla[\mathfrak{M}_\alpha,\mathfrak{M}_\beta]:\Phi$

10.1.2. Axioms, Intension

A3.01 $\mathfrak{M}\{\mathfrak{M}_\alpha\}:\mathfrak{M}_\alpha$

A3.02 $\mathfrak{M}_\alpha:\mathfrak{M}_\alpha$

A3.03 $\mathfrak{M}\{\text{C3.01}\}:\mathfrak{M}\{\text{C3.03}\}$

A3.04	$\mathfrak{M}\{\nabla[\mathfrak{M}_\alpha,\mathfrak{M}_\beta]\}:\mathfrak{M}\{\nabla[\mathfrak{M}_\beta,\mathfrak{M}_\alpha]\}$
A3.05	$\mathfrak{M}\{\nabla[\nabla[\mathfrak{M}_\alpha,\mathfrak{M}_\beta],\mathfrak{M}_\gamma]\}:\mathfrak{M}\{\nabla[\mathfrak{M}_\alpha,\nabla[\mathfrak{M}_\beta,\mathfrak{M}_\gamma]]\}$
A3.06	$\mathfrak{M}\{\text{C3.01}\}:\mathfrak{M}\{\text{C3.07}\}$
A3.07	$\mathfrak{M}\{\nabla[\mathfrak{M}_\alpha,\mathfrak{M}_\alpha]\}:\mathfrak{M}\{\mathfrak{M}_\alpha\}$
A3.08	$\mathfrak{M}\{\Delta[\mathfrak{M}_\alpha,\mathfrak{M}_\beta]\}:\mathfrak{M}\{\Delta[\mathfrak{M}_\beta,\mathfrak{M}_\alpha]\}$
A3.09	$\mathfrak{M}\{\Delta[\Delta[\mathfrak{M}_\alpha,\mathfrak{M}_\beta],\mathfrak{M}_\gamma]\}:\mathfrak{M}\{\Delta[\mathfrak{M}_\alpha,\Delta[\mathfrak{M}_\beta,\mathfrak{M}_\gamma]]\}$
A3.10	$\mathfrak{M}\{\text{C3.01}\}:\mathfrak{M}\{\text{C3.08}\}$
A3.11	$\mathfrak{M}\{\Delta[\mathfrak{M}_\alpha,\mathfrak{M}_\alpha]\}:\mathfrak{M}\{\mathfrak{M}_\alpha\}$
A3.12	$\Delta[\mathfrak{M}\{\text{C3.01}\},\mathfrak{M}\{\text{C3.09}\}]:\mathfrak{M}\{\text{C3.10}\}$
A3.13	$\Delta[\mathfrak{M}\{\nabla[\mathfrak{M}_\alpha,\mathfrak{M}_\beta]\},\mathfrak{M}\{\text{C3.09}\}]:\mathfrak{M}\{\nabla[\mathfrak{M}_\alpha,\mathfrak{M}_\gamma]\}$
A3.14	$\Delta[\mathfrak{M}\{\Delta[\mathfrak{M}_\alpha,\mathfrak{M}_\beta]\},\mathfrak{M}\{\text{C3.09}\}]:\mathfrak{M}\{\Delta[\mathfrak{M}_\alpha,\mathfrak{M}_\gamma]\}$
A3.15	$\mathfrak{M}\{\Delta[\mathfrak{M}_\alpha,\nabla[\mathfrak{M}_\beta,\mathfrak{M}_\gamma]]\}:\mathfrak{M}\{\nabla[\Delta[\mathfrak{M}_\alpha,\mathfrak{M}_\beta],\Delta[\mathfrak{M}_\alpha,\mathfrak{M}_\gamma]]\}$
A3.16	$\mathfrak{M}\{\nabla[\mathfrak{M}_\alpha,\Delta[\mathfrak{M}_\beta,\mathfrak{M}_\gamma]]\}:\mathfrak{M}\{\Delta[\nabla[\mathfrak{M}_\alpha,\mathfrak{M}_\beta],\nabla[\mathfrak{M}_\alpha,\mathfrak{M}_\gamma]]\}$
A3.17	$\mathfrak{M}\{\Delta[\mathfrak{M}_\alpha,\mathfrak{M}\{\text{C3.01}\}]:\mathfrak{M}\{\mathfrak{M}_\beta\}$

10.1.3. Definitions, Intension

10.1.3.1. Symbolism

Here our symbols are defined in terms of other symbols.

D3.01	$\mathfrak{M}\{\mathfrak{M}\}:\nabla[\nabla[\nabla[\mathfrak{M}\{\text{A3.01}\},\mathfrak{M}\{\text{A3.17}\}],$ $\nabla[\mathfrak{M}\{\text{D3.02}\},\mathfrak{M}\{\text{D3.03}\}]],\mathfrak{M}\{\text{D3.04}\}]$
D3.02	$\mathfrak{M}\{\nabla\}:\Delta[\mathfrak{M}_\nabla,\Delta[\mathfrak{M}\{\text{A3.15}\},\mathfrak{M}\{\text{A3.16}\}]]$
D3.03	$\mathfrak{M}\{\Delta\}:\Delta[\mathfrak{M}_\Delta,\Delta[\mathfrak{M}\{\text{A3.15}\},\mathfrak{M}\{\text{A3.16}\}]]$
D3.04	$\mathfrak{M}\{\text{identity format}\}:\Delta[\Delta[\mathfrak{M}\{\text{A3.02}\},\mathfrak{M}\{\text{A3.03}\}],\mathfrak{M}\{\text{A3.12}\}]$
D3.05	$\mathfrak{M}\{\blacksquare\}:\Delta[\mathfrak{M}\{\text{C3.11}\},\mathfrak{M}\{\text{C3.12}\}]$
D3.06	$\mathfrak{M}\{\mathfrak{O}\}:\mathfrak{M}\{\text{C3.13}\}$

10.1.3.2. English

This Section defines phrases of English.

E2.02	$\mathfrak{M}\{\mathfrak{M}\{d_\alpha\}\}:\mathfrak{M}\{\text{intension of } d_\alpha\}$
E3.01	$\mathfrak{M}\{\text{identity format}\}\in\mathbf{C}\{\text{reflexive relationships}\}$
E3.02	$\mathfrak{M}\{\text{C3.01}\}:\mathfrak{M}\{\text{C3.02}\}$
E3.03	$\mathfrak{M}\{\text{identity format}\}\in\mathbf{C}\{\text{symmetric relationships}\}$
E3.04	$\mathfrak{M}\{\nabla[\mathfrak{M}_\alpha,\mathfrak{M}_\beta]\}:\mathfrak{M}\{\text{the aggregation of concepts } \mathfrak{M}_\alpha \text{ and } \mathfrak{M}_\beta\}$
E3.05	$\mathfrak{M}\{\text{conjunction } \nabla\}\in\mathbf{C}\{\text{commutative relationships}\}$
E3.06	$\mathfrak{M}\{\text{conjunction } \nabla\}\in\mathbf{C}\{\text{associative relationships}\}$
E3.07	$\mathfrak{M}\{\text{C3.06}\}:\mathfrak{M}\{\text{logical implication}\}$
E3.08	$\mathfrak{M}\{\Delta[\mathfrak{M}_\alpha,\mathfrak{M}_\beta]\}:\mathfrak{M}\{\text{the coincident portion of intensions } \mathfrak{M}_\alpha \text{ and } \mathfrak{M}_\beta\}$
E3.09	$\mathfrak{M}\{\text{conjunction } \Delta\}\in\mathbf{C}\{\text{commutative relationships}\}$
E3.10	$\mathfrak{M}\{\text{conjunction } \Delta\}\in\mathbf{C}\{\text{associative relationships}\}$
E3.11	$\mathfrak{M}\{\text{A3.12}\}\in\mathbf{C}\{\text{Rules of Substitution}\}$
E3.12	$\mathfrak{M}\{\text{identity format}\}\in\mathbf{C}\{\text{transitive relationships}\}$
E3.13	$\mathfrak{M}\{\text{A3.13}\}\in\mathbf{C}\{\text{Rules of Substitution}\}$

E3.14	$\mathfrak{M}\{\text{A3.14}\}\in\mathbf{C}\{\text{Rules of Substitution}\}$
E3.15	$\mathfrak{M}\{\text{A3.17}\}\in\mathbf{C}\{\text{Rules of Substitution}\}$
E3.16	$\mathfrak{M}\{\blacksquare[\mathfrak{M}_\alpha,\mathfrak{M}_\beta]\}:\mathfrak{M}\{\mathfrak{M}_\alpha \text{ excluding any and all of } \mathfrak{M}_\beta\}$
E3.17	$\mathfrak{M}\{\oplus\}:\mathfrak{M}\{\text{nonsense}\}$
E3.18	$\mathfrak{M}\{\text{logical implication}\}\in\mathbf{C}\{\text{transitive relationships}\}$
E3.19	$\mathfrak{M}\{\text{P3.10}\}\in\mathbf{C}\{\text{Rules of Substitution}\}$
E3.20	$\mathfrak{M}\{\text{P3.11}\}\in\mathbf{C}\{\text{Rules of Substitution}\}$

10.1.4. Theorems, Intension

P3.01	$\Delta[\mathfrak{M}_\alpha,\oplus]:\oplus$
P3.02	$\mathfrak{M}\{\blacksquare[\mathfrak{M}_\alpha,\oplus]\}:\mathfrak{M}\{\mathfrak{M}_\alpha\}$
P3.03	$\Delta[\Delta[\mathfrak{M}\{\text{C3.06}\},\mathfrak{M}\{\text{C3.14}\}],\mathfrak{M}_\eta]:\mathfrak{M}\{\text{C3.15}\}$
P3.04	$\mathfrak{M}\{\text{C3.06}\}:\Delta[\mathfrak{M}\{\text{C3.16}\},\mathfrak{M}_\rho]$
P3.05	$\mathfrak{M}\{\nabla[\mathfrak{M}_\alpha,\mathfrak{M}_\beta]\}:\mathfrak{M}\{\nabla[\Delta[\mathfrak{M}_\alpha,\mathfrak{M}_\beta],\nabla[\blacksquare[\mathfrak{M}_\alpha,\mathfrak{M}_\beta],\blacksquare[\mathfrak{M}_\beta,\mathfrak{M}_\alpha]]]\}$
P3.06	$\mathfrak{M}\{\nabla[\mathfrak{M}_\alpha,\mathfrak{M}_\beta]\}:\mathfrak{M}\{\nabla[\mathfrak{M}_\alpha,\blacksquare[\mathfrak{M}_\beta,\mathfrak{M}_\alpha]]\}$
P3.07	$\mathfrak{M}\{\text{C3.01}\}:\nabla[\mathfrak{M}\{\text{C3.17}\},\mathfrak{M}_\mu]$
P3.08	$\mathfrak{M}\{\text{C3.18}\}:\nabla[\mathfrak{M}\{\text{C3.06}\},\mathfrak{M}_\rho]$
P3.09	$\blacksquare[\mathfrak{M}_\alpha,\mathfrak{M}_\alpha]:\oplus$
P3.10	$\Delta[\blacksquare[\mathfrak{M}_\alpha,\mathfrak{M}_\beta],\mathfrak{M}\{\text{C3.09}\}]:\blacksquare[\mathfrak{M}_\alpha,\mathfrak{M}_\gamma]$
P3.11	$\Delta[\blacksquare[\mathfrak{M}_\alpha,\mathfrak{M}_\beta],\mathfrak{M}\{\text{C3.10}\}]:\blacksquare[\mathfrak{M}_\gamma,\mathfrak{M}_\beta]$
P3.12	$\mathfrak{M}\{\text{C3.21}\}:\Delta[\nabla[\mathfrak{M}\{\text{C3.19}\},\mathfrak{M}\{\text{C3.20}\}],\mathfrak{M}_\rho]$

10.2. Summary of Statements, Number

10.2.1. Auxiliary Assertions, Number

C4.01	$x=y$
C4.02	The number x is identical to the number y
C4.03	$\mathfrak{M}\{x\}:\mathfrak{M}\{y\}$
C4.04	$\mathfrak{M}\{\text{C4.03}\}:\mathfrak{M}\{\text{C4.01}\}$
C4.05	$y=x$
C4.06	$\mathfrak{M}\{y\}:\mathfrak{M}\{x\}$
C4.07	$y=z$
C4.08	$x=z$
C4.09	$x\neq y$
C4.10	$\Delta[\mathfrak{M}\{x\},\mathfrak{M}\{y\}]:\oplus$
C4.11	$\mathfrak{M}\{\text{C4.10}\}:\mathfrak{M}\{\text{C4.09}\}$
C4.12	$\mathfrak{s}[x,z]=\mathfrak{s}[y,z]$
C4.13	$\mathfrak{p}[x,z]=\mathfrak{p}[y,z]$
C4.14	$\mathfrak{s}[x,0]=x$
C4.15	$\mathfrak{p}[x,1\text{»}]=x$
C4.16	$\mathfrak{s}[x,1\text{»}]=0$
C4.17	$x=(1\text{«})$

C4.18	𝔐{C4.16}:𝔐{C4.17}
C4.19	𝔰[x,𝔭[y,1«]]=z
C4.20	x=𝔰[y,z]
C4.21	𝔐{C4.19}:𝔐{C4.20}
C4.22	x=b/a
C4.23	a≠0
C4.24	𝔭[a,x]=b
C4.25	Δ[𝔐{C4.24},𝔐{C4.23}]:𝔐{C4.22}
C4.26	$f(x)=\sum_{n=0}^{N}\mathfrak{p}[a_n,x^n]$
C4.27	f(x)=0
C4.28	Number x is algebraic
C4.29	x>y
C4.30	𝔰[x,1»]>x
C4.31	x<y
C4.32	x<𝔰[x,1»]
C4.33	z=0
C4.34	y=1»
C4.35	z=1»
C4.36	δ>0

10.2.2. Axioms, Number

A4.01	Δ[𝔐{f(x)},𝔐{C4.03}]:𝔐{f(y)}
A4.02	𝔐{𝔰[x,y]}:𝔐{𝔰[y,x]}
A4.03	𝔐{𝔰[𝔰[x,y],z]}:𝔐{𝔰[x,𝔰[y,z]]}
A4.04	𝔐{C4.01}:𝔐{C4.12}
A4.05	𝔐{𝔭[x,y]}:𝔐{𝔭[y,x]}
A4.06	𝔐{𝔭[𝔭[x,y],z]}:𝔐{𝔭[x,𝔭[y,z]]}
A4.07	𝔐{C4.01}:𝔐{C4.13}
A4.08	𝔐{𝔭[x,𝔰[y,z]]}:𝔐{𝔰[𝔭[x,y],𝔭[x,z]]}
A4.09	𝔐{𝔭[1«,1«]}:𝔐{1»}

10.2.3. Definitions, Number

10.2.3.1. Symbolism

D4.01	𝔐{=}:𝔐{C4.04}
D4.02	𝔐{≠}:𝔐{C4.11}
D4.03	𝔐{𝔰}:∇[∇[𝔐{A4.02},𝔐{A4.03}],∇[𝔐{A4.04},𝔐{A4.08}]]
D4.04	𝔐{𝔭}:∇[∇[𝔐{A4.05},𝔐{A4.06}],∇[𝔐{A4.07},𝔐{A4.08}]]
D4.05	𝔐{0}:𝔐{C4.14}
D4.06	𝔐{1»}:𝔐{C4.15}
D4.07	𝔐{010»}:𝔐{𝔰[1»,1»]}
D4.08	𝔐{011»}:𝔐{𝔰[010»,1»]}

D4.09 𝕸{0100»}:𝕸{𝖘[011»,1»]}

D4.10 𝕸{0101»}:𝕸{𝖘[0100»,1»]}

D4.11 𝕸{seq(0,N)}:∇[𝕸{D4.05},∇[𝕸{D4.06},∇[𝕸{D4.07},∇[...

D4.12 𝕸{1«}:𝕸{C4.18}

D4.13 𝕸{𝖘[x,𝖕[y,1«]]}:𝕸{C4.21}

D4.14 𝕸{x/y}:𝕸{C4.25}

D4.15 𝕸{𝖕[x,x^{n}]}:𝕸{$x^{𝖘[n,1»]}$}

D4.16 𝕸{x^{0}}:𝕸{1»}

D4.17 𝕸{𝖕[x^{a},x^{b}]}:𝕸{$x^{𝖘[a,b]}$}

D4.18 𝕸{𝖕[i»,i»]}:𝕸{1«}

D4.19 𝕸{C4.29}:Δ[■[𝕸{C4.09},■[𝕸{C4.09},𝕸{C4.29}]],𝕸{C4.30}]

D4.20 𝕸{C4.31}:Δ[■[𝕸{C4.09},■[𝕸{C4.09},𝕸{C4.31}]],𝕸{C4.32}]

10.2.3.2. English

E4.01 𝕸{C4.01}:𝕸{C4.02}

E4.02 𝕸{copula =}∊**C**{reflexive relationships}

E4.03 𝕸{copula =}∊**C**{symmetric relationships}

E4.04 𝕸{copula =}∊**C**{transitive relationships}

E4.05 𝕸{P4.03}∊**C**{Rules of Substitution}

E4.06 𝕸{A4.01}∊**C**{Rules of Substitution}

E4.07 𝕸{𝖘[x,y]}:𝕸{the sum of numbers x and y}

E4.08 𝕸{conjunction 𝖘}∊**C**{commutative relationships}

E4.09 𝕸{conjunction 𝖘}∊**C**{associative relationships}

E4.10 𝕸{𝖕[x,y]}:𝕸{the product of numbers x and y}

E4.11 𝕸{conjunction 𝖕}∊**C**{commutative relationships}

E4.12 𝕸{conjunction 𝖕}∊**C**{associative relationships}

E4.13 𝕸{𝖘[x,𝖕[y,1«]]}:𝕸{the difference of x and y}

E4.14 𝕸{x/y}:𝕸{the quotient of x and y}

E4.15 Δ[𝕸{C4.26},𝕸{C4.27}]:𝕸{C4.28}

10.2.4. Theorems, Number

P4.01 x=x

P4.02 𝕸{C4.01}:𝕸{C4.05}

P4.03 ∇[𝕸{C4.01},𝕸{C4.07}]:𝕸{C4.08}

P4.04 0101»=𝖘[011»,010»]

P4.05 𝖕[x,0]=0

P4.06 𝕸{𝖕[x,010»]}:𝕸{𝖘[x,x]}

P4.07 𝖕[1»,1»]=1»

P4.08 𝖕[1«,1»]=1«

P4.09 𝕸{C4.29}:∇[𝕸{C4.10},𝕸{C4.36}]

10.3. Summary of Statements, Extension

10.3.1. Auxiliary Assertions, Extension

C5.01	$1 » \leq \mu \leq M$
C5.02	$1 » \leq \alpha \leq N(\mu)$
C5.03	$\Delta[\mathfrak{M}\{a\},\mathfrak{M}\{d_{\mu\alpha}\}]:\mathfrak{M}\{a\}$
C5.04	$\mathfrak{M}\{a_{\alpha}\}:\nabla[\mathfrak{M}\{a\},\mathfrak{M}\{k_{\alpha}\}]$
C5.05	$\Delta[\mathfrak{M}\{a\},\mathfrak{M}\{k_{\alpha}\}]:\mathfrak{O}$
C5.06	$\Delta[\mathfrak{M}\{a_{\beta}\},\mathfrak{M}\{a_{\gamma}\}]:\mathfrak{O}$
C5.07	$\beta=\gamma$
C5.08	$\Delta[\mathfrak{M}\{a_{\alpha}\},\mathfrak{M}\{\mathbf{C}\{a\}\}]:\mathfrak{M}\{a_{\alpha}\}$
C5.09	$\mathfrak{M}\{a_{\alpha}\}\in\mathbf{C}\{a\}$
C5.10	$\mathfrak{M}\{C5.09\}:\mathfrak{M}\{C5.08\}$
C5.11	$\mathbf{C}\{a\}\equiv\mathbf{C}\{b\}$
C5.12	Class $\mathbf{C}\{a\}$ contains the same members as class $\mathbf{C}\{b\}$
C5.13	$\Delta[\mathfrak{M}\{b_{\beta}\},\mathfrak{M}\{\mathbf{C}\{b\}\}]:\mathfrak{M}\{b_{\beta}\}$
C5.14	$\mathfrak{M}\{b_{\beta}\}\in\mathbf{C}\{b\}$
C5.15	$M=N$
C5.16	$\mathfrak{M}\{b_{\alpha}\}\in\mathbf{C}\{b\}$
C5.17	$\mathfrak{M}\{a_{\alpha}\}:\mathfrak{M}\{b_{\alpha}\}$
C5.18	$\mathfrak{M}\{C5.17\}:\mathfrak{M}\{C5.11\}$
C5.19	$\nabla[\nabla[\mathfrak{M}\{C5.09\},\mathfrak{M}\{C5.14\}],\nabla[\mathfrak{M}\{C5.15\},\mathfrak{M}\{C5.17\}]]:\mathfrak{M}\{C5.20\}$
C5.20	$\mathbf{C}\{b\}\equiv\mathbf{C}\{a\}$
C5.21	$\mathbf{C}\{b\}\equiv\mathbf{C}\{c\}$
C5.22	$\mathbf{C}\{a\}\equiv\mathbf{C}\{c\}$
C5.23	$\mathfrak{M}\{c_{\alpha}\}\in\mathbf{C}\{c\}$
C5.24	$\mathfrak{M}\{b_{\alpha}\}:\mathfrak{M}\{c_{\alpha}\}$
C5.25	$\mathfrak{M}\{C5.24\}:\mathfrak{M}\{C5.21\}$
C5.26	$\mathfrak{M}\{a_{\alpha}\}:\mathfrak{M}\{c_{\alpha}\}$
C5.27	$\mathfrak{M}\{C5.26\}:\mathfrak{M}\{C5.22\}$
C5.28	$\Delta[\mathfrak{M}\{a\},\mathfrak{M}\{d_{\mu\alpha}\}]:\mathfrak{M}\{a\}$
C5.29	$\Delta[\mathfrak{M}\{b\},\mathfrak{M}\{d_{\mu\alpha}\}]:\mathfrak{M}\{b\}$
C5.30	$\mathfrak{M}\{a_{\alpha}\}:\nabla[\mathfrak{M}\{h\},\nabla[\mathfrak{M}\{a\},\mathfrak{M}\{r_{\alpha}\}]]$
C5.31	$\mathfrak{M}\{b_{\beta}\}:\nabla[\mathfrak{M}\{h\},\nabla[\mathfrak{M}\{b\},\mathfrak{M}\{t_{\beta}\}]]$
C5.32	$\mathfrak{M}\{g_{\rho}\}:\Delta[\mathfrak{M}\{a_{\alpha}\},\mathfrak{M}\{b_{\beta}\}]$
C5.33	$\mathfrak{M}\{g_{\rho}\}:\nabla[\nabla[\mathfrak{M}\{a\},\mathfrak{M}\{b\}],\nabla[\mathfrak{M}\{h\},\mathfrak{M}\{s_{\gamma}\}]]$
C5.34	$\mathfrak{M}\{g_{\rho}\}\in\mathbf{C}\{a\}$
C5.35	$\mathfrak{M}\{g_{\rho}\}\in\mathbf{C}\{b\}$
C5.36	$\mathfrak{M}\{a_{\alpha}\}\in\mathbf{C}\{h\}$
C5.37	$\mathfrak{M}\{g_{\rho}\}\in\mathbf{C}\{h\}$
C5.38	$\mathfrak{M}\{b_{\beta}\}\in\mathbf{C}\{h\}$
C5.39	$\mathfrak{M}\{p_{\mu}\}\in(\mathbf{C}\{a\}\cup\mathbf{C}\{b\})$

C5.40	$\mathfrak{M}\{(\mathbf{C}\{a\}\cup\mathbf{C}\{b\})\}:\mathfrak{M}\{(\mathbf{C}\{b\}\cup\mathbf{C}\{a\})\}$
C5.41	$\mathfrak{M}\{c_\gamma\}\in\mathbf{C}\{c\}$
C5.42	$\mathfrak{M}\{q_\nu\}\in((\mathbf{C}\{a\}\cup\mathbf{C}\{b\})\cup\mathbf{C}\{c\})$
C5.43	$\mathfrak{M}\{r_\rho\}\in(\mathbf{C}\{a\}\cup(\mathbf{C}\{b\}\cup\mathbf{C}\{c\}))$
C5.44	$\mathfrak{M}\{((\mathbf{C}\{a\}\cup\mathbf{C}\{b\})\cup\mathbf{C}\{c\})\}:\mathfrak{M}\{(\mathbf{C}\{a\}\cup(\mathbf{C}\{b\}\cup\mathbf{C}\{c\}))\}$
C5.45	$\mathfrak{M}\{(\mathbf{C}\{a\}\cup\mathbf{C}\{a\})\}:\mathfrak{M}\{\mathbf{C}\{a\}\}$
C5.46	$\mathfrak{M}\{p_\mu\}\in(\mathbf{C}\{a\}\cup\mathbf{C}\{c\})$
C5.47	$\mathfrak{M}\{q_\nu\}\in(\mathbf{C}\{b\}\cup\mathbf{C}\{c\})$
C5.48	$(\mathbf{C}\{a\}\cup\mathbf{C}\{c\})\equiv(\mathbf{C}\{b\}\cup\mathbf{C}\{c\})$
C5.49	$\mathbf{C}\{a\}\supset\mathbf{C}\{b\}$
C5.50	$\mathbf{C}\{a\}\equiv(\mathbf{C}\{b\}\cup\mathbf{C}_\mu)$
C5.51	$\mathfrak{M}\{C5.49\}:\mathfrak{M}\{C5.50\}$
C5.52	Class $\mathbf{C}\{a\}$ contains all members of class $\mathbf{C}\{b\}$
C5.53	$\mathbf{C}\{a\}\subset\mathbf{C}\{b\}$
C5.54	$\mathbf{C}\{b\}\equiv(\mathbf{C}\{a\}\cup\mathbf{C}_\nu)$
C5.55	$\mathfrak{M}\{C5.53\}:\mathfrak{M}\{C5.54\}$
C5.56	Class $\mathbf{C}\{b\}$ contains all members of class $\mathbf{C}\{a\}$
C5.57	$\mathfrak{M}\{g_\rho\}\in(\mathbf{C}\{a\}\cap\mathbf{C}\{b\})$
C5.58	$\mathfrak{M}\{(\mathbf{C}\{a\}\cap\mathbf{C}\{b\})\}:\mathfrak{M}\{(\mathbf{C}\{b\}\cap\mathbf{C}\{a\})\}$
C5.59	$\mathfrak{M}\{p_\mu\}\in((\mathbf{C}\{a\}\cap\mathbf{C}\{b\})\cap\mathbf{C}\{c\})$
C5.60	$\mathfrak{M}\{q_\nu\}\in(\mathbf{C}\{a\}\cap(\mathbf{C}\{b\}\cap\mathbf{C}\{c\}))$
C5.61	$\mathfrak{M}\{((\mathbf{C}\{a\}\cap\mathbf{C}\{b\})\cap\mathbf{C}\{c\})\}:\mathfrak{M}\{(\mathbf{C}\{a\}\cap(\mathbf{C}\{b\}\cap\mathbf{C}\{c\}))\}$
C5.62	$\mathfrak{M}\{(\mathbf{C}\{a\}\cap\mathbf{C}\{a\})\}:\mathfrak{M}\{\mathbf{C}\{a\}\}$
C5.63	$\mathfrak{M}\{p_\mu\}\in(\mathbf{C}\{a\}\cap\mathbf{C}\{c\})$
C5.64	$\mathfrak{M}\{q_\nu\}\in(\mathbf{C}\{b\}\cap\mathbf{C}\{c\})$
C5.65	$(\mathbf{C}\{a\}\cap\mathbf{C}\{c\})\equiv(\mathbf{C}\{b\}\cap\mathbf{C}\{c\})$
C5.66	$\mathfrak{M}\{(\mathbf{C}\{a\}\cup\mathbf{O})\}:\mathfrak{M}\{\mathbf{C}\{a\}\}$
C5.67	$\mathfrak{M}\{\mathbf{C}\{a\}\}:\mathfrak{M}\{((\mathbf{C}\{a\}\mathbf{w}\mathbf{C}\{b\})\cup(\mathbf{C}\{a\}\cap\mathbf{C}\{b\}))\}$
C5.68	$((\mathbf{C}\{a\}\mathbf{w}\mathbf{C}\{b\})\cap(\mathbf{C}\{a\}\cap\mathbf{C}\{b\}))\equiv\mathbf{O}$
C5.69	$\mathbf{S}\{n\}\subset\mathbf{S}\{\text{natural-number}\}$
C5.70	$\mathfrak{s}[x,n]=0$
C5.71	$\mathbf{S}\{x\}\subset\mathbf{S}\{\text{negative-integer}\}$
C5.72	$\mathbf{S}\{a\}\subset\mathbf{S}\{\text{positive-integer}\}$
C5.73	$\mathbf{S}\{b\}\subset\mathbf{S}\{\text{integer}\}$
C5.74	$\mathbf{S}\{x\}\subset\mathbf{S}\{\text{rational-number}\}$
C5.75	$\mathfrak{b}\{\text{seq}(1,N)\}=N$
C5.76	$\mathfrak{b}\{\mathbf{C}\{h\}\}=N$
C5.77	$\mathfrak{M}\{C5.75\}:\mathfrak{M}\{C5.76\}$
C5.78	$\mathfrak{b}\{\mathbf{C}\{a\}\}=\mathfrak{b}\{\mathbf{C}\{b\}\}$
C5.79	Classes $\mathbf{C}\{a\}$ and $\mathbf{C}\{b\}$ are similar
C5.80	$N=\mathfrak{b}\{\mathbf{S}\{x_\alpha\}\}$
C5.81	$\mathfrak{p}[N,X]=\sum_{\alpha=1}^{N}x_\alpha$
C5.82	$\mathfrak{M}\{X\}:\mathfrak{M}\{\text{arithmetic mean of } x_\alpha\}$
C5.83	$\mathfrak{M}_1\in\mathbf{C}\{S_\alpha\}$

C5.84	$\mathfrak{M}_1$ is the selected concept from a class of $\mathfrak{M}_\alpha$
C5.85	The members S_α of the class are mutually exclusive
C5.86	$N! = \prod_{\alpha=1}^{N} \alpha$
C5.87	$\mathfrak{M}\{N!\}:\mathfrak{M}\{\text{N factorial}\}$
C5.88	$\Delta[\mathfrak{M}_\alpha,\mathfrak{M}_\beta]:\Phi$
C5.89	S_α and S_β are independent
C5.90	S_α is nonsense
C5.91	S_β is nonsense
C5.92	Both S_α and S_β are nonsense
C5.93	$(\mathbf{C}\{a\}\cap\mathbf{C}\{b\})\equiv\mathbf{O}$
C5.94	$\mathbf{C}\{a\}$ and $\mathbf{C}\{b\}$ are disjoint classes
C5.95	$\mathbf{C}\{a\}$ is a vacuous class
C5.96	$\mathbf{C}\{b\}$ is a vacuous class
C5.97	$(\mathbf{C}\{a\}\cup\mathbf{C}\{b\})$ is a vacuous class
C5.98	$x\leq y$
C5.99	$x\geq y$
C5.100	$\mathfrak{p}[x,z]>\mathfrak{p}[y,z]$
C5.101	$\mathfrak{p}[x,z]\geq\mathfrak{p}[y,z]$
C5.102	$\mathfrak{p}[x,z]\leq\mathfrak{p}[y,z]$
C5.103	$\mathbf{C}\{a\}\equiv\mathbf{O}$
C5.104	$\mathbf{C}\{b\}\equiv\mathbf{O}$
C5.105	$(\mathbf{C}\{a\}\cup\mathbf{C}\{b\})\equiv\mathbf{O}$
C5.106	$\mathbf{C}\{b\}\equiv(\mathbf{C}\{c\}\cup\mathbf{C}\{v\})$
C5.107	$\mathbf{C}\{a\}\equiv(\mathbf{C}\{c\}\cup\mathbf{C}\{r\})$
C5.108	$\mathbf{C}\{b\}\supset\mathbf{C}\{c\}$
C5.109	$\mathbf{C}\{a\}\supset\mathbf{C}\{c\}$
C5.110	$(\mathbf{C}\{a\}\cup\mathbf{C}\{c\})\equiv((\mathbf{C}\{b\}\cup\mathbf{C}\{c\})\cup\mathbf{C}\{u\})$
C5.111	$(\mathbf{C}\{a\}\mathbf{w}\mathbf{C}\{c\})\equiv(\mathbf{C}\{b\}\mathbf{w}\mathbf{C}\{c\})$
C5.112	$(\mathbf{C}\{a\}\cap\mathbf{C}\{b\})\equiv\mathbf{C}\{b\}$
C5.113	$\mathbf{C}\{v\}\equiv\mathbf{C}\{r\}$

10.3.2. Definitions, Extension

10.3.2.1. Symbolism

D5.01	$\mathfrak{M}\{\mathbf{C}\{a\}\}:\nabla[\mathfrak{M}\{a_\alpha\},\mathfrak{M}_{\mathbf{C}}]$
D5.02	$\mathfrak{M}\{\epsilon\}:\mathfrak{M}\{C5.10\}$
D5.03	$\mathfrak{M}\{\equiv\}:\mathfrak{M}\{C5.18\}$
D5.04	$\mathfrak{M}\{\cup\}:\Delta[\Delta[\mathfrak{M}\{C5.39\},\mathfrak{M}\{D5.01\}],\mathfrak{M}_\cup]$
D5.05	$\mathfrak{M}\{\supset\}:\mathfrak{M}\{C5.51\}$
D5.06	$\mathfrak{M}\{\subset\}:\mathfrak{M}\{C5.55\}$
D5.07	$\mathfrak{M}\{\cap\}:\Delta[\Delta[\mathfrak{M}\{C5.32\},\mathfrak{M}\{C5.57\}],\Delta[\mathfrak{M}\{D5.01\},\mathfrak{M}_\cap]]$
D5.08	$\mathfrak{M}\{\mathbf{O}\}:\mathfrak{M}\{C5.66\}$
D5.09	$\mathfrak{M}\{\mathbf{w}\}:\Delta[\mathfrak{M}\{C5.67\},\mathfrak{M}\{C5.68\}]$

D5.10 **N**≡**S**{natural-numbers}
D5.11 **S**{integer}≡(**S**{natural-number}∪**S**{negative-integer})
D5.12 ∇[𝕸{C5.69},𝕸{C5.70}]:𝕸{C5.71}
D5.13 **S**{natural-number}≡(**S**{0}∪**S**{positive-integer})
D5.14 ∇[∇[𝕸{C4.24},𝕸{C5.72}],𝕸{C5.73}]:𝕸{C5.74}
D5.15 **S**{rational-number}⊃**S**{integer}
D5.16 **C**{real-number}≡(**C**{rational-number}∪(**C**{irrational-number}∪**C**{transcendental-number}))
D5.17 𝕸{𝔟}:Δ[Δ[𝕸{C5.09},𝕸{C5.02}],𝕸{C5.77}]
D5.18 $\mathfrak{s}[\mathfrak{s}[x_1,x_{010}],x_{011}]=\sum_{\alpha=1}^{011}x_\alpha$
D5.19 $\sum_{\alpha=1»}^{\mathfrak{s}[n,1»]}x_\alpha=\mathfrak{s}[x_{\mathfrak{s}[n,1»]},\sum_{\alpha=1»}^{n}x_\alpha]$
D5.20 $\mathfrak{p}[\mathfrak{p}[x_1,x_{010}],x_{011}]=\prod_{\alpha=1}^{011}x_\alpha$
D5.21 $\prod_{\alpha=1}^{\mathfrak{s}[n,1»]}x_\alpha=\mathfrak{p}[x_{\mathfrak{s}[n,1»]},\prod_{\alpha=1}^{n}x_\alpha]$
D5.22 𝕸{C5.98}∊**C**{C4.01,C4.31}
D5.23 𝕸{C5.99}∊**C**{C4.01,C4.29}

10.3.2.2. English

E2.01 𝕸{**C**{d_α}}:𝕸{class of intensions of d_α}
E5.01 𝕸{∊}:𝕸{singular inclusion}
E5.02 𝕸{C5.11}:𝕸{C5.12}
E5.03 𝕸{copula ≡}∊**C**{reflexive relationships}
E5.04 𝕸{copula ≡}∊**C**{symmetric relationships}
E5.05 𝕸{copula ≡}∊**C**{transitive relationships}
E5.06 𝕸{P5.03}∊**C**{Rules of Substitution}
E5.07 𝕸{(**C**{a}∪**C**{b})}:𝕸{the union of class **C**{a} and class **C**{b}}
E5.08 𝕸{conjunction ∪}∊**C**{commutative relationships}
E5.09 𝕸{conjunction ∪}∊**C**{associative relationships}
E5.10 𝕸{C5.49}:𝕸{C5.52}
E5.11 𝕸{C5.53}:𝕸{C5.56}
E5.12 𝕸{(**C**{a}∩**C**{b})}:𝕸{the intersection of class **C**{a} and class **C**{b}}
E5.13 𝕸{conjunction ∩}∊**C**{commutative relationships}
E5.14 𝕸{conjunction ∩}∊**C**{associative relationships}
E5.15 𝕸{(**C**{a}**w**C{b})}:𝕸{**C**{a} excluding any member of **C**{b}}
E5.16 𝕸{𝔟{**C**{h}}}:𝕸{cardinality of class **C**{h}}
E5.17 𝕸{count}:𝕸{cardinality}
E5.18 𝕸{C5.78}:𝕸{C5.79}
E5.19 ∇[𝕸{C5.80},𝕸{C5.81}]:𝕸{C5.82}
E5.20 𝕸{inclusive disjunction}:𝕸{the selection of at least N alternatives}
E5.21 𝕸{exclusive disjunction}:𝕸{the selection of exactly N alternatives}
E5.22 𝕸{C5.83}:𝕸{C5.84}
E5.23 𝕸{C5.83}:𝕸{C5.85}

E5.24 𝔐{C5.86}:𝔐{C5.87}
E5.25 𝔐{C5.88}ϵ**C**{C5.89,C5.90,C5.91,C5.92}
E5.26 𝔐{C5.93}ϵ**C**{C5.94,C5.95,C5.96,C5.97}
E5.27 𝔐{copula ⊃}ϵ**C**{transitive relationships}
E5.28 𝔐{copula ⊃}ϵ**C**{reflexive relationships}

10.3.3. Theorems, Extension

P5.01 **C**{a}≡**C**{a}
P5.02 𝔐{C5.11}:𝔐{C5.20}
P5.03 ∇[𝔐{C5.11},𝔐{C5.21}]:𝔐{C5.22}
P5.04 𝔐{C5.11}:𝔐{C5.48}
P5.05 𝔐{C5.11}:𝔐{C5.65}
P5.06 𝔐{(**C**{a}∩(**C**{b}∪**C**{c}))}:𝔐{((**C**{a}∩**C**{b})∪(**C**{a}∩**C**{c}))}
P5.07 𝔐{(**C**{a}∪(**C**{b}∩**C**{c}))}:𝔐{((**C**{a}∪**C**{b})∩(**C**{a}∪**C**{c}))}
P5.08 𝔰[𝔟{(**C**{a}∪**C**{b})},𝔟{(**C**{a}∩**C**{b})}]=𝔰[𝔟{**C**{a}},𝔟{**C**{b}}]
P5.09 𝔟{**O**}=0
P5.10 𝔐{C4.29}:∇[𝔐{C5.100},$\mathfrak{M}_{\nu}$]
P5.11 𝔐{C5.99}:∇[𝔐{C5.101},$\mathfrak{M}_{\rho}$]
P5.12 𝔐{C5.98}:∇[𝔐{C5.102},$\mathfrak{M}_{\rho}$]
P5.13 𝔰[𝔭[n,x],x]=𝔭[𝔰[n,1],x]
P5.14 𝔐{C5.105}:∇[∇[𝔐{C5.103},𝔐{C5.104}],$\mathfrak{M}_{\rho}$]
P5.15 (**C**{a}∩**O**)≡**O**
P5.16 (**C**{a}**wO**)≡**C**{a}
P5.17 ∇[∇[𝔐{C5.50},𝔐{C5.106}],$\mathfrak{M}_{\eta}$]:𝔐{C5.53}
P5.18 ∇[∇[𝔐{C5.49},𝔐{C5.108}],$\mathfrak{M}_{\eta}$]:𝔐{C5.109}
P5.19 𝔐{C5.50}:∇[𝔐{C5.110},$\mathfrak{M}_{\rho}$]
P5.20 𝔐{C5.49}:𝔐{C5.110}
P5.21 𝔐{(**C**{a}∪**C**{b})}:
𝔐{((**C**{a}∩**C**{b})∪((**C**{a}**wC**{b})∪(**C**{b}**wC**{a})))}
P5.22 𝔐{(**C**{a}∪**C**{b})}:𝔐{(**C**{a}∪(**C**{b}**wC**{a}))}
P5.23 𝔐{C5.11}:∇[𝔐{C5.111},$\mathfrak{M}_{\mu}$]
P5.24 𝔐{C5.112}:∇[𝔐{C5.50},$\mathfrak{M}_{\rho}$]
P5.25 𝔐{C5.112}:∇[𝔐{C5.49},$\mathfrak{M}_{\rho}$]
P5.26 (**C**{a}**wC**{a})≡**O**
P5.27 𝔐{C5.11}:∇[∇[𝔐{C5.50},𝔐{C5.54}],$\mathfrak{M}_{\rho}$]
P5.28 𝔐{C5.11}:∇[∇[𝔐{C5.49},𝔐{C5.53}],$\mathfrak{M}_{\rho}$]
P5.29 **C**{a}⊃**C**{a}
P5.30 ∇[∇[𝔐{C5.106},𝔐{C5.107}],$\mathfrak{M}_{\mu}$]:𝔐{C5.11}
P5.31 ∇[∇[𝔐{C5.108},𝔐{C5.109}],$\mathfrak{M}_{\mu}$]:𝔐{C5.11}

10.4. Summary of Statements, Deduction

10.4.1. Auxiliary Assertions, Deduction

C6.01	$\nabla[\mathfrak{M}_\alpha,\mathfrak{M}_\beta]:\mathfrak{M}_\gamma$
C6.02	$\nabla[\mathfrak{M}_\alpha,\mathfrak{M}_\gamma]:\mathfrak{M}_\beta$
C6.03	S_γ if and only if S_β, based on S_α
C6.04	$\mathfrak{M}\{S_\alpha\}:\nabla[\mathfrak{M}\{S_\beta\},\mathfrak{M}_\mu]$
C6.05	S_α is a sufficient condition for S_β
C6.06	$\Delta[\mathfrak{M}\{S_\alpha\},\mathfrak{M}\{S_\beta\}]:\mathfrak{M}\{S_\beta\}$
C6.07	$\nabla[\mathfrak{M}\{S_\alpha\},\mathfrak{M}_\mu]:\mathfrak{M}\{S_\beta\}$
C6.08	$\blacksquare[\mathfrak{M}_\mu,\mathfrak{M}\{S_\alpha\}]:\mathfrak{M}\{S_\beta\}$
C6.09	S_α is a necessary condition for S_β
C6.10	$\Delta[\mathfrak{M}\{S_\alpha\},\mathfrak{M}\{S_\beta\}]:\mathfrak{M}\{S_\alpha\}$
C6.11	$\Delta[\mathfrak{M}\{S_\alpha\},\mathfrak{M}\{S_\beta\}]:\mathfrak{O}$
C6.12	S_α is not a necessary condition for S_β

10.4.2. Definitions, Deduction

E6.01	$\nabla[\mathfrak{M}\{C6.01\},\mathfrak{M}\{C6.02\}]:\mathfrak{M}\{C6.03\}$
E6.02	$\mathfrak{M}\{C6.04\}:\mathfrak{M}\{C6.05\}$
E6.03	$\mathfrak{M}\{C6.06\}:\mathfrak{M}\{C6.05\}$
E6.04	$\blacksquare[\mathfrak{M}\{C6.07\},\mathfrak{M}\{C6.08\}]:\mathfrak{M}\{C6.09\}$
E6.05	$\mathfrak{M}\{C6.10\}:\mathfrak{M}\{C6.09\}$
E6.06	$\mathfrak{M}\{C6.11\}:\mathfrak{M}\{C6.12\}$

10.5. Summary of Statements, Truth

10.5.1. Auxiliary Assertions, Truth

C7.01	$t_\alpha \in \mathbf{S}\{\text{real-number}\}$
C7.02	$t_\alpha \geq 0$
C7.03	$t_\alpha \leq 1$
C7.04	$t_\alpha = 0$
C7.05	S_α is false
C7.06	$t_\alpha = 1$
C7.07	S_α is true
C7.08	$t_\alpha = t_\beta$
C7.09	$t\{\nabla[\mathfrak{M}_\alpha,\mathfrak{M}_\beta]\}=(t\{\mathfrak{M}_\alpha\}\bullet t\{\mathfrak{M}_\beta\})$
C7.10	$\mathfrak{M}_\beta:\blacksquare[\mathfrak{M}_\delta,\mathfrak{M}_\gamma]$
C7.11	$\mathfrak{M}_\alpha:\mathfrak{M}_\gamma$
C7.12	$t\{\mathfrak{M}_\alpha\}\leq t\{\mathfrak{M}_\beta\}$

C7.12 $\mathfrak{M}_\gamma \epsilon \mathbf{C}\{S_\alpha\}$
C7.13 $\mathfrak{h}\{\mathbf{C}\{S_\alpha\}\}=N$
C7.14 $\mathfrak{t}\{\mathfrak{M}_\mu\}=\sum_{\alpha=1}^{N}\mathfrak{t}\{\mathfrak{M}_\alpha\}$
C7.15 $\mathfrak{t}\{\mathfrak{M}_\mu\}=1$
C7.16 The collection $\mathbf{C}\{S_\alpha\}$ is exhaustive
C7.17 p strictly implies q
C7.18 It is false that it is possible that p be true and q false
C7.19 p materially implies q
C7.20 ~(p•~q)

10.5.2. Axioms, Truth

A7.01 $\mathfrak{t}\{\mathfrak{M}\{\mathfrak{P}\}\}=1$
A7.02 $\Delta[\mathfrak{M}\{C3.01\},\mathfrak{M}\{D7.01\}]:\nabla[\mathfrak{M}\{C7.08\},\mathfrak{M}_\mu]$
A7.03 $\mathfrak{M}\{C5.88\}:\nabla[\mathfrak{M}\{C7.09\},\mathfrak{M}_\mu]$
A7.05 $\nabla[\mathfrak{M}\{C7.12\},\mathfrak{M}\{C7.13\}]:\mathfrak{M}\{C7.14\}$

10.5.3. Definitions, Truth

10.5.3.1. Symbolism

D7.01 $\mathfrak{M}\{\mathfrak{t}\{\mathfrak{M}_\alpha\}\}:\mathfrak{M}\{t_\alpha\}$
D7.02 $\mathfrak{M}\{t_\alpha\}:\Delta[\mathfrak{M}\{C7.01\},\Delta[\mathfrak{M}\{C7.02\},\mathfrak{M}\{C7.03\}]]$
D7.03 $\mathfrak{t}^c_\alpha=(1-t_\alpha)$

10.5.3.2. English

E7.01 $\mathfrak{M}\{C7.04\}:\mathfrak{M}\{C7.05\}$
E7.02 $\mathfrak{M}\{C7.06\}:\mathfrak{M}\{C7.07\}$
E7.03 $\mathfrak{M}\{P7.01\}\epsilon\mathbf{C}$\{Rules of Substitution\}
E7.04 $\mathfrak{M}\{\mathfrak{t}^c_\alpha\}:\mathfrak{M}$\{the complement of truth-value t_α\}
E7.05 $\mathfrak{M}\{P7.02\}:\mathfrak{M}$\{compound probability\}
E7.06 $\mathfrak{M}\{A7.05\}:\mathfrak{M}$\{Theorem of Total Probability\}
E7.07 $\nabla[\mathfrak{M}\{A7.05\},\mathfrak{M}\{C7.15\}]:\mathfrak{M}\{C7.16\}$
E7.08 $\mathfrak{M}\{C7.17\}:\mathfrak{M}\{C7.18\}$
E7.09 $\mathfrak{M}\{C7.19\}:\mathfrak{M}\{C7.20\}$

10.5.4. Theorems, Truth

P7.01 $\Delta[\mathfrak{M}\{\mathfrak{t}\{\mathfrak{M}_\alpha\}\},\mathfrak{M}\{C3.01\}]:\mathfrak{M}\{\mathfrak{t}\{\mathfrak{M}_\beta\}\}$
P7.02 $\mathfrak{t}\{\nabla[\mathfrak{M}_\gamma,\mathfrak{M}_\delta]\}=(\mathfrak{t}\{\mathfrak{M}_\gamma\}\bullet\mathfrak{t}\{\blacksquare[\mathfrak{M}_\delta,\mathfrak{M}_\gamma]\})$
P7.03 $\nabla[\mathfrak{M}\{C3.06\},\mathfrak{M}_\nu]:\mathfrak{M}\{C7.12\}$
P7.04 $\mathfrak{t}\{\nabla[\mathfrak{M}_\gamma,\mathfrak{M}_\delta]\}\leq\mathfrak{t}\{\mathfrak{M}_\gamma\}$
P7.05 $\mathfrak{t}\{\mathfrak{O}\}=1$

P7.06 $t_\mu=(t_\alpha+t_\beta-\mathfrak{t}\{\nabla[\mathfrak{M}_\alpha,\mathfrak{M}_\beta]\})$

P7.07 $t_\mu=(1-(1-t_\alpha)\bullet(1-t_\beta))$

10.6. Summary of Statements, Induction

10.6.1. Auxiliary Assertions, Induction

C8.01 $\delta^c_{n\alpha}$ is the observed complement of δ_α

C8.02 δ_ρ is the observation of aggregate conjunction for independence

C8.03 δ_ρ is the observation of exclusive disjunction

C8.04 δ_ρ is the observation of inclusive disjunction

C8.05 δ_ρ is the observation of identity

C8.06 δ_ρ is the observation of material implication

10.6.2. Definitions, Induction

10.6.2.1. Symbolism

D8.01 $\delta\{\mathfrak{O}\}=0$

D8.02 $\delta\{\Delta[\mathfrak{M}_\beta,\mathfrak{M}_\gamma]\}\in\mathbf{S}\{0,1\}$

D8.03 $\mathfrak{M}\{\Delta[\mathfrak{M}_\beta(x_\alpha),\mathfrak{M}_\gamma(x_\alpha)]:\mathfrak{M}_\beta\}:\nabla[\mathfrak{M}\{\delta\{\Delta[\mathfrak{M}_\beta,\mathfrak{M}_\gamma]\}=1\},\mathfrak{M}_\mu]$

D8.04 $\mathfrak{M}\{\blacksquare[\mathfrak{M}_\beta(x_\alpha),\mathfrak{M}_\gamma(x_\alpha)]:\mathfrak{M}_\beta\}:\nabla[\mathfrak{M}\{\delta\{\Delta[\mathfrak{M}_\beta,\mathfrak{M}_\gamma]\}=0\},\mathfrak{M}_\mu]$

D8.05 $N=\mathfrak{b}\{\mathbf{C}\{\delta\{\mathfrak{M}_\beta,\mathfrak{M}_\gamma\}\}\}$

D8.06 $N\bullet\mathfrak{r}\{\mathfrak{M}_\beta,\mathfrak{M}_\gamma\}=\sum_{\alpha=1}^{N}\delta\{\Delta[\mathfrak{M}_\beta(\alpha),\mathfrak{M}_\gamma(\alpha)]\}$

D8.07 $\delta^c_\alpha=(1-\delta_\alpha)$

D8.08 $\delta_\rho=(\delta_\alpha\bullet\delta_\beta)$

D8.09 $\delta_\rho=(\delta_\alpha\bullet(1-\delta_\beta)+\delta_\beta\bullet(1-\delta_\alpha))$

D8.10 $\delta_\rho=(\delta_\alpha\bullet(1-\delta_\beta)+\delta_\beta\bullet(1-\delta_\alpha)+(\delta_\alpha\bullet\delta_\beta))$

D8.11 $\delta_\rho=(\delta_\alpha\bullet\delta_\beta+(1-\delta_\alpha)\bullet(1-\delta_\beta))$

D8.12 $\delta_\rho=(1-(1-\delta_\beta)\bullet\delta_\alpha)$

10.6.2.2. English

E8.01 $\mathfrak{M}\{\delta\{\Delta[\mathfrak{M}_\beta(x_\alpha),\mathfrak{M}_\gamma(x_\alpha)]\}\}:\mathfrak{M}\{$the value (0 or 1) of the comparison made at x_α between $\mathfrak{M}_\beta$ and $\mathfrak{M}_\gamma\}$

E8.02 $\mathfrak{M}\{\mathfrak{r}\{\mathfrak{M}_\beta,\mathfrak{M}_\gamma\}\}:\mathfrak{M}\{$ratio of occurrance of S_γ on evidence $S_\beta\}$

E8.03 $\mathfrak{M}\{D8.07\}:\mathfrak{M}\{C8.01\}$

E8.04 $\mathfrak{M}\{D8.08\}:\mathfrak{M}\{C8.02\}$

E8.05 $\mathfrak{M}\{D8.09\}:\mathfrak{M}\{C8.03\}$

E8.06 $\mathfrak{M}\{D8.10\}:\mathfrak{M}\{C8.04\}$

E8.07 $\mathfrak{M}\{D8.11\}:\mathfrak{M}\{C8.05\}$

E8.08 $\mathfrak{M}\{D8.12\}:\mathfrak{M}\{C8.06\}$

BIBLIOGRAPHY

1. William P. Alston, ***Philosophy of Language***, Prentice-Hall, Inc., 1964
2. George Boole, ***An Investigation of the Laws of Thought***, Dover Publications (reprint), 1854
3. Baruch A. Brody (Ed.), ***Readings in the Philosophy of Science***, Prentice Hall, 1970
4. Rudolf Carnap, ***Introduction to Semantics***, Harvard University Press, 1948
5. Rudolf Carnap, ***Logical Foundations of Probability***, University of Chicago Press, 1950
6. Rudolf Carnap, ***Meaning and Necessity***, University of Chicago Press, 1947
7. M. R. Cohen and E. Nagel, ***An Introduction to Logic and Scientific Method***, Harcourt, Brace and Co., 1934
8. Harold Cramer, ***Mathematical Methods of Statistics***, Princeton University Press, 1951
9. George O. Curme, ***Parts of Speech and Accidence***, D. C. Heath and Co., 1935
10. John Hospers, ***An Introduction to Philosophical Analysis***, Prentice-Hall, 1967
11. John P. Hughes, ***The Science of Language***, Random House, 1963
12. Harold Jeffreys, ***Theory of Probability***, Oxford University Press, 1948
13. W. E. Johnson, ***Logic***, Cambridge University Press, 1921-24, 3 vols.
14. Maurice G. Kendall, ***The Advanced Theory of Statistics***, Vol. 1, Charles Griffin Company, 1948
15. Paul Kratochvil, ***The Chinese Language Today***, Hutchinson Co., 1968
16. Kenneth Kunen, ***Set Theory***, North-Holland, 1980
17. C. I. Lewis and C. H. Langford, ***Symbolic Logic***, Dover (reprint)
18. Jean Nicod, ***Foundations of Geometry and Induction***, The Humanities Press, 1950
19. Willard Van Orman Quine, ***Mathematical Logic***, Harvard University Press, 1947
20. Hans Reichenbach, ***Philosophic Foundations of Quantum Mechanics***, University of California Press, 1944
21. Bertrand Russell, ***The Principles of Mathematics***, W. W. Norton, 1937
22. Ivan S. Sokolnikoff, ***Advanced Calculus***, McGraw-Hill, 1939
23. John F. Sowa, ***Conceptual Structures: Information Processing in Mind and Machine***, Addison-Wesley Publishing Co., 1984
24. Danny D. Steinberg and Leon A. Jakobovits, ***Semantics***, Cambridge University Press, 1971
25. Frederick Suppe (Ed.), ***The Structure of Scientific Theories***, University of Illinois Press, 1974

26. Alfred Tarski and Steven Givant, ***A Formalization of Set Theory without Variables***, American Mathematical Society, 1987
27. Alfred M. Tozzer, ***A Maya Grammar***, Dover Publications Inc., 1977
28. Abraham Wald, ***Statistical Decision Functions***, John Wiley and Sons, 1950
29. A. N. Whitehead and B. Russell, ***Principia Mathematica***, Cambridge, England, 1925

INDEX

addition / **34**
adjective / **115**
adjective, demonstrative / **122**
adjective, descriptive / **115**
adjective, intensifying / **122**
adjective, interrogative / **122**
adjective, limiting / **118**
adjective, numeric / **118**
adjective, numeric, cardinal / **119**
adjective, numeric, ordinal / **120**
adjective, possessive / **122**
adjective, relative / **122**
adjectives, numeric / **118**
adverb / **130**
adverb, of negation / **131**
adverb, simple / **131**
adverbs of degree / **131**
algebra / **31**
ambiguity of definition / **16**
apostrophe / **137**
arithmetic mean / **56**, **104**
articles / **123**
assertion / **8**
assertions / **112**
axiom A3.03 / **17**
axiom A3.12 / **20**
axiom A3.04 / **18**
axiom A3.05 / **19**
axiom A3.07 / **19**
axiom A3.08 / **20**
axiom A3.09 / **20**
axiom A3.11 / **20**
axiom A3.15 / **21**
axiom A3.16 / **21**
axiom A3.13 / **21**
axiom A3.14 / **21**
axiom A3.17 / **21**
axiom A4.02 / **34**
axiom A4.03 / **34**
axiom A4.04 / **34**
axiom A4.05 / **35**
axiom A4.06 / **35**
axiom A4.07 / **35**
axiom A4.08 / **35**
axiom A7.02 / **80**
axiom A7.05 / **85**
axiom A7.03 / **81**
axiom A7.01 / **79**
axiom A3.02 / **17**
axiom A3.06 / **19**
axiom A3.10 / **20**
axiom, specification / **11**
axioms, intension / **138**
axioms, number / **141**
axioms, truth / **149**
Bayes Theorem / **94**
Braille / **109**
cardinal number / **118**
cardinality, class / **54**
circularity of definition / **11**
class / **5**, **7**, **42**
class, vacuous / **51**
classes, disjoint / **59**
clause: see phrase
colon / **136**
colors / **123**
comma / **136**
commands / **113**
compound probability / **81**
confirmation / **103**
conjugation, verb / **129**
conjunction / **133**
conjunction (aggregate), intension / **18**
conjunction (coincident), intension / **20**
conjunction (complement), extension / **52**
conjunction (difference), number / **37**
conjunction (disjunctive), intension / **22**
conjunction (exclusive), intension / **21**
conjunction (intersection), extension / **50**

conjunction (product), number / **35, 56**
conjunction (quotient), number / **37**
conjunction (sum), number / **34, 55**
conjunction (union), extension / **48**
conjunction, coordinating / **133**
conjunction, copulative / **133**
conjunction, disjunctive / **56, 134**
conjunction, subordinating / **133**
conjunctions, classes / **47**
conjunctions, extension / **47**
conjunctions, intension / **18**
conjunctions, number / **34**
constructive definition / **73**
continuity of existence / **98**
contradiction, proof by / **70**
copula / **16, 32, 44, 126**
counting / **55**
creativity / **101**
deduction / **68**
default assumptions / **100**
definition D4.17 / **38**
definition D3.02 / **21**
definition D3.03 / **21**
definition D3.04 / **21**
definition D3.06 / **23**
definition D3.05 / **22**
definition D3.01 / **16**
definition D5.04 / **49**
definition D5.07 / **50**
definition D5.03 / **46**
definition D5.09 / **52**
definition D5.08 / **51**
definition D5.05 / **49**
definition D5.06 / **49**
definition D4.12 / **37**
definition D5.12 / **53**
definition D4.15 / **38**
definition D4.19 / **40**
definition D4.20 / **40**
definition D4.13 / **37**
definition D4.01 / **33**
definition D4.05 / **35**
definition D4.06 / **35**
definition D4.07 / **36**
definition D4.08 / **36**
definition D4.09 / **36**
definition D4.10 / **36**
definition D5.10 / **53**
definition D5.11 / **53**
definition D5.13 / **53**
definition D5.14 / **54**
definition D5.15 / **54**
definition D5.16 / **54**
definition D4.14 / **37**
definition D4.16 / **38**
definition D5.18 / **56**
definition D5.19 / **56**
definition D5.20 / **56**
definition D5.21 / **56**
definition D5.23 / **60**
definition D5.22 / **60**
definition D5.17 / **55**
definition D4.02 / **34**
definition D4.04 / **35**
definition D4.03 / **35**
definition D4.11 / **36**
definition D7.01 / **79**
definition D7.03 / **80**
definition D7.02 / **80**
definition D4.18 / **39**
definition E2.01 / **6**
definition E2.02 / **6**
definition, specification / **14**
definitions / **4, 9**
definitions, extension / **145**
definitions, induction / **150**
definitions, intension / **139**
definitions, number / **141**
definitions, truth / **149**
deMorgan's Theorem / **85**
descriptor / **114**
descriptor, null intension / **23**
descriptor, number / **31, 32**
descriptor, real number / **38**
descriptor, vacuous class / **51**
dictionaries / **9**

difference / **37**
disjoint classes / **59**
disjunction, exclusive / **57**
disjunction, inclusive / **58**
disjunction, intension / **22, 56**
disjunction: see conjunction, disjunctive / **134**
division / **37**
ellipsis / **136**
equality / **32**
equivalence, material / **92**
exclamations / **113**
excluded middle, law of / **91**
exhaustive collection / **85**
existence / **78, 127**
extension / **5, 42**
factorial / **58**
frequency of occurrance / **89**
frequency theory of probability / **84, 89**
generalizations / **100**
greater than / **34, 40, 41**
hyphen / **137**
hypotheses / **12**
identity, extension / **45**
identity, intension / **17**
identity, number / **32**
if and only if / **71**
imperative mood / **130**
implication / **92**
implication, logical / **19**
inclusion, class / **49**
inclusion, intension / **19**
independent concepts / **59**
indicative mood / **130**
induction / **97**
induction, mathematical / **70**
inequality, number / **34**
inherent truth / **77**
integer / **53**
intension / **5, 14**
intension, null / **23**
interjections / **113**
intersection, classes / **50**
invalid argument / **94**
knowledge / **75**
Law of Excluded Middle / **79**
less than / **34, 40**
logic, modal / **95**
logic, nonmonotonic / **100**
logic, traditional / **90**
logical implication / **68**
material equivalence / **92**
material implication / **92**
mathematical induction / **70**
matrix / **52**
meaning / **14**
meaning, sentence / **14**
metric, class / **54**
metric, intension / **77**
morphemes / **16, 132**
multiplication / **35**
mutually exclusive / **57**
natural numbers / **35**
necessary condition / **72**
negation / **22, 91**
negative integers / **37, 53**
nonmonotonic logic / **100**
nonsense / **23**
noun / **115**
nouns, extension / **43**
nouns, intension / **15**
nouns, number / **32**
nouns, used as adjectives / **122**
number / **31**
number, complex / **39**
number, real / **38**
ordinal number / **118**
parentheses / **135**
parts of speech / **111**
period / **136**
philosophy / **74**
phrase, adverbial / **131**
phrase: see clause
phrases, used as adjectives / **122**
preposition / **132**
principle of indifference / **86**

probability / **78**
probability, compound / **81**
product / **35**
pronoun / **115**
proof by contradiction / **70**
proof of impossibility / **70**
punctuation / **135**
questions / **114**
quotation mark / **137**
quotient / **37**
random selection / **85**
rational decision / **97**
rational number / **54**
real numbers / **38, 54**
repeated product / **56**
repeated sum / **55**
resolution / **95**
roots of numbers / **39**
Rule of Substitution / **20, 33, 46, 70**
semantics / **111**
semicolon / **136**
semiotics / **109, 111**
sentence / **8, 109, 112**
sequence / **36**
sequencing, number / **34, 40, 60**
sets / **53**
similar classes / **55**
space / **135**
strict implication / **92**
subjunctive / **77**
subjunctive mood / **130**
substitution / **70**
subtraction / **37**
successor function / **36**
sufficient condition / **72**
sum / **34**
syllogism / **70**
syntactics / **111**
tensor / **52**
theorem P3.01 / **25**
theorem P3.07 / **27**
theorem A3.01 / **16**
theorem P5.01 / **46**
theorem P5.02 / **46**
theorem P5.03 / **46**
theorem P5.04 / **49**
theorem P5.06 / **51**
theorem P5.07 / **51**
theorem P4.02 / **33**
theorem P4.03 / **33**
theorem P4.05 / **40**
theorem A4.01 / **34**
theorem P7.01 / **80**
theorem P4.01 / **33**
theorem P3.02 / **25**
theorem P3.04 / **26**
theorem P3.05 / **26**
theorem P3.06 / **26**
theorem P3.12 / **30**
theorem P3.08 / **29**
theorem P3.09 / **29**
theorem P3.11 / **29**
theorem P3.10 / **29**
theorem P5.14 / **61**
theorem P5.15 / **62**
theorem P5.16 / **62**
theorem P5.17 / **62**
theorem P5.18 / **62**
theorem P5.19 / **63**
theorem P5.20 / **63**
theorem P5.21 / **63**
theorem P5.22 / **64**
theorem P5.23 / **64**
theorem P5.24 / **65**
theorem P5.25 / **65**
theorem P5.26 / **65**
theorem P5.27 / **67**
theorem P5.28 / **67**
theorem P5.29 / **67**
theorem P5.30 / **67**
theorem P4.09 / **41**
theorem P5.10 / **60**
theorem P5.11 / **60**
theorem P5.12 / **60**
theorem P4.04 / **36**
theorem P5.08 / **55**